STO

ALLEN COUNTY PUBLIC LIBRARY

ACPL ITEM
DISCARDED

ST THOMAS AQUINAS
SUMMA THEOLOGIÆ

ST THOMAS AQUINAS

SUMMA
THEOLOGIÆ

Latin text and English translation,
Introductions, Notes, Appendices
and Glossaries

BLACKFRIARS

IN CONJUNCTION WITH

EYRE & SPOTTISWOODE, LONDON, AND
McGRAW-HILL BOOK COMPANY, NEW YORK

PIÆ MEMORIÆ
JOANNIS
PP. XXIII
DICATUM

IN AN AUDIENCE, 13 December 1963, to a group representing the Dominican Editors and the combined Publishers of the New English *Summa*, His Holiness Pope Paul VI warmly welcomed and encouraged their undertaking. A letter from His Eminence Cardinal Cicognani, Cardinal Secretary of State, 6 February 1968, expresses the continued interest of the Holy Father in the progress of the work, 'which does honour to the Dominican Order, and the Publishers, and is to be considered without doubt as greatly contributing to the growth and spread of a genuinely Catholic culture', and communicates his particular Apostolic Blessing.

ST THOMAS AQUINAS

SUMMA THEOLOGIÆ
VOLUME 53

THE LIFE OF CHRIST
(3a. 38–45)

Latin text. English translation, Introduction,
Notes & Appendices

SAMUEL PARSONS O.P.

and

ALBERT PINHEIRO O.P.

St Albert's College, Oakland, Cal.

NIHIL OBSTAT

JANKO ZAGAR O.P.

IMPRIMI POTEST

PAUL SCANLON O.P.
Provincial of the Province of the Most Holy Name of Jesus
19 April 1971

NIHIL OBSTAT

JOHN M. T. BARTON S.T.D., L.S.S.
Censor

IMPRIMATUR

✠ VICTOR GUAZZELLI
Vic. Gen.

Westminster 26 March 1971

SBN 413 35530 6

© BLACKFRIARS 1971

[EXCEPTING LATIN TEXT OF 'DE BAPTISMO QUO CHRISTUS BAPTIZATUS EST
ET DE HIS QUÆ PERTINENT AD PROGRESSUM IPSIUS IN MUNDO']

PRINTED IN GREAT BRITAIN BY EYRE AND SPOTTISWOODE LIMITED

CONTENTS

xi   Editorial Notes
xiii Introduction

QUESTION 38. THE BAPTISM OF JOHN
3   Article 1. whether it was fitting for John to baptize
5   Article 2. whether the baptism of John was from God
9   Article 3. whether it conferred grace
11 Article 4. whether Christ alone should have been baptized by John
13 Article 5. whether the baptism of John should have ceased after Christ was baptized
17 Article 6. whether those baptized by John should afterwards have been baptized in Christ

QUESTION 39. THE BAPTIZING OF CHRIST
23 Article 1. whether it was fitting for Christ to be baptized
25 Article 2. whether he should have been baptized with the baptism of John
27 Article 3. whether the time was fitting
31 Article 4. whether he should have been baptized in the Jordan
35 Article 5. whether the heavens should have been opened
39 Article 6. whether the Holy Spirit should have descended in the form of a dove
45 Article 7. whether the dove was a real animal
47 Article 8. whether the Father's voice should have been heard bearing witness

QUESTION 40. CHRIST'S MANNER OF LIFE
53 Article 1. whether Christ should have associated with men
57 Article 2. whether he should have led an austere life
61 Article 3. and a lowly life
65 Article 4. whether he should have lived in conformity with the Law

QUESTION 41. THE TEMPTATION OF CHRIST
71 Article 1. whether Christ should have been tempted
75 Article 2. concerning the place
79 Article 3. and the time
81 Article 4. and the manner and order of temptation

QUESTION 42. CHRIST'S TEACHING
91 Article 1. whether Christ should have preached to the Jews, or to the Gentiles as well

95	Article 2.	whether he should have preached without offence to the Jews
97	Article 3.	whether he should have preached openly or secretly
101	Article 4.	and by word alone, or also by writing

QUESTION 43. CHRIST'S MIRACLES IN GENERAL

107	Article 1.	whether Christ should have worked miracles
109	Article 2.	whether he worked them by divine power
113	Article 3.	on the time when he began to work miracles
115	Article 4.	whether they sufficiently manifested his divinity

QUESTION 44. THE DIFFERENT KINDS OF MIRACLES

123	Article 1.	the miracles Christ worked concerning spiritual substances
129	Article 2.	and concerning the heavenly bodies
135	Article 3.	and concerning men
143	Article 4.	and concerning non-rational creatures

QUESTION 45. CHRIST'S TRANSFIGURATION

149	Article 1.	whether it was fitting for Christ to be transfigured
151	Article 2.	whether his splendour was the splendour of glory
155	Article 3.	on the witnesses of the Transfiguration
161	Article 4.	and the testimony of the Father's voice

APPENDICES

165	1.	The Baptism of John
171	2.	The Baptism of Christ
179	3.	The Mission of Christ
187	4.	The Temptation of Christ
195	5.	The Works and Words of Christ
204	6.	The Transfiguration

209	Index

EDITORIAL NOTES

THE LATIN text strikes a compromise between that of the Piana and of the Leonine editions, if the phrase be not too strong for a section where the differences are few and of no great moment. A few of the variations have been noted. The translation follows the order of the sentences, but, though close, has sought to avoid the crabbed effect in English of matching the original word for word.

Biblical references are to the Vulgate. Patristic references are to Migne (PG, Greek Fathers; PL, Latin Fathers). Abbreviations to St Thomas's works are as follows:

Summa Theologiæ, without title. Part, question, article, reply; e.g. 1a, 3, 2 ad 3. 1a2æ. 17, 6. 2a2æ. 180, 10. 3a. 35, 8.

Summa Contra Gentiles, CG. Book, chapter; e.g. *CG* 1, 28.

Scriptum in IV Libros Sententiarum, Sent. Book, distinction, question, article, solution or *quæstiuncula*, reply; e.g. III *Sent.* 25, 2, 3, ii ad 3.

Compendium Theologiæ, Compend. Theol.

Philosophical commentaries: On Aristotle's *De Anima, In De an.*; on his Metaphysics, *In Meta.*; on the Dionysian *De divinis nominibus, In De div. nom.*

Quæstiones de Anima, Q. de anima.

Quæstiones quodlibetales (de quolibet), Quodl.

References to the commentaries of Albert and Bonaventure on the *Sentences* take the same form as the references to Thomas's commentary. Commentaries on the *De anima* by Albert, Averroes and Themistius are given as *In De an.* The Halesian *Summa* is given as *Summa theol.*

INTRODUCTION

IN THE PROLOGUE to the *Tertia Pars* of the *Summa Theologiæ* there is a single citation from Scripture—Christ came to save his people from their sins (*Matthew* 1, 21). It is under this soteriological aspect that St Thomas offers his study of the work of Christ in human history.

Yet it must be remembered that this was done according to the method and needs of his own time, the 13th century. Prior to this the Fathers of the Church had a profound awareness of the fundamental meaning of salvation history: God revealed himself and spoke to his people in time and space. This revelation culminated in the person and mission of Jesus Christ, and it was continued and deepened in the Church which was the very living, spiritual body of Christ, the sacrament of Christ's presence in history. The Church lived in the mystery of Christ. Hence the divine-human dialogue had to be continued in the life of the Sacramental Christ, the Church. The Fathers, as leading figures of the Church, were convinced that God still spoke to his people in history. His word was preserved in the sacred writings of the Old and New Testaments and in the unwritten life of the Church and its tradition. Together both preserved and manifested the word of the living God. The Fathers were men of faith who constantly sought to make this word as revealed in and through Christ relevant to the age in which they lived.

To do this they undertook a deeper investigation of the meaning of the sacred text. They recognized the fact that the word of God as found in Scripture had a meaning in its own context, one which was given to those who first heard it. But the word of God as found in the sacred text and proclaimed in a living tradition had to speak to the faithful of all ages—to the Church which was awaiting Christ's return in glory. Accordingly the words had a deeper meaning which was both Christological and ecclesiological, and which was to be addressed to the Church in time and space. Hence the Fathers developed a basic twofold meaning, the *literal sense* and the *spiritual sense*.

The literal sense was the meaning found in the words as they were given and understood when first proclaimed in the life of the people of God, the meaning of the text in the historical situation in which it was formed. The Fathers recognized the necessity of understanding this meaning; it lay at the foundation of the divine self-revelation within salvation history. Indeed, the School of Antioch did much to assert the obligation and value of grasping the word of God in its own context. But in many ways this was seen to be inadequate and insufficient to those who sought to intensify their faith in Christ. Men wished to see how the entire Old Testament pointed to Christ and his community by way of promise; they wished to see how the Old and the New Testaments still spoke to them in their own time. The word of God had to be applied to the life and guidance of the Church in history. The spiritual sense was the meaning of the sacred text in relation to Christ's Church living in time and space. The School of Alexandria fostered the study of this spiritual sense and, constantly reassessing and reapplying God's message to new situations, made use of *analogy*; Scripture was seen to offer numerous parallels to the contemporary historical and sacramental setting. The rules of grammar, logic and rhetoric were employed to determine the literal sense; allegory and typology were the hermeneutical tools used to show how God was still speaking to his people.

The medievals were heirs of the Fathers. There was no abrupt break with the past. The desire of the men of faith was to have the sacred text speak to them in their own lives. Certainly the literal sense of Scripture was not disdained, and the more critical works of Jerome and Augustine were valued for their balance and erudition. Nevertheless, the spiritual sense was always the main interest of research and reflection. Much of the knowledge of the history of Israel had been lost, and the leaders of the Greek- and Latin-speaking Church had little understanding of the Hebrew and Judaistic mind. The literal sense was obscure and had little meaning for the faithful of the early Middle Ages. Rather God seemed to speak to them in their lives through the spiritual sense of Sacred Scripture and in the spiritual life of the Church. Great reverence was shown to the spiritual interpretations of Jerome and Augustine, Hilary and Ambrose; the influence of Origen and the School of Alexandria was predominant. A passage from the Old or New Testament would be read, and commented on with abundant parallels to the spiritual life and practice of the Church; the *Lectio Divina* and the *Homilies* of the great Fathers were ways to make the revelation of God a living reality to an age of faith. With the repetition of this process there was a reluctance to depart from established procedures.

Certain changes began to take place during the 12th and especially the 13th centuries, when men's minds became ever more impressed with the philosophical systems of classical Greece, particularly those of Plato and Aristotle. Greek philosophical thought was seen to provide a systematic non-historical understanding of man and the cosmos. Human life and conduct were based on the operations of nature and the dictates of reason rather than on the demands of God as revealed in the contingent events of history. Platonism and Aristoteleanism provided a full world-view quite independent of revelation in history. Such systems had their own natural principles based on the perceptions of a physical and metaphysical order;

they had their own solutions to the problems of man and his world. Some churchmen found this growing interest in Greek philosophy pernicious and dangerous, but others saw here no threat to faith, but rather a challenge to be faced and resolved. They sought to understand, expound and interpret the revelation of God made in salvation history and preserved in the life of Christ and his Church in terms of this non-historical, philosophical way of thought. Hence once the philosophical system was accepted it provided the thinkers of that age with certain *quæstiones* which could and should be asked of the word of God as revealed in history and contained in faith. Indeed, reason was seen to be a hermeneutic of faith, able to explain and interpret faith up to a point. It was the task of the great theologians of the 12th and 13th centuries to explain whenever possible the supernatural faith of the Church in terms of natural reason.

What did this mean with respect to the study of the word of God as found in Sacred Scripture and witnessed in the tradition of the Church? On the one hand it became subject to a new mode of analysis. The medieval doctors did not interrogate the word of God in what was taken to be the historical order of the texts. Rather, their questions were posed in the context of the system in a non-historical manner. Faith in God and his self-revelation in cosmic and human history remained the controlling factor, but the meaning of this revelation was determined by reference to a non-historical hermeneutic—the philosophical system. This development stimulated a renewed interest in the literal sense, since it was only the historical or religious situation itself—the salvation event—which was being interpreted, not its influence and significance in subsequent generations. Thus, the medieval doctors attempted to acquire more accurate texts of the Old and New Testaments and if possible to consult them in their original Hebrew and Greek. So too they stressed the study of logic and grammar as well as the proper and improper senses of words and phrases. Given the limitations of the time and the lack of source material, their efforts were praiseworthy even if not always successful.

On the other hand they did not wish to break with the older understanding and interpretation of God and his self-revelation in history. Hence they made a constant effort to connect their exposition of the word of God with the past—with the tradition of the Church as they understood it, and with the authority of its great doctors and saints. In this way they sought to preserve a continuity with the past, and an integration of the soteriological and Christological interpretation of the Bible as based on faith with the philosophical interpretation of the text as based on reason. This was a delicate balance and often difficult to preserve. Yet it was one of the crowning achievements of the high Middle Ages that the revealed word of God was co-ordinated and exposed to the philosophical mind of man as expressed in the thought of classical Greece. Systematic theology attained great insights into the meaning of the sacred text and the divine-human dialogue it recorded; revelation and reason were brought into a vast and lasting synthesis of faith and knowledge.

St Thomas Aquinas lived and died during this intellectual renaissance of the 13th century, and his work has remained as a supreme expression of its accomplishments. On the one hand he preserved continuity with the past in his mode of treating the sacred text, and certainly with respect to his presentation and exposition of the life and mission of Jesus Christ. His commentary *Super Evangelium Sancti Matthæi* (c. 1256–1259) and his commentary *Super Evangelium Sancti Joannis* (c. 1269–1272) are both traditional pieces of exegetical work in general line with the *Lectio Divina* of his age. Thus the text of the Gospel is given in whole or in part, depending upon the particular passage under consideration. Often there follows a series of remarks about the text and its structure, as well as some observations concerning the historical or religious situation described there. There is added a number of theological or spiritual reflections on the point at issue, with copious citations from both the Old and New Testaments. When appropriate, reference is made to the writings and thoughts of various distinguished Fathers of the Church, and even on occasion to theological problems or errors which might have arisen regarding a particular passage or idea found there. In this way St Thomas follows the traditional way of explaining the Gospels. He recognizes that there can be a literal and spiritual sense and both are valuable (cf 1a. 1, 10, Vol. 1 of this series). However he prefers the literal sense so far as it can best be determined, and he avoids all forms of allegorical or mystical fancy so popular in the medieval Church. To the contrary he declares that historical truth must always lie at the foundation of any spiritual interpretation of the Bible (cf 1a. 102, 1). His sobriety is evident as he comments on the life and work of Christ as recorded in the Gospel. A vast wealth of traditional and personal erudition is brought to bear on his interpretation of the word of God. In this he holds a distinguished place in the ranks of Christian exegetes.

On the other hand St Thomas was also prepared to face the challenge of his age. The faith of the Church had to be interpreted and situated in the context of a philosophical world-view which was non-historical and non-Christian. He was not the first of his age to undertake this task. Yet, in his *Summa Theologiæ* there is an impressive presentation of the confession of faith in a systematic rational whole. Reason must minister to faith, to elucidate its mystery, not to compromise or destroy it (cf 1a. 1, 8 ad 2). Accordingly, when treating of the person and mission of Christ, the point of departure remains the conviction of *faith*—that Jesus Christ is the Son of God, the Second Person of the Trinity; he is a truly divine person who became man at a given moment of time in accordance with the will of God the Father. He lived and died as a man for the salvation of all men and he was raised from the dead and exalted into a new life of eternal glory with God; he is the supreme mediator of God in cosmic and human history. Such faith is that of the primitive Church itself; it is found in the Pauline tradition, especially as represented in *Ephesians* and *Hebrews*, and in the Johannine tradition according to the witness of the Fourth Gospel.

Hence St Thomas poses certain *Quæstiones* about the meaning of the Incarnation of God as a man (3a. 1–26). Various concepts of divinity and humanity are explored, both as proclaimed by faith and clarified by reason. Then he speaks of Christ's coming into the world (3a. 27–34), his birth and childhood (3a. 35–37), his public mission (3a. 38–45), his Passion and death (3a. 46–52), his resurrection, glorification and universal judgment (3a. 53–59). Again, the mode of presentation is that of a divine figure moving into the fullness of human history and human events.

In this context, of the mission and ministry of Jesus Christ, St Thomas sees his activity as that of a divine–human figure who has come into the world to reveal the works and words of God in order to save man (3a. 44, 3). He treats John the Baptist and his ministry as a prophetic preparation and witness to the superior mission of Christ (3a. 38); the baptism of Christ as the first public manifestation of his divine sonship, one confirmed by the Father's voice and the presence of the Spirit (3a. 39); Christ's way of life from the point of view of a divine figure leading an extraordinarily humble, austere, poor human life for the sake of others (3a. 40); the temptation of Christ as an ordeal which the Son of God undergoes for the benefit of men (3a. 41); the teaching of Christ as that of a divine figure speaking to all men, Jew and Gentile alike, the salvific words of God (3a. 42); the wondrous works of Christ as showing divine power present and active in the Son of God and revealed to help and save men (3a. 43–44); and the transfiguration of Christ as yet another revelation of the divine sonship of Jesus, but one made so that his closest disciples could see the promise of their own future glorification as sons of God (3a. 45). Abundant citations from the sacred text and the writings of the Fathers support the insights which St Thomas himself had both as a man of faith and a man of reason.

Granted the overall world-view reflected here by St Thomas, his study of the human life and mission of Jesus Christ occupies a restricted position in the total presentation of his Christology. St Thomas did not wish to investigate the humanity of Christ in isolation from his divinity. Rather he writes of the divine person's activity as a man. Many features of Christ's true human character are discussed, but his divine sonship is the main underlying interest. Hence there is no effort made to trace the psychological growth of the humanity of Jesus; or to review the sociological and ethical aspects of his human mission; or to determine any precise chronological pattern for Jesus' historical ministry; or to connect his work with the history of Israel and the soteriological and eschatological hopes of contemporary Judaism. Rather he seeks to present to the inquiring minds of his age the figure of Jesus Christ, true God and true man, as the revelation of God's grace of salvation. The Son of God has entered into cosmic and human history to restore and reconcile all things to the Father. In this he remains faithful to the tradition of the Church and the Gospel itself. The evangelical and kerygmatic witness of the primitive Church reflect much the same conviction of faith. He understands the meaning of salvation history: he goes to great lengths to show that Jesus Christ was the fulfilment of God's promises to Israel as preserved in the Old Testament—and he goes on to show that Jesus Christ is still alive and active in his Church through the sacraments. However, this is expressed in a context in which the confession of faith found in the Church may be co-ordinated to the insights of men of reason. This has made the work of St Thomas a gift to posterity. The results of contemporary biblical and theological scholarship show how many of his thoughts are as vital to this as to his own age.

S. P.

ST THOMAS AQUINAS

SUMMA THEOLOGIÆ

THE LIFE OF CHRIST

DEINDE CONSIDERANDUM EST de baptismo quo Christus baptizatus est; et quia Christus baptizatus est baptismo Joannis, primo considerandum est de baptismo Joannis in communi, secundo, de baptizatione Christi.

Quæstio 38. de baptismo Joannis

Circa primum quæruntur sex:
1. utrum conveniens fuerit quod Joannes baptizaret;
2. utrum ille baptismus fuerit a Deo;
3. utrum contulerit gratiam;
4. utrum alii, præter Christum, illo baptismo debuerint baptizari;
5. utrum baptismus ille cessare debuerit Christo baptizato;
6. utrum baptizati baptismo Joannis essent postea baptizandi baptismo Christi.

articlus 1. utrum fuerit conveniens Joannem baptizare

AD PRIMUM sic proceditur:[1] 1. Videtur quod non fuerit conveniens Joannem baptizare. Omnis enim ritus sacramentalis ad aliquam pertinet legem. Sed Joannes non introduxit novam legem. Ergo inconveniens fuit quod novum ritum baptizandi introduceret.

2. Præterea, Joannes *fuit missus a Deo in testimonium*[2] tanquam propheta secundum illud *Luc.*,[3] *Tu puer propheta Altissimi vocaberis*. Sed prophetæ qui fuerunt ante Christum non introduxerunt novum ritum, sed observantiam legalium rituum inducebant, ut patet *Malach.*,[4] *Mementote legis Moysi servi mei*. Ergo nec Joannes novum ritum baptizandi introducere debuit.

3. Præterea, ubi est alicujus rei superfluitas, non est ad illud aliquid addendum. Sed Judæi excedebant in superfluitate baptismatum: dicitur enim quod *Pharisæi et omnes Judæi, nisi crebro laverint manus, non manducant, ei a foro venientes, nisi baptizentur, non comedunt; et alia multa sunt quæ tradita sunt illis servare, baptismata calicum, et urceorum, et æramentorum, et lectorum*.[5] Ergo inconveniens fuit quod Joannes baptizaret.

SED CONTRA est auctoritas Scripturæ, ubi præmissa sanctitate Joannis, subditur quod *exibant ad eum multi, et baptizabantur ab eo in Jordane*.[6]

---

[1] cf IV *Sent.* II, 2, 2 ad 5
[2] *John* 1, 6, 7   [3] *Luke* 1, 76
[4] *Malachi* 4, 4   [5] *Mark* 7, 3

THE BAPTISM OF JOHN

WE MUST NEXT CONSIDER the baptism with which Christ was baptized. And since it was with the baptism of John,[a] we must consider first the baptism of John in general, and second, his baptizing of Christ.

Question 38. The baptism of John

Here there are six points to be treated:

1. whether it was fitting for John to baptize;
2. whether that baptism was from God;
3. whether it conferred grace;
4. whether others besides Christ should have been baptized with that baptism;
5. whether that baptism should have ceased once Christ himself was baptized;
6. whether those who received the baptism of John should afterwards have had to receive the baptism of Christ.

article 1. whether it was fitting for John to baptize

THE FIRST POINT:[1] 1. It would seem not. For every sacramental rite belongs to some law. But John did not introduce the New Law. Therefore it was not fitting for him to introduce the new rite of baptism.

2. Furthermore, John *was sent by God to witness*[2] as a prophet: *And you, little child, shall be called prophet of the Most High.*[3] But the prophets who came before Christ did not introduce any new rite but urged observance of the rites of the Law: *Remember the Law of my servant Moses.*[4] Neither, then, should John have introduced any new rite of baptism.

3. Furthermore, wherever there is an overabundance of anything, nothing more should be added. But the Jews had too many ablution rites, for it is written that *the Pharisees, and the Jews in general, never eat without washing their hands frequently, and on returning from the market place they never eat without bathing themselves, and there are many other observances handed down to them concerning the washing of cups and pots and bronze dishes and beds.*[5] Therefore, it was not fitting for John to baptize.

ON THE OTHER HAND, there is the authority of Scripture, where, after having spoken of John's sanctity, it adds that *many made their way to him to be baptized by him in the Jordan.*[6]

---

[6] *Matthew* 3, 6
[a] cf Appendix 1

RESPONSIO: Dicendum quod conveniens fuit Joannem baptizare, propter quatuor. Primo quidam, quia oportebat Christum a Joanne baptizari, ut baptismum consecraret, ut Augustinus dicit.⁷ Secundo, ut Christus manifestaretur. Unde ipse Joannes Baptista dicit, *Ut manifestetur*, scilicet Christus, *in Israel, propterea veni ego in aqua baptizans*;⁸ concurrentibus enim turbis ad baptismum, annuntiabat Christum: quod quidem facilius sic factum est quam si per singulos discurrisset, ut Chrysostomus dicit.⁹ Tertio, ut suo baptismo assuefaceret homines ad baptismum Christi. Unde Gregorius dicit quod *ideo Joannes baptizavit, ut præcursionis suæ ordinem servans, qui nasciturum Dominum nascendo prævenerat, baptizando quoque baptizaturum Dominum præveniret.*¹⁰ Quarto, ut ad pœnitentiam homines inducens, homines præpararet ad digne suscipiendum baptismum Christi. Unde ibidem Beda dicit quod *quantum catechumenis nondum baptizatis prodest doctrina fidei, tantum profuit baptisma Joannis ante baptisma Christi, quia sicut ille prædicabat pœnitentiam, et baptismum Christi prænuntiabat, et in cognitionem veritatis, quæ mundo apparuit, attrahebat; sic ministri Ecclesiæ primo erudiunt, post peccata eorum redarguunt, demum in baptismo Christi remissionem peccatorum promittunt.*¹¹

1. Ad primum ergo dicendum quod baptismus Joannis non erat per se sacramentum, sed quasi quoddam sacramentale disponens ad baptismum Christi; et ideo aliqualiter pertinebat ad legem Christi, non autem ad legem Moysi.

2. Ad secundum dicendum quod Joannes non solum fuit propheta, sed *plus quam propheta*, ut dicitur *Matt.*¹² Fuit enim terminus legis et initium Evangelii.¹³ Et ideo magis pertinebat ad eum verbo et opere inducere homines ad legem Christi quam ad observantiam veteris legis.

3. Ad tertium dicendum quod baptismata illa Pharisæorum erant inania, utpote ad solam munditiam carnis ordinata; sed baptismus Joannis ordinabatur ad munditiam spiritualem: inducebat enim homines ad pœnitentiam, ut dictum est.¹⁴

articulus 2. *utrum baptismus Joannis fuerit a Deo*

AD SECUNDUM sic proceditur:¹ 1. Videtur quod baptismus Joannis non fuerit a Deo. Nihil enim sacramentale, quod est a Deo, denominatur ab homine puro; sicut baptismus novæ legis non dicitur Petri, vel Pauli, sed

---

⁷*In Joan.* XIII, 4 (*John* 3, 22) PL 35, 1494; PL 39, 2011
⁸*John* 1, 31
⁹*In Matt.* X, 2. PG 57, 186
¹⁰*In Evangelium* VII, 3. PL 76, 1101
¹¹Scotus Erigena, *Comm. on John* 3, 24. PL 122, 323; cf St Thomas, *Catena aurea*, in loc. under the name of Bede.

THE BAPTISM OF JOHN

REPLY: For John to baptize was fitting for four reasons. First of all, it was necessary for Christ to be baptized by John in order for him to sanctify baptism, as Augustine says, commenting on *John*.[7] Secondly, in order that Christ might be revealed. For which reason John the Baptist himself says: *It was to reveal him*, namely, Christ, *to Israel that I came baptizing with water*.[8] For he preached Christ to the crowds that gathered around him to be baptized, which was more easily done than if he had had to search out individuals, as Chrysostom notes, commenting on *John*.[9] Thirdly, in order that by his baptism he might accustom men to the baptism of Christ; for which reason Gregory says in one of his homilies that *John baptized in accord with his office of precursor, so that, since in birth he had preceded our Lord, he might also by baptizing precede him who would baptize*.[10] Fourthly, in order that by urging men to do penance he might prepare men to receive worthily the baptism of Christ. For this reason Bede says that *the baptism of John was as profitable before the baptism of Christ as instruction in the faith profits the catechumens not yet baptized, because, just as he preached penance and foretold the baptism of Christ, and drew men to knowledge of the truth which appeared to the world, so likewise the ministers of the Church first instruct men, then admonish them for their sins, and lastly promise them forgiveness in the baptism of Christ.*[11]

Hence: 1. The baptism of John was not a sacrament, properly speaking, but something sacramental preparatory to the baptism of Christ; and therefore, in a certain sense, belonged to the law of Christ, but not to that of Moses.

2. John was not only a prophet, but *more than a prophet*:[12] for he was the end of the Law and the beginning of the Gospel.[13] Therefore it belonged to him to lead men, both by word and deed, to the law of Christ rather than to the observance of the Old Law.[a]

3. Those ablutions of the Pharisees were vain, since they were ordered only to physical cleanliness. But the baptism of John was ordered to spiritual cleanliness, since it led men to do penance, as stated above.[14]

article 2. whether the baptism of John was from God

THE SECOND POINT:[1] 1. It would seem that the baptism of John was not from God. For nothing sacramental, which is from God, is named after a mere man; thus the baptism of the New Law is not named after Peter, or

---

[12] *Matthew* 11, 9
[13] cf *Luke* 16, 16
[14] in the corpus
[1] cf IV *Sent.* II, 2, 1, iii. *In Matt.* 21
[a] The New Law of the Gospel, cf 1a2æ. 1c6-108

Christi.² Sed ille baptismus denominatur a Joanne, secundum illud *Matt., Baptismus Joannis unde erat? e cœlo, an ex hominibus?*³ Ergo baptismus Joannis non fuit a Deo.

2. Præterea, omnis doctrina de novo a Deo procedens aliquibus signis confirmatur; unde et Dominus dedit Moysi potestatem signa faciendi;⁴ et dicitur, *Cum* fides nostra *principium accepisset enarrari a Deo, per eos qui audierunt, in nos confirmata est, contestante Deo signis et prodigiis.*⁵ Sed de Joanne Baptista dicitur, *Joannes signum fecit nullum.*⁶ Ergo videtur quod baptismus quo baptizavit, non esset a Deo.

3. Præterea, sacramenta, quæ sunt divinitus instituta, aliquibus sacræ Scripturæ præceptis continentur. Sed baptismus Joannis non præcipitur aliquo præcepto sacræ Scripturæ. Ergo videtur quod non fuerit a Deo.

SED CONTRA est quod dicitur,⁷ *Qui me misit baptizare in aqua, ille mihi dixit, Super quem videris Spiritum,* etc.

RESPONSIO: Dicendum quod, in baptismo Joannis duo possunt considerari, scilicet ipse ritus baptizandi et effectus baptismi. Ritus quidem baptizandi non fuit ex hominibus, sed a Deo, qui familiari Spiritus Sancti revelatione Joannem ad baptizandum misit. Effectus autem illius baptismi fuit ab homine, quia nihil in illo baptismo efficiebatur quod homo facere non potest. Unde non fuit a Deo nisi inquantum Deus in homine operatur.

1. Ad primum ergo dicendum quod per baptismum novæ legis homines interius per Spiritum Sanctum baptizantur; quod facit solus Deus. Per baptismum autem Joannis solum corpus mundabatur aqua. Unde dicitur *Matt.,*⁸ *Ego baptizo vos in aqua; ille vos baptizabit in Spiritu Sancto.* Et ideo baptismus Joannis denominatur ab ipso, quia scilicet nihil in eo agebatur quod ipse non ageret; baptismus autem novæ legis non denominatur a ministro, qui principalem baptismi effectum non agit, scilicet interiorem emundationem.

2. Ad secundum dicendum quod tota doctrina et operatio Joannis ordinabatur ad Christum, qui multitudine signorum et suam et Joannis doctrinam confirmavit. Si autem Joannes signa fecisset, homines ex æquo Joanni et Christo attendissent. Et ideo ut homines principaliter Christo intenderent non est datum Joanni ut faceret signum. Judæis tamen quærentibus, quare baptizaret, confirmavit suum officium auctoritate Scripturæ, dicens, *Ego vox clamantis in deserto,* etc.⁹ Ipsa etiam austeritas

---

²cf I *Corinthians* 1, 12
⁴*Exodus* 4
⁶*John* 10, 41
⁸*Matthew* 3, 11
³*Matthew* 21, 25
⁵*Hebrews* 2, 3
⁷*John* 1, 33

THE BAPTISM OF JOHN

Paul, but after Christ.[2] But that baptism is named after John, *The baptism of John, where did it come from, heaven or man?*[3] Therefore, the baptism of John was not from God.

2. Furthermore, every doctrine which proceeds anew from God is confirmed by signs; thus our Lord gave Moses the power of working signs;[4] and it is said that our faith *was first announced by the Lord himself and guaranteed to us by those who heard him, God himself confirming their witness with signs and marvels.*[5] But it is written of John the Baptist that he *worked no sign.*[6] Therefore it would seem that the baptism with which he baptized was not from God.

3. Furthermore, those sacraments which are divinely instituted are contained in certain precepts of Holy Scripture. But the baptism of John is not commanded by any precept of Holy Scripture. Therefore it would seem that it was not from God.

ON THE OTHER HAND, it is written,[7] *He who sent me to baptize with water had said to me, The man on whom you see the Spirit descend,* etc.

REPLY: In the baptism of John two aspects may be considered—namely, the rite itself of baptism and the effect of baptism. The rite of baptism was not from men, but from God, who by an interior revelation of the Holy Spirit sent John to baptize. But the effect of that baptism was from man, since it did not effect anything which man himself could not do. It was not, then, from God, except in so far as God works in all human activity.

Hence: 1. By the baptism of the New Law men are baptized interiorly by the Holy Spirit, and only God can do this. However, by the baptism of John the body alone was cleansed by water. Thus it is said, *I baptize you in water, but he will baptize you in the Holy Spirit.*[8] And therefore the baptism of John was named after him, because it effected nothing which he himself did not do. But the baptism of the New Law is not named after the minister, for he is not responsible for its main effect, which is the interior cleansing.

2. The whole teaching and work of John was ordered to Christ who, by many miracles, confirmed both his own teaching and that of John. If John, however, had worked signs, men would have paid as much attention to John as to Christ. In order that men might pay more attention to Christ, it was not given to John to work a sign. Yet when the Jews asked him why he baptized he confirmed his office by the authority of Scripture, saying, *I am the voice of one crying in the wilderness,* etc.[9] Furthermore, the very

---

[9] *John* 1, 23

vitæ ejus officium commendabat,¹⁰ quia, ut Chrysostomus dicit, *Mirabile erat in humano corpore tantam patientiam videre.*¹¹

3. Ad tertium dicendum quod baptismus Joannis non fuit ordinatus a Deo, nisi ut modico tempore duraret, propter causas prædictas:¹² et ideo non fuit commendatus aliquo præcepto communiter edito* in sacra Scriptura, sed familiari quadam revelatione Spiritus Sancti, ut dictum est.¹³

articulus 3. utrum in baptismo Joannis gratia daretur

AD TERTIUM sic proceditur.¹ 1. Videtur quod in baptismo Joannis gratia daretur. Dicitur enim, *Fuit Joannes in deserto baptizans et prædicans baptismum pœnitentiæ in remissionem peccatorum.*² Sed pœnitentia et remissio peccatorum est per gratiam. Ergo baptismus Joannis gratiam conferebat.

2 Præterea, baptizandi a Joanne confitebantur peccata sua, ut habetur *Matt.* et *Marc.*³ Sed confessio peccatorum ordinatur ad peccatorum remissionem, quæ fit per gratiam. Ergo in baptismo Joannis gratia conferebatur.

3. Præterea, baptismus Joannis propinquior erat baptismo Christi quam circumcisio. Sed per circumcisionem remittebatur peccatum originale, quia, ut Beda dicit, *idem salutiferæ curationis auxilium circumcisio in lege contra originalis peccati vulnus agebat, quod nunc baptismus agere revelatæ gratiæ tempore consuevit.*⁴ Ergo multo magi baptismus Joannis remissionem peccatorum operabatur; quod sine gratia fieri non potest.

SED CONTRA est quod *Matt.*,⁵ *Ego quidem baptizo vos in aqua in pœnitentiam*: quod exponens Gregorius dicit, *Joannes non in Spiritu, sed in aqua baptizat, quia peccata solvere non valebat.*⁶ Sed gratia est a Spiritu Sancto, et per eam peccata tolluntur. Ergo baptismus Joannis gratiam non conferebat.

RESPONSIO: Dicendum quod, sicut dictum est,⁷ tota doctrina et operatio Joannis præparatoria erat ad Christum, sicut ministri et inferioris artificis est præparare materiam ad formam quam inducit principalis artifex. Gratia autem conferenda erat hominibus per Christum, secundum illud *Joan.*,⁸ *Gratia et veritas per Jesum Christum facta est.* Et ideo baptismus Joannis gratiam non conferebat; sed solum ad gratiam præparabat tripliciter. Uno quidem modo per doctrinam Joannis inducentem homines ad fidem Christi. Alio modo assuefaciendo homines ad ritum baptismi Christi.

---

*Leonine: *tradito*, handed down
¹⁰*Matthew* 3, 4
¹²preceding art.
¹cf IV *Sent.* II, 2, 2
³*Matthew* 3, 6 and *Mark* 1, 5
⁵*Matthew* 3, 11

¹¹*In Matt.* x, 4. PG 57, 188
¹³in the corpus
²*Mark* 1, 4
⁴Homily x (*in festo Circumcis.*). PL 94, 54
⁶*In Evangelium* VII, 3. PL 76, 1101

austerity of his life commended his office,[10] because, as Chrysostom says, *it was wonderful to witness such endurance in a human body.*[11]

3. The baptism of John was ordained by God to last only for a short time for the reasons given above.[12] Therefore, it was not part of a general commandment set down in Holy Scripture, but of a certain inward revelation of the Holy Spirit, as stated above.[13]

article 3. whether the baptism of John conferred grace

THE THIRD POINT:[1] 1. It would seem so. For it is said, *John went out into the wilderness, baptizing and preaching a baptism of penance for the remission of sins.*[2] But penance and the remission of sins are accomplished through grace. Therefore, the baptism of John conferred grace.

2. Furthermore, those who were to be baptized by John *confessed their sins.*[3] But the confession of sins is ordered to their remission, which is accomplished through grace. Therefore, grace was conferred in the baptism of John.

3. Furthermore, the baptism of John is related more closely to the baptism of Christ than circumcision. But original sin was remitted through circumcision, because, as Bede says, *under the Law, circumcision brought the same saving aid to heal the wound of original sin as baptism is wont to bring now that grace is revealed.*[4] Therefore, it is all the more true that the baptism of John effected the remission of sins, which cannot be accomplished without grace.

ON THE OTHER HAND it is written, *I indeed baptize you in water for repentance:*[5] which Gregory thus explains, *John baptized, not in the Spirit, but in water, because he could not remit sins.*[6] But grace comes from the Holy Spirit, and through it sins are taken away. Therefore, the baptism of John did not confer grace.[a]

REPLY: As stated above,[7] the whole teaching and work of John was in preparation for Christ, as the helper and under-craftsman are responsible for preparing the materials for the form which the head-craftsman produces. Grace was to be conferred on men through Christ: *Grace and truth have come through Jesus Christ.*[8] And therefore, the baptism of John did not confer grace, but only prepared the way for grace in a threefold way: in one way, by John's teaching, which led men to faith in Christ; in another way, by accustoming men to the rite of Christ's baptism; and in a third

---

[7]preceding art., ad 2   [8]*John* 1, 17
[a]On the sacraments as causes of grace, cf 3a. 62. On baptismal grace, cf 3a. 69

Tertio modo per pœnitentiam præparando homines ad suscipiendum effectum baptismi Christi.

1. Ad primum ergo dicendum quod in illis verbis, ut Beda dicit,[9] super illud, *Fuit Joannes in deserto*, potest intelligi duplex baptismus. Unus quidem, quem Joannes baptizando conferebat, qui dicitur baptismus pœnitentiæ, quia scilicet ille baptismus erat quoddam inductivum ad pœnitentiam et quasi quædam protestatio, qua profitebantur homines se pœnitentiam acturos. Alius autem est baptismus Christi, per quem peccata remittuntur, quem Joannes dare non poterat, sed solum prædicabat dicens, *Ille vos baptizabit in Spiritu Sancto*.[10] Vel potest dici quod prædicabat baptismum pœnitentiæ id est, inducentem ad pœnitentiam: quæ quidem pœnitentia ducit homines in remissionem peccatorum. Vel potest dici quod per baptismum Christi, ut Hieronymus dicit super illud *Marc.*, *Prædicans baptismum pœnitentiæ, Gratia datur, qua peccata gratis dimittuntur: quod autem consummatur per sponsum, initiatur per paranymphum*,[11] scilicet per Joannem.[12] Unde dicitur quod baptizabat et prædicabat baptismum pœnitentiæ in remissionem peccatorum, non ideo quia hoc ipse perficeret, sed quia præparando ad hoc homines disponebat.

2. Ad secundum dicendum quod illa confessio peccatorum non fiebat ad remissionem peccatorum[13] statim per baptismum Joannis exhibendam, sed consequendam per pœnitentiam consequentem, et per baptismum Christi, ad quem pœnitentia illa præparabat.

3. Ad tertium dicendum quod circumcisio instituta erat ad remedium originalis peccati, sed baptismus Joannis ad hoc non erat institutus, sed solum erat præparatorius ad baptismum Christi, ut dictum est.[14] Sacramenta autem ex vi institutionis suum habent effectum.

articulus 4. utrum alii, præter Christum, baptismo Joannis baptizari debuerint

AD QUARTUM sic proceditur:[1] 1. Videtur quod baptismo Joannis solus Christus debuerit baptizari, quia, sicut dictum est,[2] *ad hoc Joannes baptizavit ut Christus baptizaretur*, sicut Augustinus dicit.[3] Sed quod est proprium Christo non debet aliis convenire. Ergo nulli alii debuerunt illo baptismo baptizari.

2. Præterea, quicumque baptizatur aut accipit aliquid a baptismo aut baptismo aliquid confert. Sed a baptismo Joannis nullus aliquid accipere poterat, quia in eo gratia non conferebatur, ut dictum est,[4] nec aliquis

---

[9] *Exposit. in Marc.*, on 1, 4. PL 92, 136
[10] *Mark* 1, 8; *Matthew* 3, 11
[11] *Exposit. in Marc.*, on 1, 4. PL 30, 592
[12] cf *John* 3, 29
[13] cf 3a. 68, 6 ad 1

way, through penance, which prepared men to receive the effect of Christ's baptism.

Hence: 1. In these words, Bede says,[9] commenting on *Mark*, *John went out into the wilderness*, a twofold baptism of penance may be understood. There is the one which John conferred by baptizing, which is called a baptism of penance, because it induced men to do penance and was a kind of protestation by which men professed their intention of doing penance. The other, however, is the baptism of Christ, by which sins are remitted, which John could not give, but only preach, saying, *He will baptize you in the Holy Spirit*.[10] Or it may be said that he preached a baptism of penance, that is, one inducing men to do penance, which penance leads men on to the remission of sins. Or it may be said, as Jerome himself says, that *through the baptism of Christ grace is given by which sins are freely remitted; but that what is completed by the bridegroom is begun by the bridesman*,[11] namely, by John.[12] For this reason it is said that *he baptized and preached a baptism of penance for the remission of sins*, not as though he himself accomplished this, but because he began the work by preparing the way.

2. The confession of sins was not made for the remission of sins,[13] to be effected immediately by the baptism of John, but to be obtained through subsequent penance and through the baptism of Christ, for which that penance was a preparation.

3. Circumcision was instituted as a remedy for original sin, while the baptism of John was not instituted for this, but was only a preparation for the baptism of Christ, as stated above.[14] [b] The sacraments, however, achieve their effect in virtue of their institution.

article 4. whether Christ alone should have been baptized by John

THE FOURTH POINT:[1] 1. It would seem so, because, as stated above,[2] *the reason why John baptized was that Christ might be baptized*, as Augustine says.[3] But what is proper to Christ should not be applied to others. Therefore no others should have received that baptism.

2. Furthermore, whoever is baptized either receives something from the baptism or confers something on the baptism. But no one could receive anything from the baptism of John, because grace was not conferred by it, as stated above.[4] Nor could anyone confer anything on baptism, excepting

---

[14]in the corpus, and art. 1
[1]cf IV *Sent.* II, 2, 3, ii
[2]art. 1
[3]*In Joan.* XIII, 6, on 3, 22. PL 35, 1495
[4]art. 3
[b]cf 3a. 37, 1 on the circumcision of Christ

baptismo aliquid conferre poterat nisi Christus, qui *tactu mundissimæ suæ carnis aquas sanctificavit.*[5] Ergo videtur quod solus Christus baptismo Joannis debuerit baptizari.

3. Præterea, si alii illo baptismo baptizabantur hoc non erat, nisi ut præpararentur ad baptismum Christi: et sic conveniens videbatur quod sicut baptismus Christi omnibus confertur, et magnis, et parvis, et gentilibus, et Judæis, ita etiam et baptismus Joannis conferretur. Sed non legitur quod ab eo pueri baptizarentur, nec etiam gentiles: dicitur enim, quod *egrediebantur ad illum Hierosolymitæ universi, et baptizabantur ab illo.*[6] Ergo videtur quod solus Christus a Joanne debuerit baptizari.

SED CONTRA est quod dicitur, *Factum est cum baptizaretur omnis populus, et Jesu baptizato, et orante, aperti sunt cœli.*[7]

RESPONSIO: Dicendum quod duplici de causa oportuit alios a Christo baptizari baptismo Joannis. Primo quidem, ut Augustinus dicit, *quia si solus Christus baptismo Joannis baptizatus esset, non deessent qui dicerent, baptismum Joannis, quo Christus esset baptizatus, digniorem esse baptismo Christi, quo alii baptizantur.*[8] Secundo, quia oportebat per baptismum Joannis alios ad baptismum Christi præparari, sicut dictum est.[9]

1. Ad primum ergo dicendum quod non propter hoc solum fuit Joannis baptismus institutus ut Christus baptizaretur, sed etiam propter alias causas, ut dictum est.[10] Et tamen si ad hoc solum esset institutus ut Christus eo baptizaretur, oportebat prædictum inconveniens vitari, aliis hoc baptismo baptizatis.[11]

2. Ad secundum dicendum quod alii qui ad baptismum Joannis accedebant non poterant quidem baptismo aliquid conferre, nec tamen a baptismo gratiam accipiebant, sed solum pœnitentiæ signum.

3. Ad tertium dicendum quod quia ille baptismus erat pœnitentiæ,[12] quæ pueris non convenit, ideo baptismo illo pueri non baptizabantur. Conferre autem gentibus viam salutis soli Christo reservabatur, qui est *expectatio gentium,* ut dicitur *Gen.*[13] Sed et ipse Christus Apostolis inhibuit gentilibus Evangelium prædicare ante passionem et resurrectionem.[14] Unde multo minus conveniebat per Joannem gentiles ad baptismum admitti.

articulus 5. utrum baptismus Joannis debuerit cessare, Christo baptizato

AD QUINTUM sic proceditur.[1] 1. Videtur quod baptismus Joannis cessare

---

[5]cf below, art. 5 note 5 [6]*Mark* 1, 5 [7]*Luke* 3, 21
[8]*In Joan.* IV, 14; V, 5. PL 35, 1412 [9]art. 1 & 3 [10]art. 1
[11]cf corpus of the art. [12]cf preceding art. [13]*Genesis* 49, 10

THE BAPTISM OF JOHN

Christ, who *sanctified the waters by the touch of his most pure flesh*.[5] Therefore, it would seem that Christ alone should have received the baptism of John.

3. Furthermore, if others were baptized with that baptism, this was only as a preparation for the baptism of Christ. And thus it would seem fitting that, just as the baptism of Christ was conferred on all, young and old, Jew and gentile, so likewise the baptism of John should be conferred on all. But we do not read that either children or gentiles were baptized by him; for it is written that *all the people of Jerusalem went out to him and were baptized by him*.[6] Therefore, it would seem that Christ alone should have been baptized by John.

ON THE OTHER HAND it is written, *Now when all the people had been baptized and while Jesus after his own baptism was at prayer, heaven was opened.*[7]

REPLY: For two reasons others should have been baptized with the baptism of John. First, as Augustine says, *if Christ alone had been baptized with the baptism of John some would have said that the baptism of John was of greater worth than the baptism of Christ, with which others are baptized.*[8] Secondly, because it was right for others to be prepared for the baptism of Christ by the baptism of John, as stated above.[9]

Hence: 1. The baptism of John was not instituted only so that Christ might be baptized, but also for other reasons, as stated above.[10] Nevertheless, even if it had been instituted only so that Christ might be baptized, it was still right for others to receive this baptism, in order to avoid the difficulty mentioned.[11]

2. Those others who went up to John to be baptized could not, certainly, confer anything on that baptism, nor did they receive any grace from the baptism; they received only the sign of penance.

3. This was a baptism of penance,[12] which made it unsuitable for children. For this reason children were not baptized with it. But it was reserved to Christ alone, who is the *expectation of the gentile peoples*, to open the way of salvation to them.[13] Indeed, Christ forbade the apostles to preach the Gospel to the gentiles before his Passion and resurrection.[14] It would have been therefore, even less fitting for the gentiles to have been admitted to baptism by John.

article 5. whether the baptism of John should have ceased after Christ was baptized

THE FIFTH POINT:[1] 1. It would seem so. For it is written, *It was to reveal*

---

[14]*Matthew* 10, 5
[1]cf below 3a. 39, 3, ad 4. IV *Sent.* II, 2, 1, i. *In Joan.* 3, 4

SUMMA THEOLOGIÆ, 3a. 38, 5

debuerit, postquam Christus fuit baptizatus. Dicitur enim *Joan.*, *Ut manifestetur in Israel, propterea veni in aqua baptizans.*[2] Sed Christo baptizato sufficienter fuit manifestatus tum per testimonium Joannis, tum per descensum columbæ, tum etiam testimonio paternæ vocis.[3] Ergo videtur quod non debuerit postea baptismus Joannis durare.

2. Præterea, Augustinus dicit, *Baptizatus est Christus, et cessavit Joannis baptismus.*[4] Ergo videtur quod Joannes post Christum baptizatum non debuerit baptizare.

3. Præterea, baptismus Joannis erat præparatorius ad baptismum Christi. Sed baptismus Christi incœpit statim Christo baptizato quia *tactu suæ mundissimæ carnis vim regenerativam contulit aquis,* ut Beda dicit.[5] Ergo videtur quod baptismus Joannis cessaverit, Christo baptizato.

SED CONTRA est quod dicitur *Joan.*, quod *venit Jesus in Judæam terram et baptizabat: erat autem et Joannes baptizans.*[6] Sed Christus non baptizavit nisi postquam fuit baptizatus. Ergo videtur quod postquam Christus fuit baptizatus, adhuc Joannes baptizabat.

RESPONSIO: Dicendum quod baptismus Joannis cessare non debuit, Christo baptizato. Primo quidem quia, ut Chrysostomus dicit, *Si cessasset Joannes baptizare, Christo baptizato, existimaretur quod zelo vel ira hoc faceret.*[7] Secundo quia si cessasset a baptizando, Christo baptizante, discipulos suos *in majorem zelum immisisset.*[8] Tertio, quia persistens in baptizando, *suos auditores mittebat ad Christum.*[9] Quarto, quia ut Beda dicit, *Adhuc permanebat umbra veteris legis, nec debuit præcursor cessare, donec veritas manifestaretur.*[10]

1. Ad primum ergo dicendum quod nondum Christus erat plene manifestatus eo baptizato: et ideo adhuc necessarium erat quod Joannes baptizaret.

2. Ad secundum dicendum quod baptizato Christo, cessavit baptismus Joannis; non tamen statim, sed eo incarcerato. Unde Chrysostomus dicit, *Æstimo propter hoc permissam esse mortem Joannis et eo sublato de medio, Christum maxime prædicare cœpisse, ut omnis multitudinis affectio ad Christum transiret, et non ultra his quæ de utroque erant, sententiis scinderetur.*[11]

3. Ad tertium dicendum quod baptismus Joannis præparatorius erat non solum ad hoc quod Christus baptizaretur, sed etiam ad hoc quod alii ad Christi baptismum accederent: quod nondum fuit impletum, Christo baptizato.

---

[2]*John* 1, 31   [3]*Matthew* 3, 11. *Mark* 1, 7. *Luke* 3, 16. *John* 1, 26
[4]*In Joan.* IV, 14. PL 35, 1412   [5]*In Luc.* I, on *Luke* 3, 21. PL 92, 358

THE BAPTISM OF JOHN

him to Israel that I came baptizing with water.[2] But once Christ was baptized he was sufficiently manifested not only by the testimony of John and by the dove coming down upon him, but also by the testimony of the Father's voice.[3] Therefore, it would seem that afterwards the baptism of John should not have been continued.

 2. Furthermore, Augustine says, *Christ was baptized, and the baptism of John ceased.*[4] Therefore, it would seem that after Christ was baptized, John should not have continued to baptize.

 3. Furthermore, the baptism of John prepared the way for the baptism of Christ. But the baptism of Christ began as soon as Christ had been baptized, because *by the touch of his most pure flesh he bestowed on the waters his regenerating power*, as Bede says.[5] Therefore, it would seem that the baptism of John should have ceased after Christ was baptized.

ON THE OTHER HAND it is written that *Jesus went into the Judaean countryside and baptized; at the same time John was baptizing.*[6] But Christ did not baptize before he himself was baptized. Therefore, it would seem that, even after Christ was baptized, John continued to baptize.

REPLY: The baptism of John did not cease after Christ was baptized. First, because, as Chrysostom says, *if John ceased to baptize*, after Christ had been baptized, *men would have concluded that he was moved by jealousy or anger.*[7] Secondly, if he had ceased to baptize while Christ continued to baptize, *he would have driven his disciples toward greater envy.*[8] Thirdly, because, while continuing to baptize, *he sent his hearers to Christ.*[9] Fourthly, because, as Bede says, *the shadow of the Old Law remained; nor should the precursor withdraw until the truth is revealed.*[10]

 Hence: 1. After his baptism, Christ was not yet fully revealed, and therefore, it was still necessary for John to continue baptizing.

 2. After Christ was baptized, the baptism of John did cease; not immediately, however, but when John was imprisoned. For this reason, Chrysostom says, *I judge that John's death was allowed to happen, and that Christ began to preach all the more after John had died, so that the allegiance of the multitude would no longer be divided among those who held different opinions regarding one or the other, but be transferred entirely to Christ.*[11]

 3. The baptism of John prepared the way not only for Christ to be baptized, but also for others to approach the baptism of Christ; and this was not established when Christ came to be baptized.

---

[6]*John* 3, 22   [7]*In Joan.* XXIX, 28. PG 59, 167   [8]ibid   [9]ibid
[10]cf *Glossa ordin.* PL 114, 369. Scotus Erigena. PL 122, 322. cf St Thomas, *Catena aurea*, on *John* 3, 23, under the name of Bede.
[11]*In Joan.* XXIX, 28, 1. PG 59, 167

articulus 6. utrum baptizati baptismo Joannis essent postea baptismo Christi baptizandi

AD SEXTUM sic proceditur:[1] 1. Videtur quod baptizati baptismo Joannis non fuerint baptizandi baptismo Christi. Joannes enim non fuit minor Apostolis; cum de eo scriptum sit *Matt.*,[2] *Inter natos mulierum non surrexit major Joanne Baptista*. Sed illi qui baptizabantur ab Apostolis, non iterum baptizabantur, sed solum modo addebatur eis impositio manuum: dicitur enim *Act.*[3] quod aliqui baptizati tantum erant a Philippo *in nomine Domini Jesu, et tunc* Apostoli, scilicet Petrus et Joannes, *imponebant manus super illos et accipiebant Spiritum Sanctum*. Ergo videtur quod baptizati a Joanne non debuerint baptizari baptismo Christi.

2. Præterea, Apostoli fuerunt baptizati baptismo Joannis: fuerunt enim quidam eorum discipuli Joannis. Sed Apostoli non videntur esse baptizati baptismo Christi: dicitur enim quod *Jesus non baptizabat, sed discipuli ejus*.[4] Ergo videtur quod baptizati baptismo Joannis non erant baptizandi baptismo Christi.

3. Præterea, minor est qui baptizatur quam qui baptizat. Sed ipse Joannes non legitur baptizatus baptismo Christi. Ergo multo minus illi qui a Joanne baptizabantur indigebant baptismo Christi.

4. Præterea, *Act.*, dicitur quod *Paulus invenit quosdam de discipulis dixitque ad eos, Si Spiritum Sanctum accepistis credentes? At illi dixerunt ad eum, Sed neque si Spiritus Sanctus est audivimus. Ille vero ait: In quo ergo baptizati estis? Qui dixerunt, In Joannis baptismate*.[5] Et sequitur quod *baptizati sunt* iterum *in nomine Domini nostri Jesu* Christi. Sic ergo videtur quod quia esse Spiritum Sanctum nesciebant, oportuit eos iterum baptizari, sicut Hieronymus dicit[6] et in epist.,[7] et Ambrosius dicit.[8] Sed quidam fuerunt baptizati baptismo Joannis, qui habebant plenam notitiam Trinitatis. Ergo non erant baptizandi iterum baptismo Christi.

5. Præterea, *Rom.*, super illud, *Hoc est verbum fidei quod prædicamus*, dicit Glossa, *Unde est ista tanta virtus aquæ, ut corpus tangat, et cor abluat, nisi faciente verbo, non quia dicitur, sed quia creditur?*[9] Ex quo patet quod virtus baptismi dependet ex fide. Sed forma baptismi Joannis significavit fidem Christi, in qua nos baptizamur: dicit enim Paulus, *Joannes baptizabat baptismo pœnitentiæ populum, dicens, in eum qui venturus est post ipsum, ut crederent, hoc est in Jesum*.[10] Ergo videtur quod non oportebat baptizatos baptismo Joannis iterum baptizari baptismo Christi.

---

[1] cf below, 3a. 66, 9, ad 2. IV *Sent.* II, 2, 4. *In Matt.* 3   [2] *Matthew* 11, 11
[3] *Acts* 8, 16 & 17   [4] *John* 4, 2   [5] *Acts* 19, 1–5
[6] *In Joel.* 2, 28. PL 25, 976   [7] Epist. LXIX, *ad Oceanum*, 6. PL 22, 660
[8] *De Spiritu Sancto* I, 3. PL 16, 713
[9] *Romans* 10, 8. Glossa ordin. PL 114, 504. cf Augustine, *In Joan.* LXXX, 3. PL 35, 1840
[10] *Acts* 19, 4

article 6. whether those baptized by John should afterwards have been baptized in Christ

THE SIXTH POINT:[1] 1. It would seem not. For John was not less than the apostles, since it is written of him, *Of all the children born of women, a greater than John the Baptist has never been seen.*[2] Now those who were baptized by the apostles were not re-baptized, but only received the imposition of hands; for it is written[3] that some were *only baptized* by Philip *in the name of the Lord Jesus;* then the apostles, namely John and Peter, *laid hands on them and they received the Holy Spirit.* Therefore, it would seem that those who received John's baptism were not obliged to receive Christ's baptism.

2. Furthermore, the apostles received John's baptism, since some of them were disciples of John.[a] But it seems that the apostles did not receive Christ's baptism, for it is written[4] that *Jesus did not baptize, but his disciples.* Therefore, it would seem that those who received John's baptism were not compelled to receive Christ's baptism.

3. Furthermore, he who is baptized is less than he who baptizes. But we do not read that John was baptized with Christ's baptism. Therefore, much less did those who had been baptized by John need to receive Christ's baptism.

4. Furthermore, it is written that Paul *found a number of disciples, and said to them: Did you receive the Holy Spirit when you became believers? And they said to him: We were never even told there was such a thing as a Holy Spirit. And he said, Then how were you baptized? And they said to him, With John's baptism.* For this reason *they were baptized* again *in the name of* our *Lord Jesus* Christ.[5] Thus it seems they needed to be re-baptized because they did not know of the Holy Spirit, as Jerome says on *Joel*,[6] and in an epistle;[7] and Ambrose too.[8] But some received John's baptism who had full knowledge of the Trinity. Therefore, these were not obliged to be baptized again with Christ's baptism.

5. Furthermore, on *Romans, This is the word of faith which we proclaim,* the *Gloss* says, *Where does this power in the water come from, that when it touches the body it also cleanses the heart, unless it be from the efficacy of the word, not because it is spoken, but because it is believed?*[9] From which it is clear that the power of baptism depends on faith. But the form of John's baptism signified the faith in which we are baptized; for St Paul says, *John baptized the people with the baptism of penance, saying that they should believe in him who was to come after him—namely, in Jesus.*[10] Therefore, it would seem that it was not necessary for those who received John's baptism to be re-baptized with Christ's baptism.

---

[a] cf *John* 1, 27

SED CONTRA est quod Augustinus dicit, *Qui baptizati sunt baptismate Joannis oportebat ut baptizarentur baptismate Christi.*[11]

RESPONSIO: Dicendum quod secundum opinionem Magistri,[12] illi qui baptizati sunt a Joanne, nescientes Spiritum Sanctum esse ac spem ponentes in illius baptismo, postea baptizati sunt baptismo Christi; illi vero qui spem non posuerunt in baptismo Joannis, et Patrem et Filium et Spiritum Sanctum credebant, non fuerunt postea baptizati, sed impositione manuum ab Apostolis super eos facta, Spiritum Sanctum receperunt.

Et hoc quidem verum est quantum ad primam partem, quod multis auctoritatibus confirmatur; sed quantum ad secundam partem est penitus irrationabile quod dicitur. Primo quidem, quia baptismus Joannis neque gratiam conferebat, neque caracterem imprimebat, sed erat solum in aqua, ut ipsemet dicit *Matt.*[13] Unde baptizati fides vel spes, quam habebat in Christum, non poterat hunc defectum supplere.

Secundo, quia quando in sacramento omittitur aliquid quod est de necessitate sacramenti, non solum oportet suppleri quod fuerat omissum, sed oportet totaliter innovari. Est autem de necessitate baptismi Christi quod fiat non solum in aqua, sed etiam in Spiritu Sancto, secundum illud *Joan., Nisi quis renatus fuerit ex aqua et Spiritu Sancto, non potest introire in regnum Dei.*[14] Unde illis qui tantum in aqua baptizati erant baptismo Joannis, non solum erat supplendum quod deerat (ut scilicet daretur eis Spiritus Sanctus per impositionem manuum), sed erant iterato totaliter baptizandi in aqua et Spiritu.

1. Ad primum ergo dicendum quod, sicut Augustinus dicit, *ideo post Joannem baptizatus est, quia non dabat baptisma Christi, sed suum: quod autem dabatur a Petro, et si quod datum est a Juda, Christi erat. Et ideo si quos baptizavit Judas, non sunt iterum baptizandi: baptisma enim tale est qualis est ille in cujus potestate datur, non qualis ille cujus ministerio datur.*[15] Et inde est etiam quod baptizati a Philippo diacono, qui baptismum Christi dabat, non sunt iterum baptizati, sed acceperunt manuum impositionem per Apostolos, sicut baptizati per sacerdotes confirmantur per episcopos.

2. Ad secundum dicendum quod, sicut Augustinus dicit ad Seleucianum, *intelligimus discipulos Christi fuisse baptizatos sive baptismo Joannis (sicut nonnulli arbitrantur), sive quod magis credibile est, baptismo Christi: neque enim ministerio baptizandi defuit, ut haberet baptizatos servos, per quos cæteros baptizaret, qui non defuit memorabilis illius humilitatis ministerio, quando eis pedes lavit.*[16]

---

[11]*In Joan.* v, 5. PL 35, 1419   [12]IV *Sent.* II, 6
[13]*Matthew* 3, 11   [14]*John* 3, 5
[15]*In Joan.* v, 18. PL 35, 1423; & v, 6. PL 35, 1417
[16]*Epistola ad Seleucianum* CCLXV. PL 33, 1088

THE BAPTISM OF JOHN

ON THE OTHER HAND Augustine says, *It was necessary for those who received John's baptism to receive the Lord's baptism.*[11]

REPLY: According to the opinion of Peter Lombard,[12] those who had been baptized by John not knowing of the existence of the Holy Spirit, and basing their hope on his baptism, were afterwards baptized with Christ's baptism; those however who did not base their hope on John's baptism, and who believed in the Father, Son and Holy Spirit, were not baptized afterwards, but received the Holy Spirit by the imposition of hands made over them by the apostles.

And this is certainly true as to the first part, and is confirmed by many authorities. But as to the second part, the assertion is thoroughly unreasonable. In the first place, because John's baptism neither conferred grace nor imprinted a character,[b] but was only *in water*, as he himself says.[13] For this reason, the faith or hope which the person baptized had in Christ could not supply for this defect.

Secondly, because, when in a sacrament something is omitted which belongs of necessity to the sacrament, not only must the omission be supplied, but the whole must be done anew. Now it is necessary for Christ's baptism that it be given not only in water, but also in the Holy Spirit: *Unless a man is born through water and the Spirit, he cannot enter the kingdom of God.*[14] For this reason, those who were baptized with John's baptism in water only, not merely had to have supplied what was lacking, namely, that the Holy Spirit be given them by the imposition of hands, but they had to be baptized all over again in water and the Spirit.

Hence: 1. As Augustine says, *For that reason, baptism was administered after John's, because he gave not Christ's baptism, but his own. That which was given by Peter, however, and if any were given by Jude, that was Christ's. And therefore, if Jude baptized anyone, these did not have to undergo re-baptism; for the baptism corresponds to him by whose authority it is given, not to him by whose ministry it is given.*[15] For this same reason those who were baptized by the deacon Philip, who gave Christ's baptism, were not re-baptized, but received the imposition of hands by the apostles, just as those who are baptized by priests are confirmed by bishops.

2. As Augustine writes to Seleucianus, *We are given to understand that Christ's disciples were baptized either with John's baptism, as some maintain, or with Christ's baptism, which is more believable. For he who did not fail in the lowly ministry of washing their feet, would not fail in the ministry of baptizing them so as to have baptized servants through whom he baptized others.*[16]

---

[b]Sacramental character, cf 3a. 63. Christian sacrament of baptism, cf 3a. 66–69

3. Ad tertium dicendum quod sicut Chrysostomus dicit, *Per hoc quod Christus Joanni dicenti, Ego a te debeo baptizari, respondit, Sine modo, ostenditur quod postea Christus baptizavit Joannem:* et hoc dicit *in quibusdam libris apocryphis manifeste scriptum esse*.[17] Certum tamen est, ut Hieronymus dicit, quod *sicut Christus fuit baptizatus in aqua a Joanne, ita Joannes a Christo erat in Spiritu baptizandus*.[18]

4. Ad quartum dicendum quod non est tota causa quare illi fuerunt baptizati post baptismum Joannis, quia Spiritum Sanctum non cognoverant, sed quia non erant baptismo Christo baptizati.

5. Ad quintum dicendum quod, sicut dicit Augustinus,[19] sacramenta nostra sunt signa præsentis gratiæ, sacramenta vero veteris legis fuerunt signa gratiæ futuræ. Unde ex hoc ipso quod Joannes baptizavit in nomine venturi, datur intelligi quod non dabat baptismum Christi, qui est sacramentum novæ legis.

---

[17] *Opus imperf. in Matt.* IV, on *Matthew* 3, 15. PG 56, 658
[18] *In Matt.* I, on 3, 13. PL 26, 30

3. As Chrysostom says, *Since, when John says, I ought to be baptized by you, Christ answers, Let it be this way for now, it follows that afterwards Christ did baptize John.* And this he says *is clearly set down in some of the apocryphal books.*[17] In any case, it is certain, as Jerome says, that *as Christ was baptized in water by John, so John had to be baptized in the Spirit by Christ.*[18]

4. The reason why they were baptized, having received already John's baptism, is not only that they did not know of the Holy Spirit, but also that they had not received Christ's baptism.

5. As Augustine says,[19] our sacraments are signs of present grace, whereas the sacraments of the Old Law were signs of future grace. From the very fact that John baptized in the name of the one who was to come, we are given to understand he did not administer Christ's baptism, which is a sacrament of the New Law.

---

[19]*Contra Faust.* XIX, 13 & 18. PL 42, 355 & 359

Quæstio 39. de baptizatione Christi

DEINDE CONSIDERANDUM est de baptizatione Christi, et circa hoc quæruntur octo:
1. utrum Christus debuerit baptizari;
2. utrum debuerit baptizari baptismo Joannis;
3. de tempore baptismi;
4. de loco;
5. de hoc quod ei sunt cœli aperti;
6. de Spiritu Sancto apparente in specie columbæ:
7. utrum illa columba fuerit verum animal;
8. de voce paterni testimonii.

articulus 1. *utrum fuerit conveniens Christum baptizari*

AD PRIMUM sic proceditur:[1] 1. Videtur quod non fuerit conveniens Christum baptizari. Baptizari enim est ablui. Sed Christo non convenit ablui, in quo nulla fuit impuritas. Ergo videtur quod Christum non decuerit baptizari.

2. Præterea, Christus circumcisionem suscepit ut impleret legem. Sed baptismus non pertinebat ad legem. Ergo non debebat baptizari.

3. Præterea, primum movens in quolibet genere est immobile secundum illum motum;[2] sicut cœlum quod est primum alterans non est alterabile. Sed Christus est primum baptizans, secundum illud *Joan.*, *Super quem videris Spiritum descendentem et manentem, hic est qui baptizat*.[3] Ergo ipsum non decuit baptizari.

SED CONTRA est quod dicitur *Matt.*, quod *venit Jesus a Galilæa in Jordanem ad Joannem, ut baptizaretur a eo*.[4]

RESPONSIO: Dicendum quod conveniens fuit Christum baptizari. Primo quidem quia, ut Ambrosius dicit, *Baptizatus est Dominus, non mundari volens sed mundare aquas, ut ablutæ per carnem Christi qui peccatum non cognovit, baptismatis vim haberent;*[5] *et ut sanctificatas aquas relinqueret postmodum baptizandis*; sicut Chrysostomus dicit super *Matt*.[6]

Secundo, quia sicut Chrysostomus dicit, *quamvis ipse non esset peccator, tamen naturam suscepit peccatricem, et similitudinem carnis peccati: propterea etsi pro se baptismate non indigebat, tamen in aliis carnalis natura opus*

---

[1] IV *Sent.* VII, 3, 2, i. *In Matt.* 3
[2] Aristotle, *Physics* VIII, 5. 256b34–257a14. St Thomas, *lect.* 9
[3] *John* 1, 33   [4] *Matthew* 3, 13
[5] *Exposit. in Luc.* II, on *Luke* 3, 21. PL 15, 1583

Question 39. the baptizing of Christ

Here[a] there are eight points of inquiry:
1. whether Christ should have been baptized;
2. whether he should have been baptized with John's baptism;
3. of the time when he was baptized;
4. of the place;
5. of the heavens being opened to him;
6. of the Holy Spirit appearing to him in the form of a dove;
7. whether that dove was a real animal;
8. of the voice of the Father testifying to him.

article 1. whether it was fitting for Christ to be baptized

THE FIRST POINT:[1] 1. It would seem that it was not. For to receive baptism is to be washed. But it is not fitting that Christ be washed, for in him there was no uncleanness. Therefore, it would seem unfitting for Christ to receive baptism.

2. Furthermore, Christ underwent circumcision in order to fulfil the Law. But baptism was not required by the Law. Therefore, he should not have received baptism.

3. Furthermore, the first cause of motion in every genus is motionless relative to that motion;[2] as the heaven, which is the first cause of change, is unchangeable. But Christ is the first cause of baptism: *The one on whom you see the Spirit come down and rest is the one who is going to baptize.*[3] Therefore, it was not fitting for Christ to be baptized.

ON THE OTHER HAND it is written, *Jesus came from Galilee to the Jordan to John to be baptized by him.*[4]

REPLY: It was fitting for Christ to receive baptism. First, because, as Ambrose says, *The Lord was baptized not because he wished to be cleansed by the waters, but in order to cleanse them, that, having been purified by the flesh of Christ that knew no sin, they might assume the power of baptism;*[5] and, as Chrysostom says, *that he might bequeath the sanctified waters to those who would be baptized afterwards.*[6]

Secondly, as Chrysostom says, *although Christ was not a sinner, nevertheless he took on a sinful nature, and the likeness of sinful flesh. For this reason, although he did not need baptism for himself, nevertheless carnal nature in*

---

[a] *Opus imperf. in Matt.* IV., on *Matthew* 3, 13. PG 56, 657
[6] cf Appendix 2

*habebat.*⁷ Et sicut Gregorius Nazianzenus dicit *baptizatus est Christus, et totum veteranum Adam immergat aquæ*.⁸

Tertio, baptizari voluit, sicut Augustinus dicit, *quia voluit facere quod faciendum omnibus imperavit*.⁹ Et hoc est quod ipse dicit, *Sic decet nos implere omnem justitiam.*¹⁰ Ut enim Ambrosius dicit, *hæc est justitia ut quod alterum facere velis, prior ipse incipias et tuo alios horteris exemplo.*¹¹

1. Ad primum ergo dicendum quod Christus non fuit baptizatus ut ablueretur, sed ut ablueret, sicut dictum est.¹²

2. Ad secundum dicendum quod Christus non solum debebat implere ea quæ erant veteris legis, sed etiam inchoare ea quæ sunt novæ legis: et ideo non solum voluit circumcidi, sed etiam baptizari.

3. Ad tertium dicendum quod Christus est primum baptizans spiritualiter, et sic non est baptizatus, sed solum in aqua.

articulus 2. *utrum Christus baptismo Joannis debuerit baptizari*

AD SECUNDUM sic proceditur:¹ 1. Videtur quod Christus non debuerit baptizari baptismo Joannis. Baptismus enim Joannis fuit *baptismus pœnitentiæ*.² Sed pœnitentia Christo non convenit, quia nullum habuit peccatum. Ergo videtur quod non debuerit baptizari baptismo Joannis.

2. Præterea, baptismus Joannis, sicut dicit Chrysostomus, *medium fuit inter baptismum Judæorum et Christi baptismum.*³ Sed medium sapit naturam extremorum.⁴ Cum ergo Christus non fuerit baptizatus baptismate legali, nec etiam baptismate suo, videtur quod pari ratione baptismate Joannis baptizari non debuerit.

3. Præterea, omne quod in rebus humanis est optimum, debet attribui Christo. Sed baptismus Joannis non tenet supremum locum inter baptismata. Ergo non convenit Christum baptizari baptismo Joannis.

SED CONTRA est quod dicitur quod *venit Jesus in Jordanem, ut baptizaretur a Joanne*.⁵

RESPONSIO: Dicendum quod, sicut dicit Augustinus, *baptizatus Dominus baptizabat, non eo baptismate quo baptizatus est.*⁶ Unde cum ipse baptizaret baptismo proprio, consequens est quod non fuerit baptizatus suo baptismate, sed baptismate Joannis. Et hoc fuit conveniens. Primo quidem

---

⁷ibid
⁸*Oration* XXXIX. PG 36, 352
⁹cf Ambrose, *Sermo de tempore* XII, 1. PL 17, 626. cf also Augustine, *Sermo supposit.* CXXXVI. PL 39, 2013
¹⁰*Matthew* 3, 15   ¹¹loc cit 90. PL 15, 1586
¹²in the corpus

*others had need of it.*⁷ And, as Gregory Nazianzen says, *Christ was baptized in order that he might plunge in the water the old Adam in his entirety.*⁸ Thirdly, he wished to be baptized, as Augustine says in a sermon on the Epiphany, *because he wished to do what he had commanded all others to do.*⁹ And this is why he says, *Thus it is fitting that we do all that justice demands.*¹⁰ For, as Ambrose says, *this is justice, that what you wish someone else to do, you do first and so encourage others by your example.*¹¹

Hence: 1. Christ was baptized, not that he might be cleansed, but that he might cleanse, as stated above.¹²

2. It was right for Christ not only to fulfil what was prescribed by the Old Law, but also to initiate what would belong to the New Law. And therefore, he wished to undergo not only circumcision, but also baptism.

3. Christ is the first cause of baptism in the Spirit. And he was not baptized in this way, but only in water.

article 2. whether it was fitting for Christ to be baptized with John's baptism

THE SECOND POINT:¹ 1. It would seem not. For John's baptism was a *baptism of penance.*² But penance is unbecoming to Christ, because he had no sin. Therefore, it would seem that he should not have been baptized with John's baptism.

2. Furthermore, John's baptism, as Chrysostom says, *was midway between the baptism of the Jews and the baptism of Christ.*³ But the midway savours of the nature of both extremes.⁴ Therefore, since Christ was not baptized with a Jewish baptism, nor yet with his own, it would seem that for the same reason he should not have been baptized with John's baptism.

3. Furthermore, whatever is best in human things should be attributed to Christ. But John's baptism does not hold the first place among baptisms. Therefore, it was not fitting for Christ to be baptized with John's baptism.

ON THE OTHER HAND it is written that *Jesus came to the Jordan to be baptized by John.*⁵

REPLY: As Augustine says, *After the Lord was baptized, he baptized not with that baptism by which he was baptized.*⁶ For which reason, since he baptized with his own baptism, it follows that he was baptized, not with his own baptism, but with John's. And this would seem fitting. First because of the

---

¹cf IV *Sent.* II, 2, 3, i. *In Matt.* 3   ²*Mark* 1, 4; *Luke* 3, 3
³Homily *de Bapt. Christi* 3. PG 49, 366
⁴Aristotle, *De part. anim.* III, 1. 661b10–11
⁵*Matthew* 3, 13   ⁶*In Joan.* XIII, 4, on *John* 3, 22. PL 35, 1494

propter conditionem baptismi Joannis, qui non baptizavit in Spiritu, sed solum in aqua.[7] Christus autem spirituali baptismate non indigebat, qui a principio suæ conceptionis gratia Spiritus Sancti repletus fuit, ut patet ex dictis.[8] Et hæc est ratio Chrysostomi.[9] Secundo, ut Beda dicit, *baptizatus est baptismo Joannis, ut baptismo suo baptismum Joannis comprobaret.*[10] Tertio, sicut Gregorius Nazianzenus dicit, *accedit Christus ad baptismum Joannis sanctificaturus baptismum.*[11]

1. Ad primum ergo dicendum quod, sicut supra dictum est,[12] Christus baptizari voluit ut nos exemplo suo induceret ad baptismum. Et ideo ad hoc quod esset efficacior ejus inductio, voluit baptizari baptismo quo manifeste non indigebat, ut homines ad baptismum accederent quo indigebant. Unde Ambrosius dicit, *Nemo refugiat lavacrum gratiæ, quando Christus lavacrum pœnitentiæ non refugit.*[13]

2. Ad secundum dicendum quod baptismus Judæorum in lege præceptus,[14] erat solum figuralis: baptismus autem Joannis aliqualiter erat realis inquantum inducebat homines ad abstinendum a peccatis; baptismus autem Christi habet efficaciam mundandi a peccato et gratiam conferendi. Christus autem neque indigebat percipere remissionem peccatorum, quæ in eo non erant, neque recipere gratiam, qua plenus erat: similiter etiam cum ipse sit veritas,[15] non competebat ei id quod in sola figura gerebatur. Et ideo magis congruum fuit quod baptizaretur baptismo medio quam aliquo extremorum.

3. Ad tertium dicendum quod baptismus est quoddam spirituale remedium: quanto autem aliquid est magis perfectum, tanto minori remedio indiget. Unde ex hoc ipso quod Christus est maxime perfectus, conveniens fuit quod non baptizaretur perfectissimo baptismo; sicut ille qui est sanus non indiget efficaci medicina.

articulus 3. utrum Christus convenienti tempore fuerit baptizatus

AD TERTIUM sic proceditur:[1] 1. Videtur quod non convenienti tempore Christus fuerit baptizatus. Ad hoc enim Christus baptizatus est ut suo exemplo alios ad baptismum provocaret. Sed fideles Christi laudabiliter baptizantur non solum ante trigesimum annum, sed etiam in infantili ætate. Ergo videtur quod Christus non debuerit baptizari in ætate triginta annorum.

2. Præterea, Christus non legitur docuisse, vel miracula fecisse ante baptismum. Sed utilius fuisset mundo si pluri* tempore docuisset,

---

* Piana: *priori*, at an earlier time.
[7]*Matthew* 3, 11   [8]3a. 34, 1
[9]loc cit. PG 49, 367
[10]*Exposit.* on *Mark* 1, 9. PL 92, 138

nature of John's baptism, that he baptized not in the Spirit, but only in water.[7] Christ, who from the very moment of his conception was filled with the grace of the Holy Spirit, did not need a baptism in the spirit, as is clear from what is said above.[8] And Chrysostom offers the same reason.[9] Secondly, as Bede says, he was baptized with John's baptism so that *through his baptism he might show his approval of John's baptism.*[10] Thirdly, as Gregory Nazianzen says, *Jesus went to receive John's baptism in order that he might sanctify baptism.*[11]

Hence: 1. As was stated above,[12] Christ wished to be baptized in order to lead us to baptism by his example. And therefore, in order that his leading us to baptism might be the more efficacious, he wished to be baptized with a baptism which he clearly did not need, that men who did need baptism might approach it. For this reason, Ambrose says, *Let no one refuse the laver of grace, since Christ did not refuse the laver of penance.*[13]

2. The Jewish baptism prescribed by the Law[14] was only figurative; on the other hand, John's baptism was, to a certain extent, real in so far as it led men to refrain from sin; Christ's baptism, however, is efficacious for cleansing from sin and conferring grace. But Christ needed neither the remission of sins, which were not in him, nor the conferral of grace, with which he was filled. And likewise, since he is *the Truth,*[15] it was not fitting for him to receive what was only a figure. And therefore, it was more fitting for him to receive the intermediate baptism than either of the extremes.

3. Baptism is a kind of spiritual remedy. Now the more perfect something is, the less remedy it needs. From this it follows that since Christ is most perfect, it is not fitting for him to receive the most perfect baptism, just as he who is healthy does not need a strong medicine.

article 3. whether the time for Christ's baptism was fitting

THE THIRD POINT:[1] 1. It would seem that Christ was not baptized at a fitting time. For Christ was baptized so that, by his example, he might induce others to receive baptism. But it is commendable that those having faith in Christ are baptized, not only before their thirtieth year, but even in infancy. Therefore, it would seem that Christ should not have been baptized when he was thirty years old.

2. Furthermore, we do not read that Christ taught or performed miracles before receiving baptism. But it would have been more beneficial to the

---

[11]Oration XXXIX. PG 36, 352. cf St Thomas, *Catena aurea,* on *Luke* 3, 21; cf also below, 3a. 66, 2
[12]preceding art.   [13]*Exposit.* on *Luke* 3, 21. PL 15, 1586
[14]*Hebrews* 9, 10   [15]*John* 14, 6
[1]cf IV *Sent.* IV, 3, 1, ii ad 1. *In Matt.* 3

incipiens a vigesimo anno vel etiam prius. Ergo videtur quod Christus, qui pro utilitate hominum venerat, ante trigesimum annum debuerit baptizari.

3. Præterea, indicium sapientiæ divinitus infusæ maxime debuit manifestari in Christo. Est autem manifestatum in Daniele tempore suæ pueritiæ, secundum illud, *Suscitavit Dominus spiritum pueri junioris cujus nomen Daniel*.[2] Ergo multo magis Christus in sua pueritia debuit baptizari et docere.

4. Præterea, baptismus Joannis ordinatur ad baptismum Christi sicut ad finem. Sed finis est prior in intentione et posterior in executione.[3] Ergo vel Christus debuit primus a Joanne baptizari, vel ultimus.

SED CONTRA est quod dicitur *Luc.*, *Factum est cum baptizaretur omnis populus, et Jesu baptizato, et orante*, etc.,[4] et infra, *Et ipse Jesus erat incipiens, quasi annorum triginta*.[5]

RESPONSIO: Dicendum quod Christus convenienter fuit in trigesimo anno baptizatus. Primo quidem quia Christus baptizabatur, quasi ex tunc incipiens docere et prædicare: ad quod requiritur perfecta ætas, qualis est triginta annorum Unde legitur quod *triginta annorum erat Joseph*, quando accepit regimen Ægypti.[6] Similiter etiam legitur de David quod *triginta annorum erat, cum regnare cœpisset*.[7] Ezechiel etiam in trigesimo anno cœpit prophetizare, ut habetur.[8]

Secundo, quia, sicut Chrysostomus dicit, futurum erat ut post baptismum Christi lex cessare inciperet. Et ideo hac ætate Christus ad baptismum venit, quæ potest omnia peccata suscipere, ut lege servata nullus dicat quod ideo eam solvit, quia implere non potuit.[9]

Tertio, quia per hoc quod Christus in ætate perfecta baptizatur, datur intelligi quod baptismus parit viros perfectos, secundum illud, *Donec occurramus omnes in unitatem fidei et agnitionis Filii Dei, in virum perfectum, in mensuram ætatis plenitudinis Christi*.[10] Unde et ipsa proprietas numeri ad hoc pertinere videtur: consurgit enim trigenarius numerus ex ductu ternarii in denarium. Per ternarium autem intelligitur fides Trinitatis, per denarium autem impletio mandatorum legis, et in his duobus perfectio vitæ christianæ consistit.

1. Ad primum ergo dicendum quod, sicut Gregorius Nazianzenus dicit, Christus non est baptizatus *quasi indigeret purgatione, nec quod aliquod illi*

---

[2]*Daniel* 13, 45
[3]cf *Sent. Philos.* PL 90, 995
[4]*Luke* 3, 21
[5]*Luke* 3, 23
[6]*Genesis* 41, 46
[7]II *Samuel* 5, 4
[8]*Ezekiel* 1, 1
[9]*In Matt.* x, 1. PG 57, 184
[10]*Ephesians* 4, 13

THE BAPTIZING OF CHRIST

world if he had taught for a longer time, beginning at his twentieth year, or even sooner. Therefore it would seem that Christ, who came for the benefit of man, should have been baptized before he was thirty years old.

3. Furthermore, the sign of wisdom divinely infused should have been most manifest in Christ. It was manifested in Daniel during his boyhood: *The Lord roused the holy spirit in a young boy, whose name was Daniel.*[2] Therefore, there is all the more reason for Christ to have been baptized or have taught in his boyhood.

4. Furthermore, John's baptism was ordered to the baptism of Christ as to its end. *But the end is first in intention and last in execution.*[3] Therefore, he should have been baptized by John either first or then last of all.

ON THE OTHER HAND, it is written, *It came to pass, when all the people had been baptized, and while Jesus after his own baptism was at prayer;*[4] and further on, *And Jesus began when he was about thirty years old.*[5]

REPLY: Christ was fittingly baptized when thirty years old. First, because Christ was baptized as though he were, thereby, beginning his work of teaching and preaching: for which purpose it is required that one be fully of age, such as thirty years old. For this reason we read that *Joseph was thirty years old*[6] when he undertook the government of Egypt. And similarly we read of David that he was *thirty years old when he began to reign.*[7] Ezekiel, too, began to prophesy when he was thirty years old.[8]

Secondly, because, as Chrysostom says, *it would happen that after the baptism of Christ the Law would begin to pass away: for this reason Christ came to receive baptism at that age which admits of all sins, in order that, by observing the Law, no one might say that he did away with the Law because he could not fulfil it himself.*[9]

Thirdly, because by Christ's being baptized when he had come fully of age, we are given to understand that baptism brings forth perfect men: *We are all to come to unity in our faith and in our knowledge of the Son of God, until we become the perfect man, fully mature with the fullness of Christ himself.*[10] And the very property of the number seems to indicate this. For thirty is arrived at by multiplying three by ten; and by the number three is implied faith in the Trinity, while ten implies the fulfilment of the commandments of the Law; and the perfection of Christian life consists of these two things.[a]

Hence: 1. As Gregory Nazianzen says, Christ was not baptized *as though he needed to be cleansed, or as though some danger would threaten him*

---

[a] The patristic allegorization of Scriptural numbers, as by Gregory, was to the taste of medieval divines.

immineret periculum differendo baptismum, sed cuivis alii non in parvum redundat periculum, si exeat ex hac vita non indutus veste incorruptionis,[11] scilicet gratia; et licet bonum sit post baptismum baptismi munditiam custodire, *potius tamen est*, ut ipse dicit, *interdum paulisper maculari quam gratia omnino carere*.[12]

2. Ad secundum dicendum quod utilitas quæ a Christo provenit hominibus præcipue est per fidem et humilitatem; ad quorum utrumque valet quod Christus in pueritia vel adolescentia non cœpit docere, sed in perfecta ætate. Ad fidem, quia per hoc apparet in eo vera natura humanitatis, quod per temporum incrementa corporaliter profecit: et ne hujusmodi profectus putaretur phantasticus noluit sapientiam suam, vel virtutem manifestare ante perfectam corporis ætatem. Ad humilitatem vero, ne ante perfectam ætatem aliquis præsumptuose prælationis gradum et docendi officium assumat.

3. Ad tertium dicendum quod Christus proponebatur hominibus in exemplum omnium: et ideo oportuit in eo ostendi id quod competit omnibus secundum legem communem, ut scilicet in ætate perfecta doceret. Sed sicut Gregorius Nazianzenus dicit, *non est lex communis quod raro contingit, sicut nec una hirundo ver facit*.[13] Aliquibus enim ex quadam speciali dispensatione secundum divinæ sapientiæ ordinem et rationem concessum est præter legem communem, ut ante perfectam ætatem officium vel præsidendi vel docendi haberent, sicut Salomon,[14] Daniel[15] et Jeremias.[16]

4. Ad quartum dicendum quod Christus nec primus nec ultimus debuit a Joanne baptizari; quia, ut Chrysostomus dicit, Christus ad hoc baptizatur *ut confirmaret prædicationem et baptismum Joannis, et ut testimonium acciperet a Joanne*.[17] Non autem creditum fuisset testimonio Joannis, nisi postquam fuerunt multi baptizati ab ipso. Et ideo non debuit primus a Joanne baptizari. Similiter etiam nec ultimus, quia, sicut ipse ibidem subdit, *sicut lux solis non expectat occasum luciferi, sed eo procedente egreditur, et suo lumine obscurat illius candorem; sic et Christus non expectavit ut cursum suum Joannes impleret, sed adhuc eo docente et baptizante apparuit.*[18]

articulus 4. utrum Christus debuerit in Jordane baptizari

AD QUARTUM sic proceditur:[1] 1. Videtur quod Christus non debuerit baptizari in Jordane. Veritas enim debet respondere figuræ. Sed figura

---

[11]Oration XL. PG 36, 400; cf St Thomas, *Catena aurea*, on *Luke* 3, 23
[12]ibid. PG 36, 384
[13]Oration XXXIX. PG 36, 352; cf Aristotle, *Ethics* I, 6. 1098a18–20; St Thomas *lect.* 10
[14]II *Kings* 3, 7   [15]*Daniel* 13, 45   [16]*Jeremiah* 1, 5

THE BAPTIZING OF CHRIST

if he were to delay baptism. But as for any other man, no small danger besets him who departs from this life without being clothed with the garment of incorruptibility,[11] namely, grace. And although it is good to remain ever clean after baptism, *nevertheless it is better,* as he says, *to be sullied for a short time now and then than to be deprived of grace altogether.*[12]

2. The benefit derived from Christ by men comes chiefly through faith and humility, to both of which he was better able to show the way by beginning to teach not in his boyhood or youth, but when he was fully mature. To faith because so his humanity is shown to be genuine, by its making bodily progress with the advance of time; and lest this progress be considered imaginary, he did not wish to show his wisdom and power before he had achieved full bodily maturity. To humility, indeed, lest anyone should presumptuously assume the position of ruling over or teaching others before reaching full maturity.

3. Christ was set before men as an example to all. And therefore it is proper that he should manifest that to which all men are subject according to the common course—namely, that he should teach after reaching full maturity. But, as Gregory Nazianzen says, *that which seldom happens is not the common law, just as 'neither does one swallow make the spring'.*[13] For, by a kind of special dispensation, in accordance with the ruling of divine wisdom, it has been granted to some, contrary to the common law, to assume the position of governing or teaching; such as Solomon,[14] Daniel[15] and Jeremiah.[16]

4. Christ should have been neither the first nor the last baptized by John. Because, as Chrysostom says, for this was Christ baptized, *that he might confirm the preaching and baptism of John, and that John might bear witness to him.*[17] But the testimony of John was not believed until after many had been baptized by him. And therefore he should not have been the first baptized by John. Similarly, he should not have been baptized last of all. For as Chrysostom says in the same passage, *As the light of the sun does not wait for the setting of the morning star, but comes forth while the latter is still above the horizon, and by its brilliance dims its shining, likewise Christ did not wait until John had run his course, but appeared while he was still teaching and baptizing.*[18]

article 4. *whether Christ should have been baptized in the Jordan*

THE FOURTH POINT:[1] 1. It would seem not. For reality should correspond to its figure. But baptism was prefigured in the crossing of the Red Sea,

---

[17]*Opus imperf. in Matt.* IV, on Matthew 3, 13. PG 56, 657
[18]loc cit   [1]cf *In Matt.* 3

baptismi præcessit in transitu maris Rubri, ubi Ægyptii sunt submersi,[2] sicut peccata delentur in baptismo. Ergo videtur quod Christus magis debuerit baptizari in mari Rubro quam in flumine Jordanis.

2. Præterea, Jordanis interpretatur descensus.[3] Sed per baptismum aliquis ascendit magis quam descendat: unde etiam *Matt.* dicitur quod *baptizatus Jesus confestim ascendit de aqua.*[4] Ergo videtur inconveniens fuisse quod Christus in Jordane baptizaretur.

3. Præterea, transeuntibus filiis Israel, aquæ Jordanis conversæ sunt retrorsum, ut legitur *Josue* et sicut etiam in *Psal.* dicitur.[5] Sed illi qui baptizantur, non retrorsum, sed in anteriora progrediuntur. Non ergo fuit conveniens quod Christus in Jordane baptizaretur.

SED CONTRA est quod dicitur *Marc.* quod *baptizatus est Jesus a Joanne in Jordane.*[6]

RESPONSIO: Dicendum quod fluvius Jordanis fuit per quem filii Israel in terram promissionis intraverunt.[7] Hoc autem habet baptismus Christi speciale præ omnibus baptismatibus, quod introducit in regnum Dei, quod per terram promissionis significatur: unde dicitur *Joan.*, *Nisi quis renatus fuerit ex aqua et Spiritu Sancto, non potest introire in regnum Dei.*[8] Ad quod etiam pertinet quod Elias divisit aquas Jordanis quando erat in curru igneo rapiendus in cœlum, ut dicitur *Reg.*,[9] quia scilicet transeuntibus per aquam baptismi per ignem Spiritus Sancti patet aditus in cœlum. Et ideo conveniens fuit ut Christus in Jordane baptizaretur.

1. Ad primum ergo dicendum quod transitus maris Rubri præfiguravit baptismum quantum ad hoc quod baptismus delet peccata; sed transitus Jordanis quantum ad hoc quod aperit januam regni cœlestis, qui est principalior effectus baptismi, est per solum Christum impletus. Et ideo convenientius fuit quod Christus in Jordane quam in mari baptizaretur.

2. Ad secundum dicendum quod in baptismo est ascensus per profectum gratiæ, qui requirit descensum humilitatis, secundum illud *Jac.*, *Humilibus autem dat gratiam;*[10] et ad talem descensum referendum est nomen Jordanis.

3. Ad tertium dicendum quod, sicut Augustinus dicit, *sicut antea aquæ Jordanis retrorsum conversæ fuerant; ita modo Christo baptizato, retrorsum peccata conversa sunt.*[11] Vel etiam per hoc significatur quod contra descensum aquarum benedictionum fluvius sursum ferebatur.

---

[2]*Exodus* 14, 22; 1 *Corinthians* 10, 2
[3]Jerome, *Epistola ad Fabiolam* LXXVIII. PL 22, 722; *De Nom. Hebr. N.T.*, on *Luke.* PL 23, 844
[4]*Matthew* 3, 16

where the Egyptians were drowned,² just as our sins are blotted out in baptism. Therefore it would seem that Christ should have been baptized in the sea rather than in the river Jordan.

2. Furthermore, *Jordan* is understood to mean *a going down*.³ But by baptism a man goes up rather than down; for this reason it is written that *as soon as Jesus was baptized he came up from the water*.⁴ Therefore it would seem unfitting for Christ to be baptized in the Jordan.

3. Furthermore, while the sons of Israel were crossing, the waters of the Jordan *were turned back*.⁵ But those who are baptized go forward, not back. Therefore it was not fitting for Christ to be baptized in the Jordan.

ON THE OTHER HAND it is written that Jesus *was baptized by John in the Jordan*.⁶

REPLY: It was by passing through the river Jordan that the sons of Israel entered the promised land.⁷ Now, this is the prerogative of Christ's baptism over all other baptisms: that it admits one to the kingdom of God, signified by the promised land. For this reason it is said, *Unless a man is born through water and the Spirit, he cannot enter the kingdom of God*.⁸ Having reference to this also is the dividing of the water of the Jordan by Elijah, who was to be snatched up into heaven in a fiery chariot;⁹ because, evidently, the approach to heaven is opened up by the fire of the Holy Spirit, to those who pass through the waters of baptism. Therefore it was fitting for Christ to be baptized in the Jordan.

Hence: 1. The crossing of the Red Sea prefigured baptism in this—that baptism blots out sin; whereas the crossing of the Jordan prefigures it in this—that it opens the gate to the kingdom of heaven: and this is the principal effect of baptism, and accomplished by Christ alone. And therefore it was more fitting for Christ to be baptized in the Jordan than in the sea.

2. In baptism one *goes up* by advancing in grace: for which it is necessary to *go down* by humility: *He gives grace to the humble*.¹⁰ And it is to this *going down* that the name of the Jordan must be referred.

3. As Augustine says in a sermon for the Epiphany, *As in the past the waters of the Jordan were turned back, so now, when Christ was baptized, sin was turned back*.¹¹ Or else this may mean that, opposing the downward flow of the waters, the river of blessings flowed upwards.

---

⁵*Joshua* 4; *Psalm* 114, 3 & 5
⁷*Joshua* 3, 4
⁹II *Kings* 2, 7
¹¹Sermon X. PL 17, 624
⁶*Mark* 1, 9
⁸*John* 3, 5
¹⁰*James* 4, 6

articulus 5. utrum, Christo baptizato, cœli debuerint aperiri

AD QUINTUM sic proceditur:[1] 1. Videtur quod Christo baptizato, non debuerint cœli aperiri. Illi enim aperiendi sunt cœli qui indiget intrare in cœlum, quasi extra cœlum existens. Sed Christus semper erat in cœlo, secundum illud *Joan.*, *Filius hominis qui est in cœlo.*[2] Ergo videtur quod non debuerint ei cœli aperiri.

2. Præterea, apertio cœlorum aut intelligitur spiritualiter aut corporaliter. Sed non potest intelligi corporaliter, quia corpora cœlestia sunt impassibilia et infrangibilia, secundum illud *Job, Tu forsitan cum eo fabricatus es cœlos, qui solidissimi quasi ære fusi sunt?*[3] Similiter etiam nec potest intelligi spiritualiter, quia ante oculos filii Dei cœli antea clausi non fuerant. Ergo videtur inconvenienter dici quod baptizato Christo, aperti fuerint ei cœli.[4]

3. Præterea, fidelibus cœlum apertum est per Christi passionem, secundum illud *Heb., Habemus fiduciam in introitu sanctorum in sanguine Christi:*[5] unde etiam nec Christi baptismo baptizati, si qui ante ejus passionem decesserint, cœlos intrare potuerunt. Ergo magis debuerunt aperiri cœli Christo patiente, quam eo baptizato.

SED CONTRA est quod dicitur *Luc., Jesu baptizato et orante, apertum est cœlum.*[6]

RESPONSIO: Dicendum quod, sicut dictum est,[7] Christus baptizari voluit, ut suo baptismo consecraret baptismum quo nos baptizaremur. Et ideo in baptismo Christi ea demonstrari debuerunt quæ pertinent ad efficaciam nostri baptismi. Circa quam tria sunt consideranda. Primo quidem principalis virtus, ex qua baptismus habet efficaciam, quæ quidem est virtus cœlestis. Et ideo, *baptizato Christo, apertum est cœlum*, ut ostenderetur quod de cætero cœlestis virtus baptismum sanctificaret.

Secundo, operatur ad efficaciam baptismi fides Ecclesiæ et ejus qui baptizatur: unde et baptizati fidem profitentur, et baptismus dicitur fidei sacramentum.[8] Per fidem autem inspicimus cœlestia, quæ sensum et rationem humanam excedunt. Et ad hoc significandum, *Christo baptizato, aperti sunt cœli.*

Tertio, quia per baptismum Christi specialiter aperitur nobis introitus

---

[1] cf below, 3a. 49, 5, ad 3. III *Sent.* XVIII, 6, iii, ad 2; XXII, 3, 1 ad 4
[2] *John* 3, 13   [3] *Job* 37, 18
[4] *Matthew* 3, 16; *Mark* 1, 10; *Luke* 3, 21
[5] *Hebrews* 10, 19
[6] *Luke* 3, 21   [7] art. 1
[8] Augustine, *Epistola ad Bonifacium* XCVIII. PL 33, 364. cf below 3a. 70, 1

article 5. whether the heavens should have been opened to Christ at his baptism

THE FIFTH POINT:[1] 1. It would seem not. For the heavens must be opened to one who needs to enter heaven, being out of it. Now Christ was always in heaven: *The Son of Man who is in heaven.*[2] Therefore, it would seem that he should not have had the heavens opened to him.

2. Furthermore, the opening of the heavens is understood either in a physical or in a spiritual sense. But it cannot be understood in a physical sense, because the heavenly bodies are impassable and unbreakable: *Have you helped him spread the vault of heaven, which is as strong as molten brass?*[3] Similarly, neither can it be understood in a spiritual sense, because the heavens were not previously closed to the eyes of the Son of God. Therefore, it would seem unfitting to say that *the heavens were opened*[4] to Christ at his baptism.

3. Furthermore, heaven was opened to the faithful through Christ's Passion: *Through the blood of Christ we have the right to enter the sanctuary.*[5] For this reason, not even those who were baptized with the baptism of Christ, and who died before his Passion, could enter heaven. Therefore, the heavens should have been opened when Christ was suffering rather than when he was baptized.

ON THE OTHER HAND it is written, *While Jesus after his own baptism was at prayer, heaven opened.*[6] [a]

REPLY: As stated above,[7] Christ wished to be baptized in order that by his baptism he might sanctify the baptism with which we were to be baptized. And therefore, in Christ's baptism there were duly manifested those things which belong to the efficacy of our baptism: concerning which efficacy there are three points to be considered. First, the principal power from which baptism derives its efficacy; now certainly, this power is from heaven. And therefore, when Christ was baptized, heaven was opened to show that, for the future, power from heaven would sanctify baptism.

Secondly, the faith of the Church and of the person baptized contributes to the efficacy of baptism; for this reason, those who are baptized make a profession of faith, and baptism is called the *sacrament of faith.*[8] Now by faith we gaze on heavenly things which surpass the senses and human reason. And in order to signify this, the heavens were opened to Christ at his baptism.

Thirdly, because the entrance to the kingdom of heaven was opened to us in a special manner by the baptism of Christ, which entrance had been

---

[a]*Mark* 1, 10 is stronger; *he saw the heavens torn apart.*

regni cœlestis, qui primo homini præclusus fuerat per peccatum.[9] Unde *baptizato Christo, aperti sunt cœli,* ut ostenderetur quod baptizatis patet via in cœlum.

Post baptismum autem necessaria est homini jugis oratio ad hoc quod cœlum introeat. Licet enim per baptismum remittantur peccata, remanet tamen fomes peccati nos impugnans interius, et mundus et dæmones qui impugnant exterius.[10] Et ideo signanter dicitur *Luc.* quod *Jesu baptizato et orante, apertum est cœlum,*[11] quia scilicet fidelibus necessaria est oratio post baptismum; vel ut detur intelligi quod hoc ipsum, quod per baptismum cœlum aperitur credentibus, est ex virtute orationis Christi. Unde signanter *Matt.* dicitur quod *apertum est ei cœlum,*[12] idest omnibus propter eum; sicut si imperator alicui pro alio petenti dicat, *Ecce hoc beneficium non illi do, sed tibi, idest, propter te illi,* ut Chrysostomus dicit super Matt.[13]

1. Ad primum ergo dicendum quod, sicut Chrysostomus dicit ibidem, *sicut Christus secundum dispensationem humanam baptizatus est, quamvis ipse propter se baptismo non indigeret; sic etiam secundum humanam dispensationem aperti sunt ei cœli; secundum autem naturam divinam semper erat in cœlis.*[14]

2. Ad secundum dicendum quod, sicut Hieronymus dicit, *cœli aperti sunt, Christo baptizato, non reseratione elementorum, sed spiritualibus oculis; sicut et Ezechiel in principio voluminis sui cœlos apertos esse commemorat.*[15] Et hoc probat Chrysostomus dicens *quod si ipsa creatura,* scilicet cœlorum, *rupta fuisset, non dixisset, aperti sunt ei: quia quod corporaliter aperitur, omnibus est apertum*[16]. Unde etiam *Marc.* expresse dicitur quod *Jesus statim ascendens de aqua vidit apertos cœlos,*[17] quasi ipsa apertio cœlorum ad visionem Christi referatur. Quod quidem aliqui[18] referunt ad visionem corporalem, dicentes quod circa Christum baptizatum tantus splendor fulsit in baptismo ut viderentur cœli aperti. Potest etiam referri ad imaginariam visionem;[19] per quem modum Ezechiel vidit cœlos apertos: formabatur enim ex virtute divina et voluntate rationis talis visio in imaginatione Christi, ad designandum quod per baptismum cœli aditus hominibus aperitur. Potest etiam ad visionem intellectualem referri,[20] prout scilicet Christus vidit, jam baptismo sanctificato, apertum esse cœlum hominibus, quod tamen etiam ante viderat esse fiendum.

3. Ad tertium dicendum quod per passionem Christi aperitur cœlum hominibus sicut per causam communem apertionis cœlorum. Oportet

---

[9]cf below 3a. 69, 7 [10]cf below 3a. 69, 3
[11]*Luke* 3, 21 [12]*Matthew* 3, 16
[13]*Opus imperf. in Matt.* IV, on *Matthew* 3, 16. PG 56, 659
[14]ibid
[15] *In Matt.* II, on *Matthew* 3, 16. PL 26, 31. *Ezekiel* 1, 1
[16] *Opus imperf. in Matt.* IV, on *Matthew* 3, 16. PG 56, 659
[17]*Mark* 1, 10

THE BAPTIZING OF CHRIST

closed to the first man through sin.⁹ For this reason, the heavens were opened to Christ at his baptism to show that the way to heaven is open to the baptized. After baptism, however, man needs to pray continually in order to enter heaven; for although sins are remitted through baptism, there still remain the inclination to sin assailing us from within, and the world and evil spirits assailing us from without.¹⁰ And therefore it is expressly stated that *while Jesus after his baptism was at prayer, heaven opened*,¹¹ because, evidently, the faithful stand in need of prayer after baptism. Or else, so we may be led to understand that it is in virtue of the prayer of Christ that heaven is opened to believers through baptism. For this reason, it is expressly stated that *heaven was opened to him*—that is, *to all for his sake*.¹² It would be as if the emperor said to one asking a favour for another, *Look, I grant this favour, not to him, but to you*—that is, *to him for your sake*, as Chrysostom says.¹³

Hence: 1. We may say with Chrysostom that *just as Christ was baptized for man's sake, though he needed no baptism for himself, so the heavens were opened to him as man, whereas in respect of his divine nature he was at all times in heaven*.¹⁴

2. As Jerome says, *the heavens were opened to Christ at his baptism, not by an unfolding of the elements, but by a spiritual vision: just as Ezekiel relates the opening of the heavens at the beginning of his book*.¹⁵ And Chrysostom proves this by saying that *if the creature*—namely, heaven—*had been sundered, he would not have said*, were opened to him, *since what is opened in a physical sense is open to all*.¹⁶ For this reason also it is said expressly that *no sooner had Jesus come up out of the water than he saw the heavens opened*;¹⁷ as though the opening of the heavens referred to a vision of Christ's. Some,¹⁸ in fact, refer this to sensory vision, and say that such a brilliant light shone round about Christ at his baptism that the heavens seemed to be opened. It can also be referred to imaginary vision,¹⁹ as the one by which Ezekiel saw the heavens opened: since such a vision was formed in Christ's imagination by the divine power and by his will, in order to signify that the entrance to heaven is opened to men through baptism. It can also be referred to intellectual vision;²⁰ inasmuch as Christ saw, after he had sanctified baptism, that heaven was opened to men; nevertheless he had also foreseen that this would be accomplished.

3. Christ's Passion is the common cause of the opening of heaven to men.ᵇ However, it is necessary to apply this cause to each one, in order that

---

¹⁸cf *Catena aurea*, on *Matthew* 3, 16. cf Origen, on *Luke* 3, 21. PG 13, 1871
¹⁹cf Jerome, on *Matthew* 3, 16. PL 26, 31. Bede, on *Mark* 1, 10. PL 92, 138
²⁰cf *Opus imperf.* on *Matthew* 3, 16. PG 56, 659
ᵇcf 3a. 49. Vol. 54, ed. T. A. R. Murphy

tamen hanc causam communem apertionis cœlorum singulis applicari, ad hoc quod cœlum introeant: quod quidem fit per baptismum, secundum illud *Rom.*, *Quicumque baptizati sumus in Christo Jesu, in morte ipsius baptizati sumus.*[21] Et ideo potius fit mentio de apertione cœlorum in baptismo quam in passione Christi.

Vel, sicut Chrysostomus dicit, *baptizato Christo cœli tantum sunt aperti; postquam vero tyrannum vicit per crucem, quia non erant necessariæ portæ cœlo nunquam claudendo, non dicunt angeli,* Aperite portas, jam enim erant apertæ, *sed,* Tollite portas.[22] Per quod dat intelligere Chrysostomus quod obstacula, quibus prius obsistentibus, animæ defunctorum introire non poterant cœlos, sunt totaliter per passionem Christi ablata; sed in baptismo Christi sunt aperta, quasi manifestata jam via per quam homines erant in cœlum intraturi.

articulus 6. utrum convenienter Spiritus Sanctus super Christum baptizatum descenderit in specie columbæ

AD SEXTUM sic proceditur:[1] 1. Videtur quod inconvenienter Spiritus Sanctus super Christum baptizatum dicatur descendisse in specie columbæ. Spiritus enim Sanctus habitat in homine per gratiam. Sed in homine Christo fuit plenitudo gratiæ a principio suæ conceptionis, quia fuit *unigenitus a Patre,*[2] ut ex supra dictis patet.[3] Non ergo debuit Spiritus Sanctus ad eum mitti in baptismo.

2. Præterea, Christus dicitur in mundum descendisse per mysterium Incarnationis, quando *exinanivit semetipsum, formam servi accipiens.*[4] Sed Spiritus Sanctus non est incarnatus. Ergo inconvenienter dicitur quod Spiritus Sanctus descenderit super eum.

3. Præterea, in baptismo Christi ostendi debuit, sicut in quodam exemplari, id quod fit in nostro baptismo. Sed in nostro baptismo non fit aliqua missio visibilis Spiritus Sancti. Ergo nec in baptismo Christi debuit fieri visibilis missio Spiritus Sancti.

4. Præterea, Spiritus Sanctus a Christo in omnes alios derivatur, secundum illud *Joan., De plenitudine ejus nos omnes accepimus.*[5] Sed super Apostolos Spiritus Sanctus descendit, non in specie columbæ, sed in specie ignis.[6] Ergo nec super Christum debuisset descendere in specie columbæ, sed in specie ignis.

SED CONTRA est quod dicitur *Luc., Descendit Spiritus Sanctus corporali specie, sicut columba, in ipsum.*[7]

---

[21] *Romans* 6, 3
[22] *loc cit,* on *Matthew* 3, 13. PG 56, 660
[1] cf below 3a. 45, 4 ad 2. 1 *Sent.* XVI, 3. *In Matt.* 3

THE BAPTIZING OF CHRIST

he enter heaven. And this is effected by baptism: *When we were baptized in Christ Jesus we were baptized in his death.*[21] For this reason, mention is made of the opening of the heavens at his baptism rather than at his Passion. Or, as Chrysostom says, *When Christ was baptized, the heavens were merely opened: but afterwards by the cross he vanquished the tyrant; since gates were no longer needed for a heaven that would never again be closed, the angels did not say, 'Open the gates,' but, 'Take them away.'*[22] In this way Chrysostom gives us to understand that the obstacles which had hitherto hindered the souls of the departed from entering into heaven were entirely removed by the Passion, but at Christ's baptism they were laid open, as though the way were now made clear by which men were to enter into heaven.

article 6. whether it is fitting that the Holy Spirit descended upon Christ in the form of a dove when he was baptized

THE SIXTH POINT:[1] 1. It would seem not. For the Holy Spirit dwells in man by grace. But in Christ the man there was the fullness of grace from the first moment of his conception, because he was the *Only-Begotten of the Father*,[2] as is clear from what has been said above.[3] Therefore the Holy Spirit should not have been sent to him at his baptism.

2. Furthermore, Christ is said to have descended into the world by the mystery of the Incarnation, when *he emptied himself, assuming the form of a slave*.[4] But the Holy Spirit did not become incarnate. Therefore it would seem unfitting to say that the Holy Spirit *descended upon him*.

3. Furthermore, that which is accomplished in our baptism should have been shown in Christ's baptism, as in an exemplar. But in our baptism the Holy Spirit is not sent in any visible way. Therefore, neither should the Holy Spirit have been sent in a visible way in Christ's baptism.

4. Furthermore, the Holy Spirit is dispensed by Christ to all others: *From his fullness we have, all of us, received.*[5] But the Holy Spirit descended on the apostles in the form, not of a dove, but of fire.[6] Therefore, neither should he have descended on Christ in the form of a dove, but in the form of fire.

ON THE OTHER HAND it is written, *The Holy Spirit descended on him in bodily shape, like a dove.*[7] [a]

---

[2] *John* 1, 14. [3] 3a. 7, 12; 34, 1
[4] *Philippians* 2, 7; cf *John* 3, 13; 6, 38 & 51
[5] *John* 1, 16 [6] *Acts* 2, 3
[7] *Luke* 3, 22
[a] cf 1a. 43, 7

RESPONSIO: Dicendum quod hoc quod circa Christum factum est in ejus baptismo sicut Chrysostomus dicit, pertinet ad mysterium omnium qui postmodum fuerant baptizandi.[8] Omnes autem qui baptismo Christi baptizantur Spiritum Sanctum recipiunt, nisi ficte accedant,[9] secundum illud *Matt., Ipse vos baptizabit in Spiritu Sancto.*[10] Et ideo conveniens fuit ut super Christum baptizatum Spiritus Sanctus descenderet.

1. Ad primum ergo dicendum quod, sicut Augustinus dicit, *absurdissimum est dicere quod Christus, cum jam triginta esset annorum, acceperit Spiritum Sanctum; sed venit ad baptismum sicut sine peccato, ita non sine Spiritu Sancto. Si enim de Joanne scriptum est quod Spiritu Sancto replebitur ab utero matris suæ; quid de homine Christo dicendum est, cujus carnis ipsa conceptio non carnalis, sed spiritualis fuit? Nunc* ergo,* idest in baptismo, *corpus suum,* idest, Ecclesiam, *præfigurare dignatus est, in qua præcipue baptizati accipiunt Spiritum Sanctum.*[11]

2. Ad secundum dicendum quod, sicut Augustinus dicit,[12] Spiritus Sanctus descendisse dicitur super Christum corporali specie sicut columba, non quia ipsa substantia Spiritus Sancti videretur, quæ est invisibilis; neque ita quod illa visibilis creatura in unitatem personæ divinæ assumeretur: neque enim dicitur quod Spiritus Sanctus sit columba, sicut dicitur quod Filius Dei est homo ratione unionis. Neque etiam hoc modo Spiritus Sanctus visus est in specie columbæ, sicut Joannes vidit agnum occisum in *Apocalypsi*;[13] illa enim visio facta fuit in spiritu per spirituales imagines corporum: de illa vero columba nullus unquam dubitavit quin oculis visa sit. Nec etiam hoc modo in specie columbæ Spiritus Sanctus apparuit, sicut dicitur I *ad Cor., Petra autem erat Christus;*[14] illa enim petra jam erat in creatura; et per significationis modum nuncupata est nomine Christi, quem significabat; illa autem columba ad hoc tantum significandum repente extitit; et postea cessavit, sicut flamma quæ in rubo apparuit Moysi.

Dicitur ergo Spiritus Sanctus descendisse super Christum non ratione unionis ad columbam, sed vel ratione ipsius columbæ significantis Spiritum Sanctum, quæ descendendo super Christum venit, vel etiam ratione spiritualis gratiæ, quæ a Deo per modum cujusdam descensus in creaturam derivatur secundum illud *Jac., Omne datum optimum, et omne donum perfectum desursum est, descendens a Patre luminum.*[15]

3. Ad tertium dicendum quod, sicut Chrysostomus dicit, *in principiis spiritualium rerum semper sensibiles apparent visiones, propter eos qui nullam intelligentiam incorporalis naturæ suscipere possunt; ut si postea non fiant, ex*

---

*Piana. *Tunc,* then
[8]*Opus imperf.*, on *Matthew* 3, 13. PG 56, 659
[9]cf below, 3a. 69, 9   [10]*Matthew* 3, 11

THE BAPTIZING OF CHRIST

REPLY: What happened with respect to Christ at his baptism, as Chrysostom says, *is connected with the mystery accomplished in all who were to be baptized afterwards.*[8] All those who are baptized with the baptism of Christ, however, receive the Holy Spirit, unless they approach it insincerely:[9] *He will baptize you in the Holy Spirit.*[10] And therefore it was fitting for the Holy Spirit to descend upon Christ at his baptism.

Hence: 1. As Augustine says, *It is most absurd to say that Christ received the Holy Spirit, when he was already thirty years old, but that when he came to be baptized, since he was without sin, he was therefore not without the Holy Spirit. For if it is written of John that, 'even from his mother's womb he shall be filled with the Holy Spirit,' what must we say of Christ the man, whose very conception in the flesh was not of the flesh, but of the spirit? Therefore now,* i.e. at his baptism, *he deigned to prefigure his body,* i.e. the Church, *in which those who are baptized receive the Holy Spirit in a special manner.*[11]

2. As Augustine says,[12] the Holy Spirit is said to have descended on Christ in bodily form, like a dove, not because the very substance of the Holy Spirit was seen, for he is invisible; nor as though that visible creature were assumed into the unity of the Divine Person; for it is not said that the Holy Spirit is a dove, as it is said that the Son of God is man by reason of union. Nor, again, was the Holy Spirit seen in the form of a dove, after the manner in which John saw the slain Lamb in the *Apocalypse*:[13] for the latter vision took place in the spirit through spiritual images of bodies; whereas no one ever doubted that the dove was seen by the eyes of the body. Nor again, did the Holy Spirit appear in the form of a dove after the manner in which it is said, *Now the rock was Christ;*[14] for the rock already had a created existence, and by way of signification was called by the name of Christ, whom it signified: whereas this dove, in order to signify on this occasion only, came suddenly into existence, and afterwards ceased to exist, like the flame which appeared in the bush to Moses.

Therefore, when it is said that the Holy Spirit descended upon Christ, it is not in the sense that the Holy Spirit was united to the dove, but rather in the sense that the dove signified the Holy Spirit which came by descending upon Christ; or again, in the sense of spiritual grace which is dispensed by God to the creature by way, as it were, of a descent: *Every good gift and every perfect gift is from above, coming down from the Father of Lights.*[15]

3. As Chrysostom says, *at the beginning of anything spiritual, sensible visions are always manifest, for the sake of those who are unable to have any understanding of what is incorporeal; so that, though afterwards no such*

---

[11]*De Trinitate* XV, 26 & 46. PL 42, 1093 & 1094
[12]ibid II, 5. PL 42, 851   [13]*Apocalypse* 5, 6
[14]I Corinthians 10, 4   [15]*James* I, 17

his quæ semel facta sunt, recipiant fidem.[16] Et ideo circa Christum baptizatum corporali specie Spiritus Sanctus visibiliter descendit, ut super omnes baptizatos* invisibiliter postea credatur descendere.

4. Ad quartum dicendum quod Spiritus Sanctus in specie columbæ apparuit super Christum baptizatum, propter quatuor. Primo quidem propter dispositionem quæ requiritur in baptizato, ut scilicet non fictus accedat,[17] quia, sicut dicitur *Sap.*, *Spiritus Sanctus disciplinæ effugiet fictum.*[18] Columba autem est animal simplex, astutia et dolo carens; unde dicitur *Matt.*, *Estote simplices, sicut columbæ.*[19]

Secundo, ad designandum septem dona Spiritus Sancti, quæ columba suis proprietatibus significat.[20] Columba enim secus fluenta habitat, ut inde, viso accipitre, mergat se et evadat: quod pertinet ad donum sapientiæ, per quam sancti secus Scripturæ divinæ fluenta resident, ut incursum diaboli evadant. Item columba meliora grana eligit: quod pertinet ad donum scientiæ, qua sancti sententias* sanas, quibus pascantur, eligunt. Item columba alienos pullos nutrit: quod pertinet ad donum consilii, quo sancti eos homines, qui fuerunt pulli, idest imitatores diaboli, doctrina nutriunt et exemplo. Item columba non lacerat rostro: quod pertinet ad donum intellectus, quo sancti bonas sententias lacerando non pervertunt, hæreticorum more. Item columba felle caret: quod pertinet ad donum pietatis, per quam sancti ira irrationabili carent. Item columba in cavernis petræ nidificat: quod pertinet ad donum fortitudinis, qua sancti in plagis mortis Christi, qui est petra firma, nidum ponunt, idest suum refugerium et spem. Item columba gemitum pro cantu habet: quod pertinet ad donum timoris, quo sancti delectantur in gemitu pro peccatis.

Tertio apparuit Spiritus Sanctus in specie columbæ propter effectum baptismi, qui est remissio peccatorum, et reconciliatio ad Deum. Columba enim est animal mansuetum: et ideo, sicut Chrysostomus dicit, *in diluvio apparuit hoc animal, ramum ferens olivæ, et communem orbis terrarum tranquillitatem annuntians: et nunc etiam columba apparet in baptismo, liberatorem nobis demonstrans.*[21]

Quarto, apparuit Spiritus Sanctus in specie columbæ super Dominum baptizatum, ad designandum communem effectum baptismi, qui est constructio ecclesiasticæ unitatis. Unde dicitur *Eph.*, quod Christus *tradidit semetipsum, ut exhiberet sibi gloriosam Ecclesiam, non habentem maculam*

---

*Piana: *baptizandos*
*Piana: *scientias*
[16]*In Matt.* XII. PG 57, 205
[17]cf below, 3a. 69, 9
[18]*Wisdom* 1, 5
[19]*Matthew* 10, 16
[20]cf *Catena aurea*, on *Matthew* 3, 16, under the name of Rabanus. cf PL 107, 777

THE BAPTIZING OF CHRIST

things occur, they may receive the faith on the basis of what has occurred once only.[16] And therefore the Holy Spirit descended visibly in bodily form, upon Christ when he was baptized, so that we may believe him to descend invisibly upon all who are baptized afterwards.

4. The Holy Spirit appeared over Christ at his baptism, in the form of a dove, for four reasons. First, because of the disposition required in the one baptized—namely, that he approach in good faith:[17] for it is written, *The holy spirit of instruction shuns deceit.*[18] For the dove is a guileless animal, void of cunning and deceit; for which reason it is said: *Be guileless as doves.*[19]

Secondly, in order to designate the seven gifts of the Holy Spirit, which the dove signifies by its properties.[20] For the dove dwells beside the running stream, in order that, on perceiving the hawk, it may plunge in and escape. This refers to the gift of wisdom, by which the saints dwell beside the running waters of Holy Scripture, in order to escape the assaults of the devil. In the same way, the dove selects choice seed. This refers to the gift of knowledge, by which the saints select sound doctrines, with which they are nourished. In the same way, the dove feeds the brood of other birds. This refers to the gift of counsel, with which the saints, by their teaching and example, feed men who have been the brood, i.e. imitators, of the devil. In the same way, the dove does not tear apart with its beak. This refers to the gift of understanding, with which the saints do not tear apart sound doctrines, as heretics do. In the same way, the dove has no gall. This refers to the gift of piety, by means of which the saints are free of unreasonable anger. In the same way, the dove makes its nest in the cleft of a rock. This refers to the gift of fortitude, with which the saints build their nest, i.e. take refuge and hope, in the death wounds of Christ, the immovable Rock. In the same way, the dove's song is plaintive rather than joyful. This refers to the gift of fear, by which the saints delight in bewailing sins.

Thirdly, the Holy Spirit appeared in the form of a dove because of the proper effect of baptism, which is the remission of sins and reconciliation with God: for the dove is a gentle animal. And therefore, as Chrysostom says, *at the deluge this animal appeared bearing an olive branch and announcing universal peace to the whole world: and now again at the baptism the dove appears, pointing to our deliverance.*[21]

Fourthly, the Holy Spirit appeared in the form of a dove over our Lord at his baptism in order to designate the common effect of baptism, which is the building up of the unity of the Church. For this reason it is written: *Christ delivered himself up in order that he might present to himself the Church in all her glory, not having spot or wrinkle or any such thing, bathing her in*

---

[21] *In Matt.* XII, 3. PG 57, 205

*aut rugam, aut aliquid hujusmodi; lavans eam lavacro aquæ in verbo vitæ.*²² Et ideo convenienter Spiritus Sanctus in baptismo demonstratus est in specie columbæ, quæ est animal amicabile et gregale.²³ Unde et *Cant.* dicitur de Ecclesia, *Una est columba mea.*²⁴

Super Apostolos autem in specie ignis Spiritus Sanctus descendit, propter duo. Primo quidem ad ostendendum fervorem, quo corda eorum erant commovenda, ad hoc quod Christum ubique inter pressuras prædicarent: et ideo etiam in igneis linguis apparuit. Unde Augustinus dicit, *Duobus modi ostendit visibiliter* Dominus Spiritum Sanctum, scilicet *per columbam super Dominum baptizatum, et per ignem super discipulos congregatos: ibi simplicitas, hic fervor ostenditur. Ergo ne spiritu sanctificati dolum habeant, in columba demonstratus est; et ne simplicitas frigida remaneat, in igne demonstratus est. Nec te moveat, quia linguæ divisæ sunt: unitatem in columba cognosce.*²⁵

Secundo, quia, sicut Chrysostomus dicit, *cum oportebat delictis ignoscere,* quod fit in baptismo, *mansuetudo necessaria erat,* quæ demonstratur in columba; *sed ubi adepti sumus gratiam, restat judicii tempus,* quod significatur per ignem.²⁶

articulus 7. utrum illa columba, in qua apparuit Spiritus Sanctus, fuerit verum anima

AD SEPTIMUM sic proceditur.¹ 1. Videtur quod illa columba in qua Spiritus Sanctus apparuit non fuerit verum animal. Illud enim videtur specie tenus apparere quod secundum similitudinem apparet. Sed *Luc.* dicitur quod *descendit Spiritus Sanctus corporali specie, sicut columba, in ipsum.*² Non ergo fuit vera columba, sed quædam similitudo columbæ.

2. Præterea, sicut natura nihil facit frustra, ita nec Deus, ut dicitur in I *de Cœlo.*³ Sed cum columba illa non advenerit, nisi *ut aliquid significaret, atque præteriret,* ut Augustinus dicit,⁴ frustra fuisset vera columba, quia hoc ipsum fieri poterat per columbæ similitudinem. Non ergo illa columba fuit verum animal.

3. Præterea, proprietates cujuslibet rei ducunt in cognitionem naturæ illius rei. Si ergo fuisset illa columba verum animal, proprietates columbæ significassent naturam veri animalis, non autem effectus Spiritus Sancti. Non ergo videtur quod illa columba fuerit verum animal.

SED CONTRA est quod Augustinus dicit, *Neque hoc ita dicimus, ut Dominum Jesum Christum dicamus solum verum corpus habuisse, Spiritum autem*

²²*Ephesians* 5, 25
²³cf below, 3a. 37, 3 ad 4
²⁴*Canticle of Canticles* 6, 8
²⁵*In Joan.* VI, 3, on *John* 1, 32. PL 35, 1426. cf 1a. 43, 7 ad 6

THE BAPTIZING OF CHRIST

water with the word of life.[22] And therefore, it was fitting for the Holy Spirit to appear at the baptism in the form of a dove, which is an animal both friendly and gregarious.[23] For this reason it is said of the Church, *One is my dove.*[24]

On the apostles, however, the Holy Spirit descended in the form of fire, for two reasons. First, to show the fervour with which their hearts would be moved to preach Christ everywhere, though surrounded by opposition. And therefore also he appeared as tongues of fire. For this reason Augustine says, our Lord *manifests* the Holy Spirit *visibly in two ways*—namely, *by the dove, over our Lord at his baptism; by fire, over the disciples gathered together. In the former case simplicity is shown, in the latter fervour. We learn, then, from the dove, that those who are sanctified by the Spirit should be without guile: and from the fire, that their simplicity should not remain cold. Nor let it disturb anyone that the tongues were divided: in the dove recognize unity.*[25]

Secondly, because, as Chrysostom says,[26] *When sins had to be forgiven*, which is effected in baptism, *meekness was necessary;* this is shown by the dove. *But when we have obtained grace we look forward to the time of judgment;* and this is signified by the fire.

article 7. whether the dove in which the Holy Spirit appeared was real

THE SEVENTH POINT:[1] 1. It would seem not. For whatever appears as a semblance would seem to be mere outward shape. But it is stated, *The Holy Spirit descended on him in bodily shape, like a dove.*[2] Therefore, it was not a real dove, but a certain semblance of a dove.

2. Furthermore, just as *nature does nothing useless*, so *neither does God*, according to the *De Cœlo*.[3] But since this dove came only *to signify something and then pass away*, as Augustine says,[4] a real dove would have been useless, since the same thing could have been achieved by using the semblance of a dove. Therefore it was not a real dove.

3. Furthermore, the properties of a thing lead to knowledge of its nature. If, therefore, this dove were real, its properties would have signified the nature of a real dove and not the effect of the Holy Spirit. Therefore it would seem that it was not a real dove.

ON THE OTHER HAND Augustine says, *Nor do we say this as if to say that our Lord Jesus Christ alone had a real body, and that the Holy Spirit*

---

[26]*Catena aurea*, on *Luke* 3, 22, under the name of Chrysostom
[1]cf I *Sent.* XVI, 3 ad 3. *In Joan.* I, lect. 14   [2]*Luke* 3, 22
[3]*De Cœlo* I, 4. 271a33. St Thomas, lect. 8
[4]*De Trinitate* II, 6. PL 42, 853

Sanctum fallaciter apparuisse oculis hominum; sed ambo illa corpora vera esse credimus.[5]

RESPONSIO: Dicendum quod, sicut supra dictum est,[6] non decebat ut Filius Dei qui est veritas Patris aliqua fictione uteretur. Et ideo non phantasticum, sed verum corpus accepit. Et quia Spiritus Sanctus dicitur *spiritus veritatis,* ut patet *Joan.*,[7] ideo etiam ipse veram columbam formavit in qua appareret, licet non assumeret ipsam in unitatem personæ. Unde post prædicta verba Augustinus subdit, *Sicut non oportebat ut homines falleret Filius Dei, sic etiam non oportebat ut falleret Spiritus Sanctus. Sed omnipotenti Deo, qui universam creaturam ex nihilo fabricavit, non erat difficile verum corpus columbæ sine aliarum columbarum ministerio figurare; sicut non fuit ei difficile verum corpus in utero Mariæ sine virili semine fabricare; cum creatura corporea et in visceribus fœminæ ad formandum hominem, et in ipso mundo ad formandam columbam, imperio Domini voluntatique serviret.*[8]

1. Ad primum ergo dicendum quod Spiritus Sanctus dicitur descendisse in specie vel similitudine columbæ, non ad excludendam veritatem columbæ, sed ad ostendendum quod ipse non apparuit in specie suæ substantiæ.

2. Ad secundum dicendum quod non fuit superfluum formare veram columbam, ut in ea Spiritus Sanctus appareret, quia per ipsam veritatem columbæ significatur veritas Spiritus Sancti et effectuum ejus.

3. Ad tertium dicendum quod proprietates columbæ eodem modo ducunt ad significandam naturam columbæ, et ad significandos effectus Spiritus Sancti. Per hoc enim quod columba habet tales proprietates, ostenditur quod columba significat Spiritum Sanctum.[9]

articulus 8. utrum convenienter, Christo baptizato, fuerit vox Patris audita Filium protestantis

AD OCTAVUM sic proceditur:[1] Videtur quod inconvenienter, Christo baptizato, fuerit vox Patris audita Filium protestantis; Filius enim et Spiritus Sanctus, secundum hoc quod sensibiliter apparuerunt, dicuntur visibiliter esse missi. Sed Patri non convenit mitti, ut patet per Augustinum.[2] Ergo etiam nec apparere.

2. Præterea, vox est significativa verbi in corde concepti.[3] Sed Pater non est Verbum. Ergo inconvenienter manifestatur in voce.

3. Præterea, homo Christus non incœpit esse filius Dei in baptismo,

---

[5]*De Agone Christiano* 22. PL 40, 303
[6]3a. 5, 1   [7]*John* 16, 13
[8]*De Agone Christiano,* loc cit
[9]cf preceding art., ad 4.

THE BAPTIZING OF CHRIST

falsely appeared to men's eyes: but we believe that both those bodies were real.[5]

REPLY: As stated above,[6] it was not becoming for the Son of God, who is the Truth of the Father, to make use of any pretence; and therefore he took, not an imaginary, but a real body. And since the Holy Spirit is called the *Spirit of Truth*,[7] therefore he too made a real dove in which to appear, though he did not assume it into the unity of his person.[a] For this reason, after the words quoted above, Augustine adds, *Just as it behoved the Son of God not to deceive men, so it behoved the Holy Spirit not to deceive. But it was easy for Almighty God, who created all creatures out of nothing, to fashion the real body of a dove without the help of other doves, just as it was easy for him to form a real body in Mary's womb without the seed of a man: since the corporeal creature obeys the command and will of its Lord, both in the mother's womb in forming a man, and in the world itself in forming a dove.*[8]

Hence: 1. When it is said that the Holy Spirit descended in the shape or semblance of a dove, it is not in order to exclude the reality of the dove, but to show that he did not appear in the form of his own substance.

2. It was not superfluous to form a real dove in which the Holy Spirit might appear, because by the very reality of the dove the reality of the Holy Spirit and his effects is signified.

3. The properties of the dove tend to signify in the same way the nature of the dove and the effects of the Holy Spirit. For it is by means of such properties that the dove happens to signify the Holy Spirit.[9]

article 8. whether it was fitting, when Christ was baptized, for the Father's voice to be heard bearing witness to the Son

THE EIGHTH POINT:[1] 1. It would seem not. For the Son and the Holy Spirit, in so far as they have appeared visibly, are said to have been visibly sent. But it is not fitting for the Father to be sent, as Augustine makes clear.[2a] Therefore, neither for him to appear.

2. Furthermore, the voice expresses the word conceived in the heart.[3] But the Father is not the Word. Therefore he is unfittingly manifested by a voice.

3. Furthermore, Christ the man did not begin to be Son of God at his

---

[1] cf below 3a. 45, 4; 66, 6. I *Sent.* XVI, 3
[2] *De Trinitate* II, 5 & 12. PL 42, 849 & 859
[3] Aristotle, *Periherm.* I, 1. 16a13–14; St Thomas, *lect.* 2
[a] The author's reluctance to give up Augustine is less pronounced in I *Sent.* XVI, 3. Cajetan comments in loc not a real dove, but a real corporeal substance.
[a] The sendings or 'missions' of the blessed Persons of the Trinity, cf 1a. 43.

sicut quidam hæretici putaverunt,[4] sed a principio suæ conceptionis fuit filius Dei. Magis ergo in nativitate debuit vox Patris protestari Christi divinitatem quam in ejus baptismo.

SED CONTRA est quod *Matt.* dicitur, *Ecce vox de cœlis dicens, Hic est Filius meus dilectus, in quo mihi complacui.*[5]

RESPONSIO: Dicendum quod, sicut supra dictum est,[6] in baptismo Christi, qui fuit exemplar nostri baptismi, demonstrari debuit quod in nostro baptismo perficitur. Baptismus autem quo baptizantur fideles consecratur in invocatione et virtute Trinitatis, secundum illud *Matt.*, *Euntes docete omnes gentes, baptizantes eos in nomine Patris, et Filii, et Spiritus Sancti.*[7] Et ideo *in baptismo Christi*, ut Hieronymus dicit, *mysterium Trinitatis demonstratur. Dominus enim in natura humana baptizatur; Spiritus Sanctus descendit in specie columbæ; Patris vox testimonium Filio perhibentis auditur.*[8] Et ideo conveniens fuit ut in illo baptismo Pater declararetur in voce.

1. Ad primum ergo dicendum quod missio visibilis addit aliquid super apparitionem, scilicet auctoritatem mittentis. Et ideo Filius et Spiritus Sanctus, qui sunt ab alio, dicuntur mitti visibiliter, et non solum apparere; Pater autem qui non est ab alio, apparere quidem potest, visibiliter autem mitti non potest.[9]

2. Ad secundum dicendum quod Pater non demonstratur in voce, nisi sicut auctor vocis vel loquens per vocem: et quia proprium est Patri producere Verbum, quod est dicere vel loqui, ideo convenientissime Pater per vocem manifestatus est, quæ significat Verbum. Unde et ipsa vox a Patre emissa filiationem Verbi protestatur. Et sicut species columbæ, in qua demonstratus est Spiritus Sanctus, non est ipsa natura Spiritus Sancti; nec species hominis, in qua demonstratus est ipse Filius, est ipsa natura Filii Dei; ita etiam ipsa vox non pertinet ad naturam Verbi vel Patris loquentis. Unde Dominus dicit, *Neque vocem ejus*, idest Patris, *unquam audistis, neque speciem ejus vidistis.*[10] Per quod, sicut Chrysostomus dicit, *paulatim eos in philosophicum dogma inducens ostendit quoniam neque vox circa Deum est, neque species; sed superior est et figuris, et loquelis talibus.*[11] Et sicut columbam et etiam humanam naturam a Christo assumptam tota Trinitas operata est, ita etiam et formationem vocis; sed tamen in voce declaratur solus Pater ut loquens; sicut naturam humanam solus Filius

---

[4]Ebion and Cerinthus; cf Epiphanius, *De Hær.* PG 41, 380, 429, 897, 925
[5]*Matthew* 3, 17   [6]art. 5
[7]*Matthew* 28, 19
[8]On *Matthew* 3, 16. PL 26, 31
[9]cf 1a. 43, 4
[10]*John* 5, 37

baptism, as some heretics have supposed:[4] but he was the Son of God from the first moment of his conception. Therefore the Father's voice should have borne witness to Christ's divinity at his birth rather than at his baptism.

ON THE OTHER HAND it is written, *Behold, a voice from the heavens said, This is my beloved Son in whom I am well pleased.*[5]

REPLY: As stated above,[6] what is accomplished in our baptism should be manifested in Christ's baptism, which was the exemplar of ours. Now the baptism which the faithful receive is sanctified by the invocation and the power of the Trinity: *Go, therefore, make disciples of all the nations; baptize them in the name of the Father and of the Son and of the Holy Spirit.*[7] And therefore, as Jerome says, *The mystery of the Trinity is manifested in Christ's baptism. Our Lord himself is baptized in his human nature; the Holy Spirit descended in the form of a dove; the Father's voice is heard bearing witness to the Son.*[8] And therefore it was fitting that in that baptism the Father should be manifested by a voice.

Hence: 1. The visible sending adds something to the appearance, namely, the authority of the sender. Therefore the Son and the Holy Spirit who are from another, are said not only to appear, but also to be sent visibly. But the Father, who is not from another, can certainly appear, but cannot be sent visibly.[9]

2. The Father is manifested by the voice, only as the originator of the voice, or speaking by means of it. And since it is proper to the Father to produce the Word—that is, to utter or to speak—therefore it was most fitting that the Father should be manifested by a voice, which signifies the Word. And for this reason, the very voice to which the Father gave utterance bore witness to the Sonship of the Word. And just as the form of the dove, in which the Holy Spirit was manifested, is not the nature of the Holy Spirit, nor is the form of man in which the Son himself was manifested, the very nature of the Son of God, so neither does the voice belong to the nature of the Word or of the Father who spoke. For this reason our Lord says of the Father, *You have never heard his voice, you have never seen his form.*[10] By which words, as Chrysostom says, *gradually leading them to knowledge of the philosophical truth, he shows them that God has neither voice nor shape, but is above all such forms and utterances.*[11] And just as the entire Trinity was operative in making both the dove and the human nature assumed by Christ, so likewise it was operative in forming the voice; yet by the voice the Father alone is manifested as speaking, just as

---

[11]*In Joan.* XL. PG 59, 232

assumpsit, et sicut in columba solus Spiritus Sanctus demonstratus est, ut patet per Augustinum.¹²

3. Ad tertium dicendum quod divinitas Christi non debuit omnibus in ejus nativitate manifestari, sed magis occultari in defectibus infantilis ætatis. Sed quando jam pervenit ad perfectam ætatem, in qua oportebat eum docere et miracula facere, et homines ad se convertere, tunc testimonio Patris erat ejus divinitas manifestanda, ut ejus doctrina credibilior fieret: unde et ipse dicit, *Qui misit me Pater, ipse testimonium perhibet de me.*¹³ Et hoc præcipue in baptismo, per quem homines renascuntur in filios Dei adoptivos. Filii autem Dei adoptivi instituuntur ad similitudinem filii naturalis, secundum illud *Rom., Quos præscivit, hos et prædestinavit conformes fieri imaginis Filii sui.*¹⁴ Unde Hilarius dicit quod *super Jesum baptizatum descendit Spiritus Sanctus, et vox Patris audita est dicentis, Hic est filius meus dilectus, ut ex his quæ consummabantur in Christo, cognosceremus post aquæ lavacrum et de cœlestibus portis* sanctum in nos Spiritum involare, et paternæ vocis adoptione Dei filios fieri.*¹⁵

---

*Leonine: *partibus*
¹²Fulgentius, *De Fide ad Petram* 9. PL 40, 770
¹³*John* 5, 37   ¹⁴*Romans* 8, 29

the Son alone assumed human nature and the Holy Spirit alone is manifested in the dove, as Augustine makes clear.[12]

3. It was not proper for the divinity of Christ to be manifested to all at his birth, but rather to remain hidden in the deficiencies of infancy. But as soon as he came of age, when it was opportune for him to teach, to work miracles and to direct men to himself, then his divinity had to be pointed out by the testimony of the Father, so that his teaching might become the more credible. For this reason he also says, *The Father who sent me bears witness to me himself.*[13] And this especially at the time of baptism, by which men are born again as adopted sons of God; for the adopted sons of God are made to be like unto his natural Son: *Those whom he has foreknown he has also predestined to become conformed to the image of his Son.*[14] For which reason Hilary says that the Holy Spirit descended upon Jesus at his baptism, and the voice of the Father was heard saying, This is my beloved Son, *in order that we might know from what was accomplished in Christ, that after being washed in the waters of baptism, the Holy Spirit comes down upon us from on high and the voice of the Father declares us to have become sons of God by adoption.*[15]

---

[15] *In Matt.* 2, 6. PL 9, 927

CONSEQUENTER POST EA QUÆ pertinent ad ingressum Christi in mundum vel ad ejus principium, considerandum restat de his quæ pertinent ad progressum ipsius.

Et primo considerandum est de modo conversationis ipsius;
secundo, de tentatione ejus;
tertio, de doctrina;
quarto, de miraculis.

Quæstio 40. de modo conversationis Christi

Circa primum quæruntur quatuor:

1. utrum Christus debuerit solitariam vitam ducere, an inter homines conversari;
2. utrum debuerit austeram vitam ducere in cibo, et potu, et vestitu, an cum aliis communem;
3. utrum debuerit abjecte vivere in hoc mundo, an in divitiis et honore;
4. utrum debuerit secundum legem vivere.

articulus 1. *utrum conveniens fuerit Christum inter homines conversari*

AD PRIMUM sic proceditur.[1] 1. Videtur quod Christus non debuerit inter homines conversari, sed solitariam vitam agere. Oportebat enim quod Christus sua conversatione non solum se hominem ostenderet esse, sed etiam Deum. Sed Deum non convenit cum hominibus conversari: dicitur enim *Dan.*, *Exceptis diis quorum non est cum hominibus conversatio;*[2] et Philosophus dicit quod *ille qui solitarius vivit, aut est bestia,* si scilicet propter sævitiam hoc faciat, *aut est Deus,*[3] si hoc faciat propter contemplandam veritatem. Ergo videtur quod non fuerit conveniens Christum inter homines conversari.

2. Præterea, Christus, dum in carne mortali vixit, debuit perfectissimam vitam ducere. Perfectissima autem vita est contemplativa, ut in secunda parte habitum est.[4] Ad vitam autem contemplativam maxime competit solitudo, secundum illud, *Ducam eam in solitudinem, et loquar ad cor ejus.*[5] Ergo videtur quod Christus debuerit solitariam vitam ducere.

3. Præterea, conversatio Christi debuit esse uniformis, quia semper in

---

[1] cf 2a2æ. 25, 6 ad 5   [2] *Daniel* 2, 11
[3] *Politics* 1. 1253a29. St Thomas, *lect.* 1   [4] 2a2æ. 182, 1 & 2

CHRIST'S MANNER OF LIFE

FOLLOWING THE MATTERS which relate to Christ's coming into the world or to the beginning of his life, it remains for us to consider those which relate to his life as it advanced.

We must first consider his manner of life (40);[a]
secondly, his temptation (41);
thirdly, his teaching (42);
and fourthly, his miracles (43).

Question 40. Christ's manner of life

Here there are four points to be considered:

1. whether Christ should have led a solitary life, or have associated with men;
2. whether he should have led an austere life as regards food, drink and clothing, or as is common with others;
3. whether he should have undertaken a lowly kind of life, or one of wealth and honour;
4. whether he should have lived in conformity with the Law.

article 1. whether Christ should have associated with men

THE FIRST POINT:[1] 1. It would seem that Christ should not, but have led a solitary life. For it was proper for Christ to show by his manner of life that he was not only man, but also God. But it is not fitting for God to associate with men, for it is written, *Except the gods, whose dwelling is not with men*;[2] and Aristotle says that he who lives alone *is either a beast—* that is, if he does this because he is wild—*or a god*,[3] if he does this in order to contemplate truth. Therefore it would seem that it was not fitting for Christ to associate with men.

2. Furthermore, while he lived in mortal flesh, Christ ought to have led a most perfect life. But the most perfect is the contemplative life, as we have agreed.[4] Now, solitude belongs most properly to the contemplative life, according to the prophet, *I am going to lead her out into the wilderness and speak to her heart*.[5] Therefore it would seem that Christ should have led a solitary life.

3. Furthermore, Christ's manner of life ought to have been uniform,

---

[5] *Hosea* 2, 14
[a] cf Appendix 3

eo debuit apparere id quod optimum est. Sed quandoque Christus solitaria loca quærebat, turbas declinans; unde Remigius dicit super *Matt.*, *Tria refugia legitur Dominus habuisse, navim, montem, et desertum: ad quorum alterum, quotiescumque a turbis comprimebatur, conscendebat.*[6] Ergo et semper debuit solitariam vitam agere.

SED CONTRA est quod dicitur *Baruch, Post hæc in terris visus est, et cum hominibus conversatus est.*[7]

RESPONSIO: Dicendum quod conversatio Christi talis debuit esse ut conveniret fini incarnationis, secundum quam venit in mundum. Venit autem in mundum primo quidem ad manifestandum veritatem, sicut ipse dicit *Joan.*, *In hoc natus sum, et ad hoc veni in mundum, ut testimonium perhibeam veritati.*[8] Et ideo non debebat se occultare, vitam solitariam agens, sed in publicum procedere, publice prædicando. Unde dixit illis qui volebant eum detinere, *Quia et aliis civitatibus oportet me evangelizare regnum Dei, quia ideo missus sum.*[9]

Secundo, venit ad hoc ut homines a peccato liberaret, secundum illud I ad *Tim.*, *Christus Jesus venit in hunc mundum peccatores salvos facere.*[10] Et ideo, ut Chrysostomus dicit, licet *in eodem loco manendo posset Christus ad se omnes attrahere, ut ejus prædicationem audirent; non tamen hoc fecit, præbens nobis exemplum ut perambulemus, et requiramus pereuntem, sicut pastor ovem perditam, et medicus accedit ad infirmum.*[11]

Tertio, venit ut per ipsum habeamus accessum ad Deum, ut dicitur *Rom.*[12] Et ideo familiariter cum hominibus conversando, conveniens fuit ut hominibus fiduciam daret ad se accedendi. Unde dicitur *Matt.*, *Factum est, discumbente eo in domo, ecce multi publicani et peccatores venientes discumbebant cum Jesu et discipulis ejus*[13]*;* quod exponens Hieronymus dicit, *Peccatores viderunt publicanum, a peccatis ad meliora conversum, locum invenisse pœnitentiæ; et ob id etiam ipsi non desperant salutem.*[14]

1. Ad primum ergo dicendum quod Christus per humanitatem suam voluit manifestare divinitatem: et ideo conversando cum hominibus (quod est proprium hominis), manifestavit omnibus suam divinitatem, prædicando et miracula faciendo, et innocenter et juste inter homines conversando.

2. Ad secundum dicendum quod, sicut in secunda parte dictum est,[15] vita contemplativa simpliciter est melior quam activa, quæ occupatur circa corporales actus; sed vita activa, secundum quam aliquis prædicando et

---
[6]cf *Catena aurea*, on *Matthew* 5, 1, under the name of Remigius; cf also Isidore, PL 83, 206
[7]*Baruch* 3, 38   [8]*John* 18, 37   [9]*Luke* 4, 42–3   [10]I *Timothy* 1, 15
[11]cf *Catena aurea*, on *Luke* 4, 42, under the name of Chrysostom

because there ought to be manifest in him always what is best. But at times Christ, avoiding the crowds, sought out lonely places; for which reason Remigius says, *We read that our Lord had three places of refuge: the ship, the mountain and the desert; he went off to one or other of these whenever he was pressed by the crowd.*[6] Therefore he ought always to have led a solitary life.

ON THE OTHER HAND it is written, *After this he appeared on earth and moved among men.*[7]

REPLY: Christ's manner of life had to be in keeping with the end of the incarnation, according to which end he came into the world. Now he came into the world, first, in order to manifest the truth, as he himself says, *I was born for this, I came into the world for this: to bear witness to the truth.*[8] And therefore he should not have hidden himself by leading a solitary life, but have moved about openly by preaching in public. For which reason he says to those who would hold him back, *I must proclaim the Good News of the kingdom of God to the other towns too, because that is what I was sent to do.*[9]

Secondly, he came in order to free men from sin: *Christ Jesus came into the world to save sinners.*[10] And therefore, as Chrysostom says, *although Christ might, by remaining in the same place, have drawn all men to himself to hear his preaching, yet he did not do so; he showed us by his example that we should go about and search for those who are perishing, like the shepherd who searches for the lost sheep, and the physician who attends to the sick.*[11]

Thirdly, he came so that through him *we might have access to* God, as it is written.[12] And thus, it was fitting for him to give men confidence in approaching him by associating familiarly with them. For this reason it is written, *It happened that while he was at dinner in the house a number of tax collectors and sinners came to sit at table with Jesus and his disciples.*[13] Jerome comments, *They had seen the tax collector who, having become repentant, had been converted from a sinful to a better life: and because of this they too did not despair of their own salvation.*[14]

Hence: 1. Christ wished to manifest his divinity through his humanity. And therefore, by associating with men, as is proper to man, he manifested to all his divinity by preaching and working miracles and by leading among men a blameless and righteous life.

2. As stated in the second part,[15] the contemplative life is, absolutely speaking, more perfect than the active life which is taken up with bodily actions; but the active life according to which a man, by preaching and

---

[12]*Romans* 5, 2; cf *Ephesians* 2, 18   [13]*Matthew* 9, 10
[14]*In Matt.* I, on 9, 10. PL 26, 56   [15]2a2æ. 181, 1; 188, 6

docendo contemplata aliis tradit, est perfectior quam vita quæ solum est contemplativa, quia talis vita præsupponit abundantiam contemplationis. Et ideo Christus talem vitam elegit.

3. Ad tertium dicendum quod actio Christi fuit nostra instructio.[16] Et ideo ut daret exemplum prædicatoribus, quod non semper se darent in publicum, quandoque Dominus se a turbis retraxit. Quod quidem legitur fecisse propter tria. Quandoque quidem propter corporalem quietem: unde dicitur quod Dominus dixit discipulis, *Venite seorsum in desertum locum, et requiescite pusillum: erant enim qui veniebant et redibant multi, et nec spatium manducandi habebant.*[17] Quandoque vero causa orationis. Unde dicitur, *Factum est in illis diebus, exiit in montem orare, et erat pernoctans in oratione Dei;*[18] ubi ait Ambrosius quod *ad præcepta virtutis suo nos informat exemplo.*[19] Quandoque vero, ut doceret favorem humanum vitare. Unde super illud *Matt.*, *Videns Jesus turbas, ascendit in montem,*[20] dicit Chrysostomus, *Per hoc quod non in civitate et foro, sed in monte, et solitudine sedit, erudivit nos nihil ad ostentationem facere, et a tumultibus abscedere et maxime cum de necessariis disputare oportet.*[21]

articulus 2. *utrum Christus austeram vitam in hoc mundo ducere debuerit*

AD SECUNDUM sic proceditur:[1] Videtur quod Christus debuerit austeram vitam ducere in hoc mundo. Christus enim multo magis prædicavit perfectionem vitæ quam Joannes. Sed Joannes austeram vitam duxit, ut suo exemplo homines ad perfectionem vitæ provocaret: dicitur enim *Matt.* quod *ipse Joannes habebat vestimentum de pilis camelorum et zonam pelliceam circa lumbos suos; esca autem ejus erant locustæ et mel sylvestre;*[2] quod exponens Chrysostomus dicit, *Erat mirabile in humano corpore tantam patientiam videre; quod et Judæos magis attrahebat.*[3] Ergo videtur quod multo magis Christum decuerit austeritas vitæ.

2. Præterea, abstinentia ad continentiam ordinatur: dicitur enim, *Comedent, et non saturabuntur; fornicati sunt, et non cessaverunt.*[4] Sed Christus continentiam et in se servavit, et aliis servandam proposuit cum dixit *Matt.*, *Sunt eunuchi qui se castraverunt propter regnum cœlorum: qui potest capere capiat.*[5] Ergo videtur quod Christus in se et in suis discipulis austeritatem vitæ servare debuerit.

3. Præterea, ridiculum videtur ut aliquis districtiorem vitam incipiat,

---

[16]*Instruct. Sacerdot.* 6. PL 184, 777. Innocent III, Sermon XXII. PL 217, 411
[17]*Mark* 6, 31 [18]*Luke* 6, 12
[19]*Exposit. in Luc.* V, on *Luke* 6, 12. PL 15, 1647
[20]*Matthew* 5, 1
[21]*In Matt.* XV, 1. PG 57, 223
[1]cf *In Matt.* 11

teaching, gives to others the fruits of his contemplation is more perfect than the life by which a man contemplates alone, because such a life presupposes an abundance of contemplation. And therefore, Christ chose such a life.

3. *What Christ did he did for our instruction.*[16] And therefore, in order to show preachers by his example that they ought not always to be before the public, at times our Lord withdrew himself from the crowds. We read that he did this for three reasons. Sometimes he did it for bodily rest. For this reason it is written, '*You must come away to some lonely place all by yourselves and rest for a while*', *for there were so many coming and going that they had no time even to eat.*[17] At other times he did it for the sake of prayer. For this reason it is written, *It happened at that time that he went out into the hills to pray, and he spent the whole night in prayer to God.*[18] On this Ambrose remarks that *by his example he instructs us in the precepts of virtue.*[19] And sometimes in order to teach us to avoid the favour of men. For this reason Chrysostom, commenting on the text, *Jesus, seeing the crowds, went up the mountain,*[20] says, *By sitting not in the city and in the market-place, but on a mountain and in a lonely place, he taught us to do nothing for show, and to withdraw from the crowd, especially when it is opportune to speak of needful things.*[21]

article 2. *whether it was becoming for Christ to lead an austere life in this world*

THE SECOND POINT:[1] 1. It would seem that it was. For Christ preached the life of perfection much more than John did. But John led an austere life in order to persuade men by his example to embrace the life of perfection; for it is written that *this man John wore a garment of camel's hair with a leather belt round his waist, and his food was locusts and wild honey;*[2] on which Chrysostom comments, *It was marvellous to see such austerity in a human frame: which thing also particularly attracted the Jews.*[3] Therefore it would seem much more becoming for Christ to lead a life of austerity.

2. Furthermore, abstinence is ordained to continence; for it is written, *They will eat but never be satisfied; they will commit fornication, but remain sterile.*[4] But Christ himself observed continence, and proposed that it be observed by others when he said, *There are eunuchs who have made themselves that way for the sake of the kingdom of heaven. Let anyone accept this who can.*[5] Therefore it would seem that Christ should have observed a life of austerity both in himself and in his disciples.

3. Furthermore, it would seem ridiculous for a man to begin a stricter

---

[2]*Matthew* 3, 4
[4]*Hosea* 4, 10
[3]*In Matt.* x. PG 57, 188
[5]*Matthew* 19, 12

et ab ea in laxiorem revertatur: potest enim dici contra eum quod habetur *Luc.*, *Hic homo cœpit ædificare, et non potuit consummare.*[6] Christus autem districtissimam vitam incœpit post baptismum, manens in deserto, et jejunans quadraginta diebus et quadraginta noctibus.[7] Ergo videtur non fuisse congruum quod post tantam vitæ districtionem ad communem vitam rediret.

SED CONTRA est quod dicitur in *Matt.*, *Venit Filius hominis manducans et bibens.*[8]

RESPONSIO: Dicendum quod, sicut dictum est,[9] congruum erat incarnationis fini, ut Christus non ageret solitariam vitam, sed cum hominibus conversaretur. Qui autem cum aliquibus conversatur, convenientissimum est ut se eis in conversatione conformet, secundum illud Apostoli, *Omnibus omnia factus sum.*[10] Et ideo convenientissimum fuit ut Christus in cibo et potu communiter se, sicut alii, haberet. Unde Augustinus dicit quod *Joannes dictus est non manducans, neque bibens, quia illo victu quo Judæi utebantur, non utebatur. Hoc ergo nisi Dominus uteretur, non in ejus comparatione manducans bibensque diceretur.*[11]

1. Ad primum ergo dicendum quod Dominus in sua conversatione exemplum perfectionis dedit in omnibus quæ per se pertinent ad salutem. Ipsa autem abstinentia cibi et potus non per se pertinet ad salutem, secundum illud *Rom.*, *Non est regnum Dei esca et potus.*[12] Augustinus dicit exponens illud *Matt.*, *Justificata est sapientia a filiis suis,*[13] quia scilicet *sancti Apostoli intellexerunt regnum Dei non esse in esca et potu, sed in æquanimitate tolerandi, quos nec copia sublevat, nec deprimit egestas;*[14] et dicit quod *in omnibus talibus non usus rerum, sed libido utentis in culpa est.*[15] Utraque autem vita est licita et laudabilis, ut scilicet aliquis a communi consortio hominum segregatus abstinentiam servet, et ut in societate aliorum positus communi vita utatur. Et ideo Dominus voluit utriusque vitæ exemplum dare hominibus.

Joannes autem, sicut Chrysostomus dicit, *nihil plus ostendit præter vitam et justitiam; Christus autem et a miraculis testimonium habebat. Dimittens ergo Joannem jejunio fulgere, ipse contraria incessit via, ad mensam intrans publicanorum, et manducans, et bibens.*[16]

2. Ad secundum dicendum quod sicut alii homines per abstinentiam consequuntur virtutem continendi; ita etiam Christus in se et in suis discipulis per virtutem suæ divinitatis carnem comprimebat. Unde, sicut *Matt.*

---

[6]*Luke* 14, 30
[7]*Matthew* 4, 1–2; *Mark* 1, 13; *Luke* 4, 1–2
[8]*Matthew* 11, 19
[9]preceding art.
[10]1 *Corinthians* 9, 22
[11]*Contra Faust.* XVI, 31. PL 42, 337
[12]*Romans* 14, 17
[13]*Matthew* 11, 19

form of life and then revert to an easier one; for you might quote against him what is written, *Here was a man who began to build, and could not finish.*⁶ Now Christ began a most strict form of life after his baptism, remaining in the desert and fasting for *forty days and forty nights.*⁷ Therefore it would seem odd, after leading such a strict life, for him to return to an ordinary form of life.

ON THE OTHER HAND it is written, *The Son of Man came eating and drinking.*⁸

REPLY: As stated above,⁹ it was in keeping with the purpose of the incarnation for Christ not to lead a solitary life, but to associate with men. Now it is most fitting that he who associates with others should conform to their manner of living; according to what St Paul says *I became all things to all men.*¹⁰ And therefore it was most fitting for Christ to conform to others as regards eating and drinking. For which reason Augustine says that *John is described as neither eating nor drinking, because he did not take the same food as the Jews did. Therefore, unless our Lord had taken it, it would not be said of him, in contrast, 'eating and drinking'.*¹¹

Hence: 1. In his manner of living our Lord gave an example of perfection in all those things which of themselves relate to salvation. But abstinence from food and drink does not of itself relate to salvation: *The kingdom of God does not mean eating and drinking.*¹² And Augustine says, *Wisdom has been proved right by her children,*¹³ because, evidently, the holy apostles *understood that the kingdom of God does not consist in eating and drinking, but in enduring with equanimity, for they are neither uplifted by abundance, nor distressed by want.*¹⁴ Again he says that in all such things *it is not the making use of them, but the inordinate desire of the one using them, that is blameworthy.*¹⁵ Now both forms of life are lawful and praiseworthy— namely, that a man cut himself off from ordinary association with other men and observe abstinence; and that he continue to live the ordinary life in association with others. And therefore our Lord wished to give men an example of both forms of life.

John, however, as Chrysostom says, *exhibited no more than his life and righteousness. But Christ gave testimony also by his miracles. Leaving, therefore, John to be illustrious by his fasting, he himself went in the opposite way, coming to sit at table with tax-collectors and eating and drinking.*¹⁶

2. Just as by abstinence other men acquire the power of self-restraint, so also Christ, in himself and in his own, subdued the flesh by the power of his divinity. For this reason, as we read, the Pharisees and the disciples

---

¹⁴*De Quæst.* II, 11, on *Luke* 7, 37. PL 35, 1337. cf 2a2æ. 146, 1 ad 1 & 2
¹⁵*De Doctr. Christ.* III, 12. PL 34, 73   ¹⁶*In Matt.* XXXVII. PG 57, 423

dicitur, Pharisæi et discipuli Joannis jejunabant, non autem discipuli Christi.[17] Quod exponens Beda illud *Luc.*, *Ne timeas, Maria*, dicit quod *Joannes vinum et siceram non bibit, quia illi abstinentia meritum auget cui potentia nulla inerat naturæ. Dominus autem, cui naturaliter supsetebat delicta donare, cur eos declinaret quos abstinentibus poterat reddere puriores?*[18]

3. Ad tertium dicendum quod, sicut Chrysostomus dicit, *ut discas quam magnum bonum est jejunium et quale scutum est adversus diabolum, et quoniam post baptismum non lasciviæ, sed jejunio intendere oportet, et ipse jejunavit, non eo indigens, sed nos instruens; non autem ultra processit jejunando quam Moyses et Elias, ne incredibilis videretur carnis assumptio.*[19] Secundum mysterium autem, ut Gregorius dicit, *quadragenarius numerus exemplo Christi in jejunio custoditur, quia virtus Decalogi per libros quatuor Evangelii impletur: denarius enim quater ductus in quadragenarium surgit. Vel quia in hoc mortali corpore ex quatuor elementis subsistimus, per cujus voluptates præceptis Dominicis contrahimus, quæ per Decalogum sunt accepta.*[20] Vel secundum Augustinum, *omnis sapientiæ disciplina est, Creatorem creaturamque cognoscere. Creator est Trinitas, et Pater, et Filius, et Spiritus Sanctus. Creatura vero partim est invisibilis, sicut anima, cui ternarius numerus attribuitur; diligere enim Deum tripliciter jubemur ex toto corde, et ex tota anima, et ex tota mente; partim visibilis, sicut corpus, cui quaternarius debetur, propter calidum, humidum, frigidum et siccum. Denarius ergo numerus, qui totam insinuat disciplinam, quater ductus, idest numero, qui corpori tribuitur multiplicatus, quadragenarium conficit numerum, et ideo tempus quo ingemiscimus et dolemus, quadragenario numero celebratur.*[21]

Nec tamen incongruum fuit ut Christus post jejunium et desertum ad communem vitam rediret. Hoc enim convenit vitæ, secundum quam aliquis contemplata aliis tradit, quam Christus dicitur assumpsisse, ut primo contemplationi vacet, et postea ad publicum actionis descendat, aliis convivendo.[22] Unde et Beda dicit, *Jejunavit Christus, ne præceptum declinares; manducavit cum peccatoribus, ut gratiam cernens, agnosceres potestatem.*[23]

articulus 3. utrum Christus in hoc mundo debuerit pauperem vitam ducere

AD TERTIUM sic proceditur:[1] 1. Videtur quod Christus in hoc mundo non debuerit pauperem vitam ducere. Christus enim debuit eligibilissimam

---

[17]*Matthew* 9, 14   [18]*In Marc.* I, on 2, 18. PL 92, 151. cf Ambrose. PL 15, 1556
[19]*In Matt.* XIII, 1. PG 57, 209
[20]*In Evangelium* XVI, 5. PL 76, 1137; cf 2a2æ. 147, 5
[21]*LXXXIII Quæst.* 81. PL 40, 96. cf 2a2æ. 147, 5
[22]cf preceding art. ad 2; and 2a2æ. 188, 6 & 7
[23]*In Marc.* I, on 2, 18. PL 92, 151; cf Ambrose, *Exposit. in Luc.* II, 11. PL 15, 1556

of John fasted, but not the disciples of Christ.¹⁷ Bede comments upon this, saying that *John drank neither wine nor strong drink: because abstinence increases the merit of those whose nature is weak.* But why should our Lord, whose right it is by nature to forgive sins, avoid those whom he could make holier than such as abstain?¹⁸

3. As Chrysostom says, *that you might learn how great a good it is to fast, and how it is a shield against the devil, and that after baptism you should give yourself up, not to luxury, but to fasting—for this reason he fasted, not as needing it himself, but as teaching us.* But in fasting he went no further than Moses and Elijah, lest his assumption of our flesh might seem incredible.¹⁹ The mystical meaning, as Gregory says, is that the number *forty* is observed by Christ's example of fasting, because the power of the *decalogue is fulfilled by the four books of the Holy Gospel: since ten multiplied by four results in forty.* Or, because *we subsist in a mortal body composed of the four elements, and by its desires we transgress the commandments of the Lord, which are presented to us by means of the decalogue.*²⁰ Or, according to Augustine, *The entire teaching of wisdom consists in knowing the Creator and the creature. The Creator is the Trinity, the Father, the Son, and the Holy Spirit. Now the creature is partly invisible, as the soul, to which is attributed the number three, for we are commanded to love God in a threefold way, with all our heart, with all our soul, and with all our mind; and partly visible, as the body, to which the number four is applicable on account of its being subject to heat, moisture, cold, and dryness. Therefore if the number ten, which may be referred to the entire moral code, is multiplied by four, which may be attributed to the body, because it is by means of the body that the law is executed, the result is the number forty.* And therefore, *the time during which we sigh and grieve is symbolized by the number forty.*²¹

And yet it was not odd for Christ to return to an ordinary form of life after the time spent fasting in the desert. For it is fitting to the form of life which we say was taken up by Christ, according to which a man gives to others the fruits of his contemplation, that he devote himself first of all to contemplation, and that afterwards he come down to the common sphere of action by associating with other men.²² For this reason Bede says, *Christ fasted so that you might not disobey the commandment; he ate with sinners so that, discerning his sanctity, you might acknowledge his power.*²³

article 3. whether Christ should have led a life of poverty in this world

THE THIRD POINT:¹ 1. It would seem not. For Christ should have embraced the most eligible form of life. But the most eligible form of life is one

---

¹cf *CG* IV, 55. *Contra Græcos* 7; *Contra retrahentes* 15

vitam assumere. Sed eligibilissima vita est quæ est mediocris inter divitias et paupertatem: dicitur enim *Prov., Mendicitatem et divitias ne dederis mihi, tribue tantum victui meo necessaria.*² Ergo Christus non debuit pauperem vitam ducere, sed moderatam.

2. Præterea, exteriores divitiæ ad usum corporis ordinantur quantum ad victum et vestitum. Sed Christus in victu et vestitu communem vitam duxit, secundum modum aliorum quibus convivebat. Ergo videtur quod in divitiis et paupertate communem modum vivendi servare debuerit, et non uti maxima paupertate.

3. Præterea, Christus maxime homines invitavit ad exemplum humilitatis, secundum illud *Matt., Discite a me, quia mitis sum et humilis corde.*³ Sed humilitas maxime commendatur in divitibus: unde dicitur 1 ad *Tim., Divitibus hujus seculi præcipe, non altum sapere.*⁴ Ergo videtur quod Christus non debuerit ducere pauperem vitam.

SED CONTRA est quod dicitur *Matt., Filius hominis non habet ubi caput reclinet:*⁵ quasi dicat, secundum Hieronymum, *Cur me propter divitias et seculi lucra cupis sequi, cum tantæ sim paupertatis, ut nec hosiptiolum quidem habeam, et tecto utar non meo?*⁶ Et super illud *Matt., Ut non scandalizemus eos, vade ad mare,* dicit Hieronymus, *Hoc simpliciter intellectum ædificat auditorem; dum audit tantæ Dominum fuisse paupertatis, ut unde tributa pro se, et Apostolo redderet, non habuerit.*⁷

RESPONSIO: Dicendum quod Christum decuit in hoc mundo pauperem vitam ducere. Primo quidem, quia hoc erat congruum prædicationis officio, propter quod venisse se dicit *Marc., Eamus in proximos vicos et civitates, ut et ibi prædicem: ad hoc enim veni.*⁸ Oportet autem prædicatores verbi Dei, ut omnino vacent prædicationi, omnino a secularium rerum cura esse absolutos; quod facere non possunt qui divitias possident. Unde et ipse Dominus Apostolos ad prædicandum mittens, dicit eis *Matt., Nolite possidere aurum, neque argentum:*⁹ et ipsi Apostoli dicunt *Act., Non est æquum nos relinquere verbum Dei et ministrare mensis.*¹⁰

Secundo, quia sicut mortem corporalem assumpsit, ut nobis vitam largiretur spiritualem, ita corporalem paupertatem sustinuit, ut nobis divitias spirituales largiretur, secundum illud 2 ad *Cor., Scitis gratiam Domini nostri Jesu Christi, quoniam propter vos egenus factus est, ut illius inopia vos divites essetis.*¹¹

Tertio, ne si divitias haberet, cupiditati ejus prædicatio adscriberetur. Unde Hieronymus dicit quod *si discipuli ejus divitias habuissent, viderentur*

---

²*Proverbs* 30, 8
⁴1 *Timothy* 6, 17
⁶*In Matt.* I. PL 26, 53
³*Matthew* 11, 29
⁵*Matthew* 8, 20
⁷*In Matt.* III, on *Matthew* 17, 26. PL 26, 127-8

lying between the extremes of wealth and poverty; for it is written, *Give me neither poverty nor riches, grant me only what is necessary.*[2] Therefore Christ should have led a life, not of poverty, but of moderation.

2. Furthermore, external wealth is ordained to bodily use as food and clothing. But Christ, as regards food and clothing, led an ordinary life in the manner of those among whom he lived. Therefore it would seem also that as regards wealth and poverty he should have observed an ordinary form of life, and not one of extreme poverty.

3. Furthermore, Christ specially invited men to follow his example of humility: *Learn from me, for I am meek and humble.*[3] But humility is specially commended to the rich; as it is written, *Warn those who are rich in this world's goods not to be high-minded.*[4] Therefore it would seem that Christ should not have led a life of poverty.

ON THE OTHER HAND it is written, *The Son of Man has nowhere to lay his head,*[5] as if to say, according to Jerome, *Why would you follow me for the sake of riches and worldly gain; since I am so poor that I have not even a small dwelling-place, and I am sheltered by a roof that is not my own?*[6] And on the text, *So that we may not offend them, go to the sea,* Jerome says, *This incident, taken literally, is edifying to those who hear it when they are told that our Lord was so poor that he had not the wherewithal to pay the tax for himself and his apostle.*[7] [a]

REPLY: Fittingly Christ led a life of poverty in this world. First, of course, because this was in keeping with the office of preaching, for which purpose he said he came, *Let us go to the neighbouring towns and cities, so that I can preach there too, for that is why I came.*[8] Now, in order that the preachers of the word of God might devote all their time to preaching, they must be entirely free from worldly concerns: which is impossible for those who are wealthy. For this reason, our Lord himself, when sending the apostles out to preach, said to them, *Keep neither gold nor silver.*[9] And the apostles say, *It would not be right for us to neglect the word of God in order to serve at tables.*[10]

Secondly, because just as he took upon himself the death of the body in order to confer on us spiritual life, so he endured bodily poverty in order to confer on us spiritual riches; *You know how generous the Lord Jesus was . . . he became poor for our sakes, to make us rich through his poverty.*[11]

Thirdly, lest his preaching might have been ascribed to cupidity if he had possessed wealth. For which reason Jerome says, if the disciples had

---

[8] *Mark* 1, 38   [9] *Matthew* 10, 9   [10] *Acts* 6, 2   [11] II *Corinthians* 8, 9
[a] The poverty of Christ was to be a cardinal issue in the 14th and 15th centuries, above all for Franciscan theologians.

non causa salutis hominum, sed causa lucri prædicare;[12] et eadem ratio est de Christo.

Quarto, ut tanto major virtus divinitatis ejus ostenderetur quanto per paupertatem videbatur abjectior. Unde dicitur in quodam sermone Ephesini concilii, *Omnia paupera et vilia elegit, omnia mediocria, et plurimis obscura, ut divinitas cognosceretur orbem transformasse terrarum: propterea pauperculam elegit matrem, pauperiorem patriam, egens fuit pecuniis; et hoc tibi exponit præsepe.*[13]

1. Ad primum ergo dicendum quod superabundantia divitiarum, et mendicitas vitanda videntur ab his qui volunt vivere secundum virtutem, inquantum sunt occasiones peccandi. Abundantia namque divitiarum est superbiendi occasio; mendicitas autem est occasio furandi et mentiendi, aut etiam perjurandi.[14] Quia vero Christus peccati capax non erat, propter hanc causam, ex qua Salomon hoc vitabat, Christo vitanda non erant. Neque tamen quælibet mendicitas est furandi et perjurandi occasio, ut ibidem Salomon subdere videtur; sed sola illa quæ est contraria voluntati, ad quam vitandam homo furatur et perjurat. Sed paupertas voluntaria hoc periculum non habet: et talem paupertatem Christus elegit.[15]

2. Ad secundum dicendum quod communi vita uti quantum ad victum et vestitum, potest aliquis non solum divitias possidendo, sed etiam a mulieribus et divitibus necessaria accipiendo: quod etiam circa Christum factum est. Dicitur enim *Luc.* quod *mulieres quædam* sequebantur Christum, *quæ ministrabant ei de facultatibus suis.*[16] Ut enim Hieronymus dicit super illud, Erant ibi mulieres, *consuetudinis Judaicæ fuit, nec ducebatur in culpam more gentis antiquo, ut mulieres de substantia sua victum atque vestitum præceptoribus suis ministrarent. Sed quia hoc scandalum facere poterat in nationibus, Paulus se abjecisse commemorat.*[17] Sic ergo communis victus poterat esse sine sollicitudine impediente prædicationis officium, non autem divitiarum possessio.

3. Ad tertium dicendum quod in eo qui ex necessitate pauper est, humilitas non multum commendatur; sed in eo qui voluntarie pauper est (sicut fuit Christus) ipsa paupertas est maximæ humilitatis indicium.

articulus 4. utrum Christus in hac vita secundum legem conversatus fuerit

AD QUARTUM sic proceditur:[1] 1. Videtur quod Christus non fuerit conversatus secundum legem. Lex enim præcipiebat ut nihil operis in sabbato fieret,[2] sicut Deus *die septimo requievit ab omni opere quod patrarat.*[3] Sed

---

[12]*In Matt.* I, on 10, 9. PL 26, 62
[13]Mansi III, 9. cf Theodotus, 1, 8. PG 77, 1360
[14]cf *Proverbs* 30, 9   [15]cf 2a2æ. 186, 3, 2   [16]*Luke* 8, 2
[17]*Contra Vigilantium;* cf *In Matt.* IV, on *Matthew* 27, 55. PL 26, 214. cf also I *Thessalonians* 2, 9; II *Thessalonians* 3, 8

had wealth, *they would have seemed to preach for profit, not for the salvation of mankind.*¹² And the same reason applies to Christ.

Fourthly, that the more abject he seemed by reason of his poverty, the greater might the power of his divinity be shown to be. For this reason we read in a sermon of the Council of Ephesus, *He chose all that was poor and despicable, all that was of small account and hidden from the majority, so we might recognize that his divinity transformed the whole world. For this reason he chose a poor maid for his mother, chose a poorer fatherland, and lived in want. Learn this from the manger.*¹³

Hence: 1. It seems that those who wish to live virtuously must avoid excessive wealth and mendicity, in so far as these are occasions of sin: since abundant wealth is the occasion for being proud; and mendicity is the occasion of thieving and lying, and even of swearing falsely.¹⁴ But because Christ was incapable of sin, these things did not have to be avoided by Christ for the same reason that Solomon avoided them. However, neither is every form of mendicity the occasion of thieving and swearing falsely, as Solomon seems to add in the same place, but only that form which is involuntary; it is in order to avoid this form of mendicity that a man thieves and swears falsely. But voluntary poverty is not open to this danger. And such was the poverty that Christ chose.¹⁵

2. A man can lead an ordinary life as regards food and clothing, not only by possessing wealth, but also by receiving what is necessary from women and the wealthy. This is what happened in regard to Christ: for it is written, that certain women followed Christ and *provided for him out of their own resources.*¹⁶ For, as Jerome says, *It was a Jewish custom, nor was it thought wrong for women, following the ancient tradition of their nation, out of their private means to provide their teachers with food and clothing. But because it might give scandal to the gentiles, Paul writes that he gave it up:*¹⁷ in this way, therefore, it was possible for them to have a common fund in which anxiety did not hinder their office of preaching, since it was not a question of possessing wealth.

3. Humility is not to be praised much in one who is poor of necessity. But in one who is poor voluntarily, as Christ was, poverty itself is a sign of very great humility.

article 4. whether Christ abided by the Law

THE FOURTH POINT:¹ 1. It would seem that Christ did not. For the Law commanded that no work be done on the Sabbath,² since God *rested on the seventh day from all the work he had been doing.*³ But our Lord healed a man

---

¹cf III *Sent.* XIV, 3, vi ad 3; IV, 1, 2, 2, iii. *In Matt.* 5
²*Exodus* 20, 8; 31, 13. *Deuteronomy* 5, 12   ³*Genesis* 2, 2

ipse in sabbato curavit hominem, et ei mandavit ut tolleret lectum suum. Ergo videtur quod non fuerit secundum legem conversatus.

2. Præterea, eadem Christus fecit et docuit secundum illud *Act.*, *Cœpit Jesus facere et docere*.[4] Sed ipse *Matt.* docuit quod *omne quod intrat in os, non coinquinat hominem*;[5] quod est contra præceptum legis, quæ per usum et contactum quorumdam animalium dicebat hominem immundum fieri, ut patet *Lev.*[6] Ergo videtur quod ipse non fuerit secundum legem conversatus.

3. Præterea, idem judicium videtur esse facientis et consentientis, secundum illud *Rom.*, *Non solum illi qui faciunt, sed et qui consentiunt facientibus.*[7] Sed Christus consensit discipulis suis solventibus legem in hoc quod sabbato spicas vellebant, excusando eos, ut habetur *Matt.*[8] Ergo videtur quod Christus non conversatus fuerit secundum legem.

SED CONTRA est quod dicitur *Matt.*, *Nolite putare quoniam veni solvere legem aut prophetas:*[9] quod exponens Chrysostomus dicit, *Legem implevit, primo quidem nihil transgrediendo legalium, secundo justificando per fidem, quod lex per litteram facere non valebat.*[10]

RESPONSIO: Dicendum quod Christus in omnibus secundum legis præcepta conversatus est. In cujus signum etiam voluit circumcidi: circumcisio enim est quædam protestatio legis implendæ, secundum illud *Gal.*, *Testificor omni homini circumcidenti se, quoniam debitor est universæ legis faciendæ.*[11]

Voluit autem Christus secundum legem conversari. Primo quidem ut legem veterem approbaret. Secundo, ut eam observando, in seipso consummaret et terminaret, ostendens quod ad seipsum erat ordinata. Tertio, ut Judæis occasionem calumniandi subtraheret. Quarto, ut homines a servitute legis liberaret; secundum illud *Gal.*, *Misit Deus Filium suum factum sub lege, ut eos qui sub lege erant redimeret.*[12]

1. Ad primum ergo dicendum quod Dominus super hoc se excusat a transgressione legis tripliciter. Uno quidem modo quia per præceptum de sanctificatione sabbati non interdicitur opus divinum, sed opus humanum. Quamvis enim Deus die septimo cessaverit a novis creaturis condendis, semper tamen operatur in rerum conservatione et gubernatione. Quod autem Christus miracula faciebat, erat operis divini. Unde ipse dicit *Joan.*, *Pater meus usque modo operatur, et ego operor.*[13]

Secundo, excusat se per hoc quod illo præcepto non prohibentur opera quæ sunt de necessitate salutis, etiam corporalis. Unde ipse dicit *Luc.*,

[4]*Acts* 1, 1
[5]*Matthew* 15, 11
[6]*Leviticus* 11
[7]*Romans* 1, 32
[8]*Matthew* 12, 1–8
[9]*Matthew* 5, 17
[10]*In Matt.* XVI, 2. PG 57, 241

on the Sabbath, and commanded him to take up his mat. Therefore it would seem that he did not abide by the Law.

2. Furthermore, what Christ taught, that he also did: *Jesus undertook to do and to teach.*[4] But he taught that *what goes into the mouth does not make a man unclean*:[5] and this goes against the precept of the Law, which declared that a man was made unclean by eating and touching certain animals.[6] Therefore it would seem that he did not abide by the Law.

3. Furthermore, he who consents to anything is of the same mind as he who does it: *Not only they who do such things, but they who consent to others doing them.*[7] But Christ, by excusing his disciples, consented to their breaking the Law by plucking the ears of corn on the sabbath.[8] Therefore it would seem that Christ did not abide by the Law.

ON THE OTHER HAND it is written, *Do not think that I have come to abolish the Law or the Prophets.*[9] Chrysostom comments upon this, saying, *He fulfilled the Law, in one way, by transgressing none of the precepts of the Law; secondly, by justifying us through faith, which the Law, in the letter, was unable to do.*[10 a]

REPLY: Christ abided by all the precepts of the Law. In token of this he wished even to be circumcised; for circumcision is a kind of protestation of one's intent to keep the Law: *I testify to every man who accepts circumcision, that he is obliged to keep the whole Law.*[11]

Now Christ willed to abide by it, first, certainly, to show his approval of the Old Law. Secondly, so that by observing it he might perfect it and bring it to an end in himself, showing that it was ordained to him. Thirdly, to deprive the Jews of the occasion to calumniate him. Fourthly, in order to free men from subjection to the Law: *God sent his Son, born a subject of the Law, to redeem those subject to the Law.*[12]

Hence: 1. Our Lord excuses himself from any transgression of the Law concerning this matter in three ways. First, because the precept of keeping holy the sabbath forbids not divine work, but human work, for although God on the seventh day ended his work of creating new creatures, yet as regards conserving and governing his creatures he never stops working. Now that Christ worked miracles was a divine work. For this reason he says, *My Father goes on working, and so do I.*[13]

Secondly, he excuses himself on the ground that this precept does not forbid works which are necessary for bodily health. For this reason he says,

---

[11]*Galatians* 5, 3
[12]*Galatians* 4, 4–5
[13]*John* 5, 17. cf 1a. 73, 2; 118, 3 ad 1; 1a2æ. 107, 2 ad 3. *Suppl.* 88, 1
[a]The Old Law, cf 1a2æ. 98–105. Vol. 29, ed. D. Bourke.

Unusquisque vestrum sabbato non solvit bovem suum aut asinum a præsepio, et ducit adaquare?[14] Et infra, *Cujus vestrum asinus aut bos in puteum cadet, et non continuo extrahet illum die sabbati?*[15] Manifestum est autem quod opera miraculorum, quæ Christus faciebat, ad salutem corporis et animæ pertinebant.

Tertio, quia illo præcepto non prohibentur opera quæ pertinent ad Dei cultum. Unde dicitur *Matt.*, *An non legistis in lege, quia sabbatis sacerdotes in templo sabbatum violant, et sine crimine sunt?*[16] Et *Joan.* dicitur quod *circumcisionem accepit homo in sabbato.*[17] Quod autem Christus paralytico mandavit ut lectum suum sabbato portaret, ad cultum Dei pertinebat, idest ad laudem virtutis divinæ.

Et sic patet quod sabbatum non solvebat; quamvis hoc ei Judæi falso objicerent, dicentes *Joan.*, *Non est hic homo a Deo, qui sabbatum non custodit.*[18]

2. Ad secundum dicendum quod Christus voluit ostendere per illa verba quod homo non redditur immundus secundum animam ex usu ciborum quorumcumque secundum suam naturam, sed solum secundum quamdam significationem. Quod autem in lege quidam cibi dicuntur immundi hoc est per quamdam significationem. Unde Augustinus dicit, *Si de porco et agno requiratur, utrumque natura mundum est, quia omnis creatura Dei bona est, quadam vero significatione agnus mundus, porcus immundus est.*[19]

3. Ad tertium dicendum quod etiam discipuli, quando esurientes spicas sabbato vellebant, a transgressione legis excusantur propter necessitatem famis; sicut et David non fuit transgressor legis, quando propter famis necessitatem comedit sanctos panes, quos ei edere non licebat.

---

[14]*Luke* 13, 15
[15]*Luke* 14, 5; cf 2a2æ. 122, 4
[16]*Matthew* 12, 5
[17]*John* 7, 23
[18]*John* 9, 16

Is there one of you who does not untie his ox or his donkey from the manger on the sabbath and lead it to water?[14] And farther on, *Which of you, if his donkey or his ox falls into a pit, will not pull him out immediately on a sabbath day?*[15] Now it is manifest that the miraculous works done by Christ related to health of body and soul.

Thirdly, because this precept does not forbid works which relate to the worship of God. For this reason he says, *Or again, have you not read in the Law that on the sabbath day the Temple priests break the sabbath without being blamed for it?*[16] And it is written that *a man can be circumcised on the sabbath.*[17] Now when Christ commanded the paralytic to carry his mat on the sabbath, this related to the worship of God, that is, to the praise of God's power.

And thus it is clear that he did not break the sabbath, although the Jews threw this false accusation at him, saying, *this man cannot be from God, since he does not keep the sabbath.*[18]

2. By these words Christ wished to show that man is not rendered unclean as to his soul by the use of any kind of food considered according to its nature, but only according to some signification read into it. That certain foods are in the Law called 'unclean' is due to some signification; for this reason Augustine says, *If a question be raised about pork and lamb, both are clean by nature, since 'all God's creatures are good'; but by a certain signification lamb is clean and pork unclean.*[19]

3. The disciples who, when they became hungry, plucked the ears of corn on the sabbath, are likewise to be excused from transgressing the Law, since they were compelled by hunger: just as David did not transgress the Law when, compelled by hunger, he ate the loaves which it was not lawful for him to eat.

---

[19]*Contra Faust.* VI, 7. PL 42, 233. cf 1a2æ. 102, 6 ad 1; 103, 4 ad 3; 107, 2; 2a2æ. 148, 1, 1; 149, 3

Quæstio 41. de tentatione Christi

DEINDE CONSIDERANDUM est de tentatione Christi: et circa hoc quæruntur quatuor:

1. utrum fuerit conveniens Christum tentari:
2. de loco tentationis;
3. de tempore;
4. de modo et ordine tentationis.

articulus 1. *utrum conveniens fuerit Christum tentari*

AD PRIMUM sic proceditur:[1] 1. Videtur quod Christum tentari non conveniebat.[2] Tentare enim est experimentum sumere;[3] quod quidem non fit nisi de re ignota. Sed virtus Christi erat nota etiam dæmonibus: dicitur enim *Luc.*, quod *non sinebat dæmones loqui quia sciebant eum esse Christum.*[4] Ergo videtur quod non debuerit Christum tentari.

2. Præterea, Christus ad hoc venerat ut opera diaboli dissolveret, secundum illud 1 *Joan.*, *In hoc apparuit Filius Dei, ut dissolvat opera diaboli.*[5] Sed non est ejusdem dissolvere opera alicujus, et ea pati: et ita videtur inconveniens fuisse quod Christus pateretur se tentari a diabolo.

3. Præterea, triplex est tentatio, scilicet a carne, a mundo, et a diabolo.[6] Sed Christus non fuit tentatus nec a carne, nec a mundo. Ergo nec etiam debuit tentari a diabolo.

SED CONTRA est quod dicitur *Matt.*, *Ductus est Jesus a Spiritu in desertum, ut tentaretur a diabolo.*[7]

RESPONSIO: Dicendum quod Christus tentari voluit. Primo quidem ut nobis contra tentationes auxilium ferret; unde Gregorius dicit, *Non erat indignum Redemptori nostro quod tentari voluit, qui venerat occidi: justum quippe erat ut sic tentationes nostras suis tentationibus vinceret, sicut mortem nostram venerat sua morte superare.*[8]

Secundo, propter nostram cautelam, ut nullus quantumcumque sanctus se æstimet securum et immunem a tentatione. Unde et post baptismum tentari voluit quia, sicut Hilarius dicit, *in sanctificatis nobis maxime diaboli*

---

[1] cf *In Matt.* 4
[2] *Matthew* 4; *Mark* 1, 12–13; *Luke* 4
[3] cf Hugh of St Victor, *Quæst. in Epist. ad Heb.* 38. PL 175, 618. cf 1a. 114, 2; 2a2æ. 97, 1
[4] *Luke* 4, 41 [5] 1 *John* 3, 8
[6] cf *Medit. de Hum. Condit.* 12 & 13. PL 184, 503 & 504

Question 41. Christ's temptation

There are four points of inquiry:
1. whether it was fitting for Christ to be tempted;
2. concerning the place of temptation;
3. concerning the time;
4. concerning the mode and order of temptation.[a]

article 1. whether it was fitting for Christ to be tempted

THE FIRST POINT:[1] 1. It would seem not.[2] For to tempt is to put to the test,[3] which is done only in regard to something unknown. But the power of Christ was known even to the evil spirits; for it is written that *he would not allow them to speak because they knew he was the Christ*.[4] Therefore it would seem unbecoming for Christ to be tempted.

2. Furthermore, Christ came in order to undo the works of the devil: *It was to undo the works of the devil that the Son of God appeared*.[5] But to undo someone's works is not the same as to submit to them. Therefore it would seem unfitting for Christ to submit himself to temptation by the devil.

3. Furthermore, temptation is threefold: of the flesh, the world, and the devil.[6] But Christ was not tempted by the flesh or the world. Therefore neither should he have been tempted by the devil.

ON THE OTHER HAND it is written, *Jesus was led by the Spirit out into the wilderness to be tempted by the devil*.[7]

REPLY: Christ willed to be tempted; first, in order to strengthen us against temptations. For this reason Gregory says in a homily, *It was not improper for our Redeemer to wish to be tempted, who came also to be slain; in order that by his temptations he might conquer our temptations, just as by his death he overcame our death*.[8]

Secondly, in order to warn us, so that nobody, however holy, may think himself safe or free from temptation. For this reason also he willed to be tempted after his baptism, because, as Hilary says, *The temptations of the devil are mounted especially against those who have been sanctified, for he*

---

[7] *Matthew* 4, 1
[8] *In Evangelium* XVI, 1. PL 76, 1135
[a] cf Appendix 4. The devil as cause of sin, cf 1a2æ. 78. For 'the kingdom of evil', cf 3a. 8, 7 & 8.

*tentamenta grassantur, quia victoria magis est ei exoptata de sanctis.*⁹ Unde et *Eccl.* dicitur, *Fili, accedens ad servitutem Dei, sta in justitia et timore, et præpara animam tuam ad tentationem.*¹⁰

Tertio propter exemplum, ut scilicet nos instrueret, qualiter diaboli tentationes vincamus: unde Augustinus dicit quod *Christus diabolo se tentandum præbuit, ut ad superandas tentationes ejus mediator esset, non solum per adjutorium, verum etiam per exemplum.*¹¹

Quarto, ut nobis fiduciam de sua misericordia largiretur: unde dicitur *Heb.*, *Non habemus pontificem qui non possit compati infirmitatibus nostris; tentatum autem per omnia pro similitudine absque peccato.*¹²

1. Ad primum ergo dicendum quod, sicut Augustinus dicit, *Christus tantum innotuit dæmonibus, quantum voluit, non per id quod est vita æterna, sed per quædam temporalia suæ virtutis effecta,*¹³ ex quibus quamdam conjecturam habebant, Christum esse Filium Dei. Sed quia rursus in eo quædam signa humanæ infirmitatis videbant, non pro certo cognoscebant eum esse Filium Dei, et ideo eum tentare voluerunt. Et hoc significatur *Matt.* ubi dicitur quod *postquam esuriit, accessit tentator ad eum,*¹⁴ quia, ut Hilarius dicit, *tentare Christum diabolus non fuisset ausus, nisi in eo per esuritionis infirmitatem, quæ sunt hominis recognosceret.*¹⁵ Et hoc etiam patet ex ipso modo tentandi, cum dixit, *Si Filius Dei es,* quod exponens Ambrosius* dicit, *Quid sibi vult talis sermonis exorsus, nisi quia cognoverat Dei Filium esse venturum, sed venisse per hanc infirmitatem corporis non putabat.*¹⁶

2. Ad secundum dicendum quod Christus venerat dissolvere opera diaboli, non potestative agendo, sed magis ab eo et ejus membris patiendo, ut sic diabolum vinceret justitia, non potestate; sicut Augustinus dicit quod *diabolus non potentia Dei, sed justitia superandus fuit.*¹⁷ Et ideo circa tentationem Christi considerandum est, quid propria voluntate fecit, et quid a diabolo passus fuit. Quod enim tentatori se offerret, fuit propriæ voluntatis. Unde dicitur *Matt.*, *Ductus est Jesus in desertum a Spiritu, ut tentaretur a diabolo;*¹⁸ quod Gregorius intelligendum dicit de Spiritu Sancto, ut scilicet *illuc eum Spiritus suus duceret, ubi eum ad tentandum spiritus malignus inveniret.*¹⁹ Sed a diabolo passus est ut assumeretur vel *supra pinnaculum templi,* vel etiam *in montem excelsum valde.* Nec est mirum, ut Gregorius dicit, *si se ab illo permisit in montem duci, quie se*

---

*Leonine: Gregorius

⁹*In Matt.* 3. PL 9, 928
¹⁰*Sirach* 2, 1
¹¹*De Trinitate* IV, 13, 17. PL 42, 899
¹²*Hebrews* 4, 15
¹³*De Civitate Dei* IX, 21. PL 41, 273
¹⁴*Matthew* 4, 2-3
¹⁵*In Matt*, 3, 2. PL 9, 929
¹⁶Ambrose, *Exposit. in Luc.* IV, 18, on *Luke* 4, 3. PL 15, 1617
¹⁷*De Trinitate* XIII, 13. PL 42, 1026
¹⁸*Matthew* 4, 1

THE TEMPTATION OF CHRIST

desires, above all, to overcome the holy.[9] For this reason also, it is written, *My son, if you aspire to serve the Lord, be steadfast and sincere of heart, and prepare yourself for temptation.*[10]

Thirdly, in order to give us an example: to teach us, namely, how to overcome the temptations of the devil. For this reason Augustine says that Christ *allowed himself to be tempted* by the devil, *so that, in overcoming these temptations, he might be our Mediator, not only as one who helps us, but also as one who gives us the example.*[11]

Fourthly, in order to fill us with confidence in his mercy. For which reason it is written, *We have not a high priest incapable of having compassion on our weaknesses, but one who has been tempted in every way that we are, though he is without sin.*[12]

Hence: 1. As Augustine says, *Christ was known to the evil spirits only so far as he willed; not as the source of eternal life, but as the cause of certain temporal effects,*[13] from which they formed some sort of conjecture that Christ was the Son of God.[a] On the other hand, because they also observed in him certain signs of human weakness, they did not know with certitude that he was the Son of God. And therefore the devil wished to tempt him. This is the meaning of the text that *after he was very hungry, the tempter came to him,*[14] because, as Hilary says, *the devil would not have dared to tempt Christ, had not his weakness in hungering betrayed his human nature.*[15] And this is also clear from the very manner of the temptation, when he said, *If you are the Son of God.* Which Ambrose explains saying, *Why did he address him in this way, unless it were because although he knew that the Son of God was to come, yet he did not think that he had come in the weakness of the flesh?*[16]

2. Christ came to undo the works of the devil, not by mighty deeds, but rather by submitting to him and his cohorts, so as to conquer the devil by righteousness, not by might; as Augustine says, *the devil had to be overcome, not by the power of God, but by righteousness.*[17] And therefore in regard to Christ's temptation we must consider what he did of his own will and how he submitted to the devil. For that he allowed himself to be tempted was due to his own will. For which reason it is written, *Jesus was led by the Spirit out into the wilderness to be tempted by the devil;*[18] and Gregory says that, as regards the Holy Spirit, this must be interpreted as saying that *his spirit led him out where the evil spirit would find him and tempt him.*[19] But he submitted to the devil in being *taken up on to the parapet of the Temple,* and again, *up to a very high mountain.* Nor is it strange, as Gregory remarks, *that he who allowed himself to be crucified by his*

---

[19]*In Evangelium* XVI, 1. PL 76, 1135
[a]cf Luke 4, 41.

permisit a membris ipsius crucifigi.[20] Intelligitur autem a diabolo assumptus, non quasi ex necessitate; sed quia, ut Origines dicit super *Luc.*, *sequebatur eum ad tentationem, quasi athleta sponte procedens.*[21]

3. Ad tertium dicendum quod, sicut Apostolus dicit *Hebr.*, *Christus in omnibus tentari voluit absque peccato.*[22] Tentatio autem quæ est ab hoste potest esse sine peccato, quia fit per solam exteriorem suggestionem. Tentatio autem quæ est a carne non potest esse sine peccato, quia hujusmodi tentatio fit per delectationem et concupiscentiam: et sicut Augustinus dicit, *nonnullum peccatum est quando caro concupiscit adversus spiritum.*[23] Et ideo Christus tentari voluit ab hoste, sed non a carne.

articulus 2. utrum Christus in deserto tentari debuerit

AD SECUNDUM sic proceditur:[1] 1. Videtur quod Christus non debuerit tentari in deserto. Christus enim tentari voluit propter exemplum nostrum, ut dictum est.[2] Sed exemplum debet manifeste proponi illis qui sunt per exemplum informandi. Non ergo debuit in deserto tentari.

2. Præterea, Chrysostomus dicit quod *tunc maxime instat diabolus ad tentandum, cum viderit solitarios; unde et in principio mulierem tentavit, sine viro eam inveniens;*[3] et sic videtur per hoc quod in desertum ivit ut tentaretur, quod tentationi se exposuit. Cum ergo ejus tentatio sit nostrum exemplum, videtur quod etiam alii debeant se ingerere ad tentationes suscipiendas; quod tamen videtur esse periculosum, cum magis tentationum occasiones vitare debeamus.

3. Præterea, *Matt.* ponitur secunda Christi tentatio, qua *diabolus Christum assumpsit in sanctam civitatem, et statuit eum super pinnaculum templi;*[4] quod quidem non erat in deserto. Non ergo tentatus est solum in deserto.

SED CONTRA est quod dicitur *Marc.* quod *erat Jesus in deserto quadraginta diebus, et quadraginta noctibus, et tentabatur a Satana.*[5]

RESPONSIO: Dicendum quod, sicut dictum est,[6] Christus propria voluntate se diabolo exhibuit ad tentandum, sicut etiam propria voluntate membris ejus se exhibuit ad occidendum; alioquin diabolus venire ad eum non auderet. Diabolus autem magis attentat aliquem, cum est solitarius, quia,

---

[20] ibid, PL 76, 1135
[21] *In Luc.* XXXI, on Luke 4, 9. PG 13, 1879 (cf PL 26, 286)
[22] *Hebrews* 4, 15
[23] *De Civitate Dei* XIX, 4. PL 41, 629. cf 1a2æ. 74, 3
[1] cf *In Matt.* 4   [2] preceding art.   [3] *In Matt.* XIII, 1. PG 57, 209
[4] *Matthew* 4, 5   [5] *Mark* 1, 13   [6] preceding art., ad 2

own, should allow himself to be led up a mountain.[20] We understand, however, that he was taken up by the devil, not, as it were, by force, but because, as Origen says, *he followed him in the course of his temptation like an athlete advancing of his own accord.*[21]

3. As the Apostle says, Christ wished to be *tempted in every way, without sin.*[22] Now temptation which comes by way of an enemy can be without sin, because it comes about by mere outward suggestion. But temptation which comes by way of the flesh cannot be without sin,[b] because such a temptation is brought about by pleasure and concupiscence; and, as Augustine says *there is some sin whenever 'the desire of the flesh opposes the spirit.'*[23] And so Christ wished to be tempted by an enemy, but not by the flesh.

article 2. whether Christ should have been tempted in the wilderness

THE SECOND POINT:[1] 1. It would seem not. For Christ willed to be tempted in order to give us an example, as stated above.[2] But an example should be set openly before those who are to follow it. Therefore he should not have been tempted in the wilderness.

2. Furthermore, Chrysostom says, *It is when he sees us alone that the devil most especially assails us by tempting us. Thus did he tempt the woman in the beginning when he found her apart from her husband.*[3] And thus it would seem that, by going into the wilderness to be tempted, he exposed himself to temptation. Therefore, since his temptation is an example to us, it would seem that others too should take such steps as will lead them into temptation. However, this would seem to be dangerous, since we should, on the contrary, avoid the occasions of temptation.

3. Furthermore, it is written that in Christ's second temptation, *the devil took* Christ *to the Holy City and made him stand on the parapet of the Temple,*[4] which is certainly not in the wilderness. Therefore he was not tempted in the wilderness only.

ON THE OTHER HAND it is written that Jesus *was in the wilderness forty days and forty nights, and was tempted by Satan.*[5]

REPLY: As stated above,[6] Christ of his own will submitted himself to the devil to be tempted, just as by his own will he submitted himself to his own people to suffer death; otherwise the devil would not have dared to approach him. For the devil prefers to tempt a man who is alone, because,

---

[b]Sin in the 'sensual' part of man, cf 1a2æ. 74, 3 & 4; sin from passion, cf 1a2æ 77, 2, 3 & 6. Vol. 25, ed. J. Fearon.

ut dicitur *Eccles.*, *si quispiam prævaluerit contra unum, duo resistunt ei.*⁷ Et inde est quod Christus in desertum exivit quasi ad campum certaminis, ut ibi a diabolo tentaretur. Unde Ambrosius dicit quod *Christus agebatur in desertum consilio, ut diabolum provocaret. Nam nisi ille certasset,* scilicet diabolus, *non iste mihi vicisset,*⁸ idest Christus. Addit autem et alias rationes, dicens hoc Christum fecisse mysterio, ut Adam de exilio liberaret, qui scilicet de paradiso in desertum ejectus est;⁹ et exemplo, ut ostenderet nobis diabolum ad meliora tendentibus invidere.¹⁰

1. Ad primum ergo dicendum quod Christus proponitur omnibus in exemplum per fidem, secundum illud *Heb.*, *Aspicientes in auctorem fidei et consummatorem Jesum.*¹¹ *Fides* autem, ut dicitur *Rom.*, *est ex auditu,*¹² non autem ex visu. Quinimo *Joan.* dicitur, *Beati qui non viderunt, et crediderunt.*¹³ Et ideo ad hoc quod tentatio Christi esset nobis in exemplum non oportuit quod ab hominibus videretur; sed sufficiens fuit quod hominibus narraretur.

2. Ad secundum dicendum quod duplex est tentationis occasio. Una quidem ex parte hominis, puta cum aliquis se peccato propinquum facit, occasiones peccandi non evitans: et talis occasio tentationis est vitanda, sicut dictum est Loth, *Gen.*, *Ne steteris in omni regione circa Sodomam.*¹⁴

Alia vero tentationis occasio est ex parte diaboli, qui *semper invidet ad meliora tendentibus,* ut Ambrosius dicit,¹⁵ et talis tentationis occasio non est vitanda. Unde dicit Chrysostomus quod non solum Christus ductus est in desertum a Spiritu, sed *omnes filii Dei habentes Spiritum Sanctum: non enim sunt contenti sedere otiosi; sed Spiritus Sanctus urget eos aliquod magnum apprehendere opus; quod est esse in deserto quantum ad diabolum, quia non est ibi injustitia, in qua diabolus delectatur. Omne etiam bonum opus est desertum, quantum ad carnem et mundum, quia non est secundum voluntatem carnis et mundi.*¹⁶ Talem autem occasionem tentationis dare diabolo non est periculosum, quia magis est consilium Spiritus Sancti, qui est perfecti operis auctor, quam impugnatio diaboli invidentis.

3. Ad tertium dicendum quod quidam dicunt omnes tentationes factas fuisse in deserto: quorum quidam¹⁷ dicunt quod Christus ductus est in sanctam civitatem non realiter, sed secundum imaginariam visionem: quidam¹⁸ autem dicunt quod etiam ipsa civitas sancta, idest Jerusalem, desertum dicitur, quia erat derelicta a Deo. Sed hoc non est necessarium, quia Marcus dicit quod in deserto tentabatur a diabolo; non autem dicit quod solum in deserto.

---

⁷*Ecclesiastes* 4, 12 ⁸*In Luc.* IV, 14, on 4, 1. PL 15, 1616
⁹*Genesis* 3, 23 ¹⁰*In Luc.*, loc cit ¹¹*Hebrews* 12, 2
¹²*Romans* 10, 17 ¹³*John* 20, 29 ¹⁴*Genesis* 19, 17
¹⁵*In Luc.*, loc. cit. PL 15, 1617
¹⁶*Opus imperf.* v, on *Matthew* 4, 1. PG 56, 662

as it is written, *where one man alone would be overcome, two will put up resistance*.⁷ And so it was that Christ went out into the wilderness, as to a field of battle, to be tempted there by the devil. For this reason Ambrose says that Christ *was led into the wilderness for the purpose of provoking the devil. For had the devil not fought, Christ would not have conquered*.⁷ He adds other reasons as well, saying that Christ in this way enacted *the mystery of Adam's delivery from exile*, who had been expelled from paradise into the wilderness,⁹ and *he intended to show us by his example that the devil envies those who strive for better things*.¹⁰

Hence: 1. Christ is set forth to all as an example through faith: *We look on Jesus, who is the source of faith and who brings it to perfection*.¹¹ Now faith, as it is written, *comes by hearing*,¹² and not by seeing; on the contrary, it is even said, *Happy are those who have not seen and yet believe*.¹³ And therefore, in order that Christ's temptation might be an example to us, it was not necessary for men to see it, but it was sufficient for men to hear it related.

2. The occasions of temptation are twofold. One is on the part of man—for instance, when a man comes close to sinning by not avoiding the occasion of sin. And such occasions of temptation should be avoided, as in the warning to Lot, *Do not stay anywhere near Sodom*.¹⁴

Another occasion of temptation is on the part of the devil, who always *envies those who strive for better things*, as Ambrose says.¹⁵ And such occasions of temptation are not to be avoided. For this reason Chrysostom says, *It was not Christ alone who was led into the wilderness by the Spirit, but all God's children who have the Holy Spirit. For it is not enough for them to sit idle; but the Holy Spirit urges them to undertake something great: which is for them to be in the wilderness from the devil's standpoint, because there can be found there no unrighteousness, in which the devil delights. Again, every good work, compared to the flesh and the world, is the wilderness, because it is not according to the will of the flesh and of the world*.¹⁶ Now it is not dangerous to give the devil such an occasion of temptation: since the help of the Holy Spirit, who is the author of the perfect work, is more powerful than the assault of the envious devil.

3. Some say that all the temptations took place in the wilderness. Of these some¹⁷ say that Christ was led to the Holy City, not really, but in an imaginary vision. While others¹⁸ say that the Holy City itself, i.e. Jerusalem, is called *a wilderness*, because it was abandoned by God. But this explanation is unnecessary. For Mark says that he was tempted in the wilderness by the devil, but not that he was tempted in the wilderness only.

---

¹⁷Ernaldus Bonaevallis, *De cardinalibus operibus Christi*, 5. PL 189, 1637. Paschasius Radbertus. *In Matt*. 4. PL 120, 194   ¹⁸cf St Thomas, *In Matt*., on 4, 5

articulus 3. *utrum Christi tentatio debuerit esse post jejunium*

AD TERTIUM sic proceditur:[1] 1. Videtur quod Christi tentatio non debuerit esse post jejunium. Dictum enim est supra,[2] quod Christum non decebat conversationis austeritas. Sed maximæ austeritatis fuisse videtur quod quadraginta diebus et quadraginta noctibus nihil comederit: sic enim intelligitur quadraginta diebus et noctibus jejunasse, quia scilicet *illis diebus nullum omnino cibum sumpsit*, ut Gregorius dicit.[3] Ergo non videtur quod debuerit hujusmodi jejunium tentationi præmittere.

2. Præterea, *Marc.* dicitur quod *erat in deserto quadraginta diebus et quadraginta noctibus, et tentabatur a Satana*.[4] Sed quadraginta diebus et quadraginta noctibus jejunavit. Ergo videtur quod non post jejunium, sed simul dum jejunaret, sit tentatus a diabolo.

3. Præterea, Christus non legitur nisi semel jejunasse. Sed non solum semel fuit tentatus a diabolo; dicitur enim *Luc.* quod *consummata omni tentatione, diabolus recessit ab illo usque ad tempus*.[5] Sicut ergo secundæ tentationi non præmisit jejunium, ita nec primæ præmittere debuit.

SED CONTRA est quod dicitur *Matt.*, *Cum jejunasset quadraginta diebus et quadraginta noctibus, postea esuriit: et tunc accessit ad eum tentator*.[6]

RESPONSIO: Dicendum quod convenienter Christus post jejunium tentari voluit. Primo quidem propter exemplum, quia cum omnibus, sicut dictum est,[7] immineat se contra tentationes tueri, per hoc quod ipse ante tentationem futuram jejunavit docuit quod per jejunium nos oportet contra tentationes armari. Unde inter arma justitiæ Apostolus jejunia connumerat, 2 ad *Cor.*[8]

Secundo, ut ostenderet quod etiam jejunantes diabolus aggreditur ad tentandum, sicut alios qui bonis operibus vacant: et ideo sicut post baptismum, ita post jejunium Christus tentatur.[9] Unde Chrysostomus dicit, *Ut discas quam magnum bonum est jejunium, et quale scutum est adversus diabolum, et quoniam post baptismum non lasciviæ, sed jejunio intendere opcrtet; ideo Christus jejunavit, non jejunio indigens, sed nos instruens.*[10]

Tertio, quia post jejunium secuta est esuries, quæ dedit diabolo audaciam eum aggrediendi, sicut dictum est.[11] *Cum autem esuriit Dominus, ut Hilarius dicit, non fuit ex surreptione inediæ, sed naturæ suæ hominem dereliquit: non enim erat a Deo diabolus, sed a carne vincendus*.[12] Unde

---

[1] cf *In Matt.* 4
[2] 3a. 40, 2
[3] *In Evang.* XVI, 5. PL 76, 1137
[4] *Mark* 1, 13
[5] *Luke* 4, 13
[6] *Matthew* 4, 2–3
[7] art. 1
[8] II *Corinthians* 6, 5 & 7
[9] cf art. 1
[10] *In Matt.* XIII, 1. PG 57, 209
[11] art. 1 ad 1

THE TEMPTATION OF CHRIST

article 3. whether Christ's temptation should have taken place after his fast

THE THIRD POINT:[1] 1. It would seem not. For it was said above[2] that an austere mode of life was not becoming to Christ. But it would seem to be a mark of extreme austerity that he did not eat anything for forty days and forty nights, for this is how we understand the fact that *he fasted for forty days and forty nights*, since, evidently, as Gregory says, *during that time he took no food at all.*[3] Therefore it would seem that he should not have undertaken a fast of this sort before his temptation.

2. Furthermore, it is written that *he was in the wilderness forty days and forty nights, and was tempted by Satan.*[4] Now he fasted for forty days and forty nights. Therefore it would seem that he was tempted by the devil, not after, but during, his fast.

3. Furthermore, we read that Christ fasted once only. But he was not tempted by the devil once only, for it is written that *having exhausted all ways of tempting him, the devil left him, to return at the appointed time.*[5] Therefore, as he did not fast before the second temptation, so he should not have fasted before the first.

ON THE OTHER HAND it is written, *He fasted for forty days and forty nights, after which he was very hungry,* and then *the tempter came* to him.[6]

REPLY: It was fitting that Christ should wish to be tempted after having fasted. First, in order to give us an example. Because, as said above,[7] it is incumbent upon us all to shield ourselves against temptation; thus, by his having fasted before being tempted, he teaches us the need of fasting in order to arm ourselves against temptation. For this reason St Paul reckons *fasting* among the *weapons of righteousness.*[8]

Secondly, in order to show that the devil assails with temptations those also who fast, just as he assails anyone else who is given to good works. And therefore, just as it was after his baptism that Christ was tempted,[9] so also it was after his fast. For this reason Chrysostom says, *That you might learn how great a good it is to fast, and how it is a shield against the devil, and that after baptism you should give yourself up, not to luxury, but to fasting—for this reason Christ fasted, not as needing it himself, but as teaching us.*[10]

Thirdly, because after the fast, hunger followed, which made the devil dare to attack him, as said above.[11] Now, *when our Lord was hungry,* says Hilary, *it was not because he was overcome by want of food, but because he abandoned his manhood to its nature. For the devil was to be conquered, not by God, but by the flesh.*[12] For this reason also, as Chrysostom says, *In*

---

[12]*In Matt.* 3. PL 9, 928

etiam, ut Chrysostomus dicit, *non ultra processit in jejunando quam Moyses et Elias, ne incredibilis videretur carnis assumptio.*[13]

1. Ad primum ergo dicendum quod Christum non decuit conversatio austerioris vitæ, ut se communem exhiberet illis quibus prædicavit. Nullus autem debet assumere prædicationis officium, nisi prius fuerit purgatus et in virtute perfectus; sicut et de Christo dicitur *Act.* quod *cœpit Jesus facere et docere.*[14] Et ideo Christus statim post baptismum austeritatem vitæ assumpsit, ut doceret, post carnem edomitam oportere alios ad prædicationis officium transire, secundum illud Apostoli 1 *Cor.*, *Castigo corpus meum, et in servitutem redigo, ne forte cum aliis prædicavero, ipse reprobus efficiar.*[15]

2. Ad secundum dicendum quod verbum illud *Marci* potest sic intelligi, quod *erat in deserto quadraginta diebus et quadraginta noctibus*, quibus scilicet jejunavit. Quod autem dicitur, *Et tentabatur a Satana*, intelligendum est non in illis quadraginta diebus et quadraginta noctibus quibus jejunavit, sed post illos, eo quod Matthæus dicit quod *cum jejunasset quadraginta diebus et quadraginta noctibus, postea esuriit:*[16] ex quo sumpsit tentator occasionem accendendi ad ipsum. Unde et quod subditur, *Et angeli ministrabant ei*, consecutive intelligendum esse ostenditur ex hoc quod Matt. dicitur, *Tunc reliquit eum diabolus*, scilicet post tentationem, *et ecce angeli accesserunt et ministrabant ei.*[17] Quod vero interponit *Marc.*, *Eratque cum bestiis*,[18] inducitur, secundum Chrysostomum, ad ostendendum quale erat desertum, quia scilicet erat invium hominibus, et bestiis plenum.[19]

Tamen secundum expositionem Bedæ, Dominus tentabatur quadraginta diebus et quadraginta noctibus.[20] Sed hoc intelligendum est non de illis tentationibus visibilibus, quas narrant Matthæus et Lucas, quæ manifeste factæ sunt post jejunium, sed de quibusdam aliis impugnationibus, quas forte illo jejunii tempore Christus est a diabolo passus.

3. Ad tertium dicendum quod, sicut Ambrosius dicit, *recessit diabolus a Christo usque ad tempus, quia postea non tentaturus, sed aperte pugnaturus advenit*,[21] tempore scilicet passionis: et tamen per illam impugnationem videbatur Christum tentare de tristitia et odio proximorum, sicut in deserto de delectatione gulæ, et contemptu Dei per idololatriam.

articulus 4. utrum fuerit conveniens ordo et modus tentationis Christi

AD QUARTUM sic proceditur:[1] 1. Videtur quod non fuerit conveniens tentationis modus et ordo. Tentatio enim diaboli ad peccandum inducit.

---

[13]*In Matt.* XIII, 2. PG 57, 209
[14]*Acts* I, 1
[15]1 *Corinthians* 9, 27
[16]*Matthew* 4, 2
[17]*Matthew* 4, 11
[18]*Mark* 1, 13
[19]*In Matt.* XIII, 1. PG 57, 209
[20]*In Marc.* I, on 1, 12. PL 92, 140
[21]*In Luc.* IV, on 4, 13. PL 15, 1623

fasting he went no further than Moses and Elijah, lest his assumption of our flesh might seem incredible.[13]

Hence: 1. It was becoming for Christ not to adopt an austere mode of life, so that he might show himself in conformity with those to whom he preached. Now, no one should assume the office of preaching, unless he have first been cleansed and perfected in virtue, according to what is said of Christ that *Jesus undertook to do and to teach*.[14] And therefore, immediately after his baptism Christ assumed an austere form of life, in order to teach others that they should pass on to the office of preaching only after having tamed the flesh, according to St Paul, *I chastise my body, and bring it into subjection, lest perhaps, having been a preacher to others, I myself should be cast out.*[15]

2. These words of Mark may be understood as meaning that *he was in the wilderness forty days and forty nights*, during which time he fasted: and the words, *and he was tempted by Satan*, must be understood as referring, not to those forty days and forty nights, but to the time that followed: because Matthew says that *he had fasted for forty days and forty nights, after which he was very hungry*,[16] which provided the tempter with the occasion to approach him. And so the words that follow, *and the angels ministered to him*, must be taken in sequence, which is clear from what Matthew writes, *Then the devil left him*, i.e. after the temptation, *and angels appeared and ministered to him.*[17] As for the words inserted by Mark, *he was with the wild beasts*,[18] these are, according to Chrysostom, set down in order to describe what kind of wilderness it was:[19] namely, that it was impassable to man and full of beasts.

However, according to Bede's explanation of Mark, our Lord was tempted for forty days and forty nights.[20] But this is not to be understood of those visible temptations which are related by Matthew and Luke, and took place after the fast, but of certain other assaults which perhaps Christ endured from the devil during the time of the fast.

3. As Ambrose says, the devil left Christ *for a time*, because, *later on he returned, not to tempt him, but to assail him openly*—namely, at the time of his Passion.[21] Nevertheless, in this later assault he seemed to tempt Christ to dejection and hatred of his neighbour; just as in the wilderness he had tempted him to gluttonous pleasure and idolatrous contempt of God.

article 4. whether the mode and order of temptation were fitting

THE FOURTH POINT:[1] 1. It would seem not. For temptation by the devil leads to sin. But if Christ had assuaged his bodily hunger by changing the

---

[1]cf *In Matt.* 4

Sed si Christus subvenisset corporali fami convertendo lapides in panem, non peccasset; sicut non peccavit, cum panes multiplicavit, quod non fuit minus miraculum, ut turbæ esurienti subveniret.² Ergo videtur quod nulla fuerit illa tentatio.

2. Præterea, nullus persuasor convenienter suadet contrarium ejus quod intendit. Sed diabolus statuens Christum supra pinnaculum templi, intendebat eum de superbia, seu vana gloria tentare. Ergo inconvenienter persuadet ei ut se mittat deorsum, quod est contrarium superbiæ, vel vanæ gloriæ, quæ semper quærit ascendere.

3. Præterea, una tentatio conveniens est ut sit de uno peccato. Sed in tentatione quæ fuit in monte duo peccata persuasit, scilicet cupiditatem et idololatriam. Non ergo conveniens videtur fuisse tentationis modus.

4. Præterea, tentationes ad peccata ordinantur. Sed septem sunt vitia capitalia, ut in secunda parte habitum est.³ Non autem tentavit nisi de tribus, scilicet gula, vana gloria et cupiditate. Non ergo videtur sufficiens tentationis modus fuisse.

5. Præterea, post victoriam omnium vitiorum remanet homini tentatio superbiæ vel vanæ gloriæ, quia *superbia etiam bonis operibus insidiatur, ut pereant*, sicut dicit Augustinus.⁴ Inconvenienter ergo Matthæus ultimam ponit tentationem cupiditatis in monte, mediam autem inanis gloriæ in templo, præsertim cum Lucas ordinet e converso.

6. Præterea, Hieronymus dicit quod *propositum Christi fuit diabolum humilitate vincere, non potestate*.⁵ Ergo non imperiose et objurgando eum repellere debuit, dicens, *Vade retro, Satana*.

7. Præterea, narratio Evangelii videtur falsum continere: non enim videtur possibile quod Christus supra pinnaculum templi statui potuerit quin ab aliis videretur: neque aliquis mons tam altus invenitur ut inde totus mundus inspici possit, ut sic ex eo potuerint Christo omnia regna mundi ostendi. Inconvenienter ergo videtur descripta Christi tentatio.

SED CONTRA est sacræ Scripturæ auctoritas *Matt.* et *Luc.*⁶

RESPONSIO: Dicendum quod tentatio quæ est ab hoste, fit per modum suggestionis, ut Gregorius dicit.⁷ Non autem eodem modo potest aliquid omnibus suggeri; sed unicuique suggeritur aliquid ex his circa quæ est affectus. Et ideo diabolus hominem spiritualem non statim tentat de

---

²*Matthew* 14, 15; 15, 32
³1a2æ. 84, 4
⁴*Epist.* CCXI, *ad Sanctimonial.* 6. PL 33, 960
⁵*In Matt.* I, on 4, 4. PL 26, 31
⁶*Matthew* 4, 1–11; *Luke* 4, 1–13
⁷*In Evang.* XVI, 1. PL 76, 1135

stones into loaves of bread, he would not have sinned; just as he did not sin when he multiplied the loaves, which was no less a miracle, in order to assuage the hungry crowd.² Therefore it would seem that this was in no way a temptation.

2. Furthermore, it is not fitting for a counsellor to encourage the contrary of what he wishes done. But the devil, by setting Christ on the parapet of the Temple, wished to tempt him to pride and vainglory. Therefore it would seem unfitting to encourage Christ to throw himself down from there, for this would be contrary to pride or vainglory which always seeks to rise.

3. Furthermore, it is fitting for a single temptation to result in a single sin. But in the temptation on the mountain he encouraged two sins—namely, cupidity and idolatry. Therefore it would seem that the mode of temptation was unfitting.

4. Furthermore, temptations are ordered to sins. But there are seven deadly sins, as stated in the second part.³ But the tempter only deals with three, namely, gluttony, vainglory and cupidity. Therefore it would seem that the temptation was incomplete.

5. Furthermore, after overcoming all the vices, man is still tempted to pride or vainglory, *because pride insidiously creeps even into good works, in order to destroy them,* as Augustine says.⁴ Therefore, that Matthew should place last the temptation to cupidity on the mountain, while he places second the temptation to vainglory in the Temple, is unfitting, especially since Luke reverses the order.

6. Furthermore, Jerome says that it was Christ's *intent to overcome the devil by humility, not by might.*⁵ Therefore he should not have repulsed him with the imperious rebuke, *Begone, Satan.*

7. Furthermore, the Gospel narrative appears to be false, for it seems impossible that Christ could be placed on a parapet of the Temple without being seen by others. Nor is there any mountain to be found which is so high that the whole world can be seen from it, such that from it all the kingdoms of the world could be shown to Christ. Therefore it would seem that Christ's temptation is unfittingly described.

ON THE OTHER HAND stands the authority of the Scriptures.⁶ ᵃ

REPLY: When the devil tempts us he does it by way of a suggestion, as Gregory says.⁷ Now a suggestion cannot be made to everybody in the same way; it arises from those things towards which one is inclined. And so the

---

ᵃThe sequence of the temptations differs in *Matthew* and in *Luke*; the latter probably seeks to reduce scene-shifting in telling the story.

gravibus peccatis, sed paulatim a levioribus incipit ut postmodum ad graviora perducat. Unde Gregorius exponens illud *Job, Procul odoratur bellum, exhortationem ducum et ululatum exercitus,*⁸ dicit, Bene duces exhortari dicti sunt, exercitus ululare, quia prima vitia deceptæ menti quasi sub quadam ratione se inserunt: sed innumera quæ sequuntur, dum hanc ad omnem insaniam pertrahunt, quasi bestiali clamore confundunt.⁹

Et hoc idem diabolus observavit in tentatione primi hominis:¹⁰ nam primo sollicitavit mentem primi hominis de ligni vetiti esu, dicens, *Cur præcepit vobis Deus ut non comederetis de omni ligno paradisi?*¹¹ Secundo, de inani gloria, cum dixit, *Aperientur oculi vestri.*¹² Tertio, perduxit tentationem ad extremam superbiam, cum dixit, *Eritis sicut Dei, scientes bonum et malum.*¹³

Et hunc etiam tentandi ordinem servavit in Christo. Nam primo tentavit ipsum de eo quod appetunt quantumcumque spirituales viri, scilicet de sustentatione corporalis naturæ per cibum. Secundo, processit ad id in quo spirituales viri quandoque deficiunt, ut scilicet aliqua ad ostentationem operentur, quod pertinet ad inanem gloriam. Tertio, perduxit tentationem ad id quod jam non est spiritualium virorum, sed carnalium, scilicet ut divitias, et gloriam mundi concupiscant usque ad contemptum Dei.¹⁴ Et ideo in primis duabus tentationibus dixit, *Si filius Dei es,* non autem in tertia, quæ non potest convenire spiritualibus viris qui sunt per adoptionem filii Dei, sicut duæ primæ.

His autem tentationibus Christus restitit testimoniis legis, non potestate virtutis, *ut hoc ipso et plus hominem honoraret, et adversarium plus puniret, cum hostis generis humani non quasi a Deo, sed quasi ab homine vinceretur,* sicut dicit Leo papa.¹⁵

1. Ad primum ergo dicendum quod uti necessariis ad sustentationem non est peccatum gulæ; sed quod ex desiderio hujus sustentationis homo aliquid inordinatum faciat, ad vitium gulæ pertinere potest. Est autem inordinatum quod aliquis ubi potest recursus haberi ad humana subsidia, pro solo corpore sustentando, miraculose sibi cibum quærere velit. Unde et Dominus filiis Israel miraculose manna præbuit in deserto ubi aliunde cibus haberi non poterat:¹⁶ et similiter Christus in deserto turbas pavit miraculose ubi aliter cibi haberi non poterant. Sed Christus ad subveniendum fami poterat aliter sibi providere quam miracula faciendo, sicut et

---

⁸*Job* 39, 25
⁹*Moral.* XLV, 17, 32. PL 76, 622
¹⁰*Genesis* 3, 1–6   ¹¹*Genesis* 3, 1
¹²*Genesis* 3, 5   ¹³*Genesis* 3, 5
¹⁴cf Augustine, *De Civitate Dei* XIV, 28. PL 41, 436. Also 1a2æ. 77, 4. 2a2æ. 25, 7 ad 1; 153, 5, 3
¹⁵*Sermones* XXXIX (I de Quadrag.), 3. PL 54, 265

devil does not immediately tempt the spiritual man to grave sins; but he begins little by little with lighter sins, so as to lead him shortly to more serious ones. For this reason, while explaining the text, *From afar he smells the battle, the encouraging words of the captains and the shouting of the army*,[8] Gregory says, *The captains are well described as encouraging, and the army as shouting. Because, at first, vices present themselves to the mind in forms which beguile it, but then those that follow become so numerous that they drive it on to every sort of madness, confounding it, as it were, with brutal clamour.*[9]

This is the very way in which the devil set out to tempt the first man.[10] For at first he enticed the mind of the first man to eat from the forbidden tree, saying, *Why did God command you not to eat from every tree in paradise?*[11] Secondly, he tempted him to vainglory, saying, *Your eyes will be opened.*[12] Thirdly, he directed the temptation to extreme pride, saying, *You will be like gods, knowing good and evil.*[13]

He observed this order also in tempting Christ. For at first he tempted him to that which men desire, however spiritual they may be—namely, the sustenance of the natural body by food. Secondly, he advanced to that in which spiritual men are sometimes found wanting, in so far as they do certain things for show, which pertains to vainglory. Thirdly, he directed the temptation to that in which spiritual men no longer have a part, while carnal men do—namely, to desire worldly riches and renown, even to the point of holding God in contempt.[14] And so in the first two temptations he said, *If you are the Son of God*; but not in the third, which cannot apply, as do the first two, to spiritual men who are sons of God by adoption.

And Christ resisted these temptations by appealing to the Law as witness, and not in virtue of his power, *so that, by this, he might both give greater honour to man and mete out greater punishment to his adversary, since the enemy of the human race was conquered, not as by God, but as by man*, as Pope Leo says.[15]

Hence: 1. To make use of what is necessary for sustenance is not the sin of gluttony; but if a man does anything inordinate out of desire for such sustenance, it can pertain to the vice of gluttony. Now it is inordinate for anyone, where recourse can be had to human means, to seek food for himself miraculously for the mere sustenance of body. And so the Lord miraculously provided the children of Israel with manna in the wilderness, where food could not be obtained otherwise.[16] Similarly, Christ miraculously provided food for the crowds in the wilderness, where food could not be obtained otherwise. But in order to assuage his hunger he could have provided for himself otherwise than by working a miracle, just as

---

[16]*Exodus* 16

Joannes Baptista fecit, ut legitur *Matt.*,[17] vel etiam ad loca proxima properando: et ideo reputabat diabolus quod Christus peccaret, si ad subveniendum fami miracula facere attentaret, si esset purus homo.

2. Ad secundum dicendum quod per humiliationem exteriorem frequenter quærit aliquis gloriam, qua exaltetur circa spiritualia bona. Unde Augustinus dicit, *Animadvertendum est, non in solo rerum corporearum nitore atque pompa, sed etiam in ipsis sordibus luctuosis esse posse jactantiam.*[18] Et ad hoc significandum diabolus Christo suasit, ut ad quærendum gloriam spiritualem corporaliter mitteret se deorsum.

3. Ad tertium dicendum quod divitias et honores mundi appetere peccatum est, quando hujusmodi inordinate appetuntur. Hoc autem præcipue manifestatur ex hoc quod pro hujusmodi adipiscendis homo aliquid inhonestum facit. Et ideo non fuit contentus diabolus persuadere cupiditatem divitiarum et honorum; sed induxit ad hoc quod propter hujusmodi adipiscenda Christus eum adoraret, quod est maximum scelus et contra Deum.[19] Nec solum dixit, *Si adoraveris me,* sed addidit, *Si cadens,* quia, ut dicit Ambrosius, *habet ambitio domesticum periculum: ut enim dominetur aliis, prius servit, et curvatur obsequio, ut honore donetur: et dum vult esse sublimior, fit remissior.*[20]

Et similiter etiam in præcedentibus tentationibus ex appetitu unius peccati in aliud peccatum inducere est conatus; sicut ex desiderio cibi conatus est inducere in vanitatem sine causa miracula faciendi; et ex cupiditate gloriæ conatus est inducere ad tentandum Deum per præcipitium.

4. Ad quartum dicendum quod, sicut dicit Ambrosius, *Non dixisset Scriptura quod consummata omni tentatione, diabolus recessit ab illo, nisi in tribus præmissis esset omnium materia delictorum; quia causæ tentationum causæ sunt cupiditatum,* scilicet *carnis oblectatio, spes gloriæ et aviditas potentiæ.*[21]

5. Ad quintum dicendum quod, sicut Augustinus dicit, *incertum est quid prius factum sit, utrum regna terræ prius demonstrata sint ei, et postea in pinnaculum templi locatus sit; an hoc prius, et illud postea; nihil tamen ad rem, dum omnia facta esse manifestum sit.*[22] Videntur autem Evangelistæ diversum ordinem tenuisse, quia quandoque ex inani gloria venitur ad cupiditatem, quandoque e converso.

6. Ad sextum dicendum quod Christus, cum passus fuisset tentationis injuriam, dicente sibi diabolo, *Si Filius Dei es, mitte te deorsum,* non est turbatus, nec diabolum increpavit. Quando vero diabolus Dei sibi

---

[17]*Matthew* 3, 4
[18]*De Sermone Domini in Monte* II, 12. PL 34, 1287
[19]*Job* 31, 28
[20]*In Luc.* IV, on 4, 5. PL 15, 1621

John the Baptist did, as we read;[17] or even by hastening to neighbouring places. Consequently the devil reckoned that if Christ were a mere man, he would sin by attempting to work a miracle in order to assuage his hunger.

2. It often happens that a man will, by submitting himself to external humiliation, seek glory whereby he is exalted as regards spiritual good. For this reason Augustine says, *It must be noted that it is possible to boast not only of the splendour and magnificence of material things, but also of their filthy squalor.*[18] And to signify this, the devil encouraged Christ to seek spiritual glory by throwing himself down bodily.

3. It is a sin to desire worldly riches and honours when things of this sort are desired inordinately. And this is especially clear in the case of a man who does something wrong in order to acquire such things. And so the devil was not satisfied with encouraging cupidity for riches and honours, but he went on to tempt Christ to acquire such things by worshipping him, which is a very serious offence, and against God.[19] He does not say only, *if you will worship me*, but he adds, *if, falling down*; because, as Ambrose says, *Ambition harbours a danger within itself: for, while seeking to rule, it will serve; it will bow in submission that it may be crowned with honour; and the higher it aims, the lower it abases itself.*[20]

And so, as in the preceding temptations, he tried to lead him from desiring one sin to committing a second one; thus he tried to lead him from desiring food to working a needless miracle in vain; and from desiring glory inordinately to tempting God by throwing himself down headlong.

4. As Ambrose says, *Scripture would not have said that 'having exhausted all ways of tempting him, the devil left him', unless the matter of all sins were included in the three temptations already mentioned. For the causes of temptations are the causes of inordinate desires*—namely, *lust of the flesh, hope of glory, vehement desire for power.*[21]

5. As Augustine says, *It is not certain which happened first; whether the kingdoms of the world were first shown to him, and afterwards he was set on the parapet of the Temple; or the latter first, and the former afterwards. However, it does not matter, provided that it be made clear that all these things did take place.*[22] It would seem that the Evangelists present them in a different order, because sometimes vainglory leads to cupidity, and sometimes the reverse happens.

6. After Christ had suffered the insult of being tempted by the devil's saying to him, *If you are the Son of God, throw yourself down*, he was not disturbed, nor did he rebuke the devil. But when the devil usurped the

---

[21]ibid, on 4, 13. PL 15, 1622
[22]*De Consensu Evang.* II, 16. PL 34, 1093

usurpavit honorem, dicens, *Hæc omnia tibi dabo, si cadens adoraveris me*, exasperatus est et repulit eum, dicens, *Vade, Satana*: ut nos illius discamus exemplo, nostras quidem injurias æquanimiter sustinere, Dei autem injurias nec usque ad auditum sufferre.

7. Ad septimum dicendum quod, sicut Chrysostomus dicit, *forsitan diabolus, quantum ad se, sic Christum assumebat in pinnaculum templi, ut ab omnibus videretur; ipse autem, nesciente diabolo, sic agebat ut a nemine videretur.*[23]

Quod autem dicit, *Et ostendit ei omnia regna mundi, et gloriam eorum*, non est intelligendum quod videret ipsa regna, vel civitates eorum, vel populos, vel aurum vel argentum; sed partes terræ, in quibus unumquodque regnum, vel civitas posita est, diabolus Christo digito demonstrabat, et uniuscujusque regni honores et statum verbis exponebat.[24] Vel secundum Origen em, ostendit ei quomodo ipse per diversa vitia regnabat in mundo.[25]

---

[23]*Opus imperf.* v, on *Matthew* 4, 5. PG 56, 665–6   [24]ibid, on 4, 8. PG 56, 667
[25]*In Luc.* xxx, on *Luke* 4, 5. PG 13, 1877. cf PL 26, 285

THE TEMPTATION OF CHRIST

honour due to God, saying, *I will give you all these, if you fall at my feet and worship me,* he became exasperated, and repulsed him, saying, *Begone, Satan*: that we might learn from his example to suffer magnanimously the insults aimed at us, but not to allow ourselves even so much as to listen to those which are aimed at God.

7. As Chrysostom says: *The devil set him* on the parapet of the Temple[b] *that he might be seen by all, whereas, unknown to the devil, he acted so as not to be seen by anyone.*[23]

In regard to the words, '*He showed him all the kingdoms of the world and their splendour*', *we are not to understand the very kingdoms, with the cities and inhabitants, their silver and gold: but that the devil pointed out the direction in which each kingdom or city lay, and set forth to him in words their splendour and worth.*[24] Or, as Origen says, he showed him how by giving himself up to divers vices he could rule over the world.[25]

---

[b]*pinnaculum Templi*, probably the top of the wall of the Temple enclave overlooking the Kedron chasm.

Quæstio 42. de doctrina Christi

DEINDE CONSIDERANDUM est de doctrina Christi, et circa hoc quæruntur quatuor:

1. utrum Christus debuerit prædicare solum Judæis, an etiam gentilibus;
2. utrum in sua prædicatione debuerit turbationem Judæorum vitare;
3. utrum debuerit prædicare publice vel occulte;
4. utrum debuerit docere solum verbo vel etiam scripto.

De tempore autem quo docere incœpit, supra dictum est,[1] cum de baptismo ejus ageretur.

articulus 1. utrum conveniens fuerit Christum Judæis, et non gentilibus prædicare

AD PRIMUM sic proceditur:[2] 1. Videtur quod Christus non solum Judæis, sed etiam gentilibus debuerit prædicare. Dicitur enim *Isa.*, *Parum est ut sis mihi servus ad suscitandas tribus Israel, et fæces Jacob convertendas: dedi te in lucem gentium, ut sis salus mea usque ad extremum terræ*.[3] Sed lumen et salutem Christus præbuit per suam doctrinam. Ergo videtur parum fuisse, si solum Judæis et non gentilibus prædicavit.

2. Præterea, sicut dicitur *Matt.*, *Erat docens eos, sicut potestatem habens*.[4] Sed major potestas doctrinæ ostenditur in instructione illorum qui penitus nihil audierant, quales erant gentiles: unde Apostolus dicit *Rom.*, *Sic prædicavi Evangelium hoc, non ubi nominatus est Christus, ne super alienum fundamentum ædificarem*.[5] Ergo multo magis Christus prædicare debuit gentilibus quam Judæis.

3. Præterea, utilior est instructio multorum quam unius. Sed Christus aliquos gentilium instruxit, sicut mulierem Samaritanam, *Joan.*[6] et Chananæam, *Matt.*[7] Ergo videtur quod multo fortius Christus debuerit multitudini gentium prædicare.

SED CONTRA est quod Dominus dicit *Matt.*, *Non sum missus nisi ad oves, quæ perierunt domus Israel*.[8] Sed *Rom.* dicitur: *Quomodo prædicabunt, nisi mittantur?*[9] Ergo Christus non debuit prædicare nisi Judæis.

---

[1] 3a. 39, 3
[2] cf III *Sent.* 1, *Expos. litt. In Matt.* 10, 15; *In Rom.* 15, 1
[3] *Isaiah* 49, 6
[4] *Matthew* 7, 29
[5] *Romans* 15, 20
[6] *John* 4, 7
[7] *Matthew* 15, 22
[8] *Matthew* 15, 24
[9] *Romans* 10, 15

Question 42. Christ's teaching

WE MUST NEXT CONSIDER Christ's teaching,[a] regarding which there are four points of inquiry:

1. whether Christ should have preached to the Jews only, or to the gentiles as well;
2. whether in his preaching he should have avoided stirring up the Jews;
3. whether he should have preached openly or secretly;
4. whether he should have preached by word only, or by writing also.

The time when he began to teach has already been discussed above when his baptism was considered.[1]

article 1. whether Christ should have preached not only to the Jews, but to the gentiles as well

THE FIRST POINT:[2] 1. It would seem that he should not have preached only to the Jews. For it is written, *It is not enough for you to be my servant that you restore the tribes of Israel and bring back the survivors of Jacob: I have given you to be the light of the gentiles, so that my salvation may reach to the very ends of the earth.*[3] But Christ gave light and salvation through his teaching. Therefore it would seem that it was not enough for him to preach to the Jews alone, and not to the gentiles.

2. Furthermore, as it is written, *he taught them as one having power.*[4] Now the power of his teaching is made more manifest in the instruction of those who, like the gentiles, have not heard anything at all. For this reason St Paul says, *I have made it a rule not to preach where Christ's name has already been heard, lest I build upon another man's foundation.*[5] Therefore Christ should have much rather preached to the gentiles than to the Jews.

3. Furthermore, it is more useful to instruct many than one. But Christ instructed some individual gentiles, such as the Samaritan woman,[6] and the Canaanite woman.[7] Therefore, it would seem there was all the more reason for Christ to preach to the gentiles in general.

ON THE OTHER HAND our Lord says, *I was sent only to the lost sheep of the House of Israel.*[8] And it is written, *And how shall they have a preacher unless one is sent?*[9] Therefore Christ should not have preached to the gentiles.

---

[a] cf Appendix 5. On human teaching. cf 1a. 117. Vol. 15, ed. M. Charlesworth.

RESPONSIO: Dicendum quod conveniens fuit prædicationem Christi tam per ipsum quam per Apostolos a principio solis Judæis exhiberi.

Primo quidem ut ostenderet per suum adventum impleri promissiones antiquitus factas Judæis, non autem gentilibus. Unde Apostolus dicit *Rom.*, *Dico Christum Jesum ministrum fuisse circumcisionis*, idest apostolum et prædicatorem Judæorum, *propter veritatem Dei, ad confirmandas promissiones patrum.*[10]

Secundo, ut ejus adventus ostenderetur esse a Deo. *Quæ* enim *a Deo sunt, ordinata sunt*, ut dicitur *Rom.*[11] Hoc autem debitus ordo exigebat, ut Judæis, qui Deo erant propinquiores per fidem et cultum unius Dei, prius doctrina Christi proponeretur et per eos transmitteretur ad gentes; sicut etiam in cœlesti hierarchia per superiores angelos ad inferiores divinæ illuminationes deveniunt.[12] Unde super illud *Matt.*, *Non sum missus, nisi ad oves, quæ perierunt domus Israel*,[13] dicit Hieronymus, *Non hoc dicit, quin et ad gentes missus sit, sed quod primum ad Israel missus est.*[14] Unde *Isa.* dicitur, *Mittam ex eis, qui salvati fuerunt*, scilicet ex Judæis, *ad gentes, et annuntiabunt gloriam meam gentibus.*[15]

Tertio, ut Judæis auferret calumniandi materiam: unde super illud *Matt.*, *In viam gentium ne abieritis*,[16] dicit Hieronymus, *Oportebat primum adventum Christi nuntiari Judæis, ne justam haberent excusationem, dicentes, ideo se Dominum rejecisse, quia ad gentes et Samaritanos apostolos miserit.*[17]

Quarto, quia Christus per crucis victoriam meruit potestatem et dominium super gentes, unde dicitur *Apoc.*, *Qui vicerit, dabo illi potestatem super gentes sicut et ego accepi a Patre meo;*[18] et *Phil.* dicitur quod quia *factus est obediens usque ad mortem crucis. Deus exaltavit illum, ut in nomine Jesu omne genu flectatur, et omnis lingua ei confiteatur.*[19] Et ideo ante passionem suam noluit gentibus prædicari suam doctrinam; sed post passionem dixit discipulis *Matt.*, *Euntes docete omnes gentes.*[20] Propter quod, ut legitur *Joan.*, cum imminente passione quidam gentiles vellent Jesum videre, respondit, *Nisi granum frumenti cadens in terram mortuum fuerit, ipsum solum manet; si autem mortuum fuerit, multum fructum affert;*[21] et, sicut Augustinus dicit ibidem, *se dicebat granum mortificandum in infidelitate Judæorum, et multiplicandum in fide omnium populorum.*[22]

1. Ad primum ergo dicendum quod Christus fuit in lumen et salutem gentium per discipulos suos quos ad prædicandum gentibus misit.

2. Ad secundum dicendum quod non est minoris potestatis, sed majoris

---

[10]*Romans* 15, 8
[11]*Romans* 13, 1
[12]Dionysius, *De cæl. hier.* 7. PG 3, 209. cf also 1a. 106, 1, 3 & 4
[13]*Matthew* 15, 24
[14]*In Matt.* II, on 15, 24. PL 26, 110
[15]*Isaiah* 66, 19
[16]*Matthew* 10, 5
[17]*In Matt.* I, on 10, 5. PL 26, 62
[18]*Apocalypse* 2, 26 & 28
[19]*Philippians* 2, 8
[20]*Matthew* 28, 19

REPLY: It was fitting in the beginning for Christ's preaching, through himself as well as through his apostles, to be directed to the Jews alone. First of all, to show that by his coming the promises were fulfilled which had been made of old to the Jews, and not to the gentiles. For which reason St Paul says, *I say that Christ became the servant of the circumcised*, that is, the apostle and preacher of the Jews, *so that God could faithfully carry out the promises made to the patriarchs.*[10]

Secondly, in order to show that his coming was from God. For, as it is written, *Those things which are from God are well ordered.*[11] Now right order demanded that Christ's teaching should first be presented to the Jews, who, by reason of their believing in and worshipping one God, were nearer to God, and that it should be transmitted through them to the gentiles: just as in the heavenly hierarchy the divine illuminations come to the lower angels through the higher ones.[12] For this reason, writing on, *I was sent only to the lost sheep of the House of Israel*,[13] Jerome says, *He does not mean by this that he was not sent to the gentiles, but that he was sent to the Jews first.*[14] For which reason it is written, *I will send some of their survivors*, i.e. the Jews, *to the gentiles, and they will proclaim my glory to the gentiles.*[15]

Thirdly, in order to deprive the Jews of ground for misrepresenting him. For this reason, on *Do not turn your steps to gentile territory*,[16] Jerome says, *It was necessary for Christ's coming to be announced to the Jews first, lest they should have a valid excuse, and say that they had rejected our Lord because he had sent his apostles to the gentiles and Samaritans.*[17]

Fourthly, because it was through the victory of the cross that Christ merited power and dominion over the gentiles. For which reason it is written, *To those who prove victorious I will give them power over the gentiles which I myself have been given by my Father;*[18] and because *he was humbler yet, even to accepting death on a cross, God raised him high, so that every one should bend the knee at the name of Jesus, and every tongue acclaim him.*[19] And so, before his passion he did not wish his teachings to be preached to the gentiles; but after his passion he said to his disciples, *Go, therefore, make disciples of all the gentiles.*[20] For this reason, as it is written, when, shortly before his passion, certain disciples wished to see Jesus, he answered, *Unless the grain of wheat falls on the ground and dies, it remains a single grain; but if it dies, it yields a rich harvest.*[21] And as Augustine says regarding this passage, *He called himself the grain of wheat which must be made to die by the Jews' lack of faith, multiplied by the faith of the gentiles.*[22]

Hence: 1. Christ was given to be the light and salvation of the gentiles through his disciples, whom he sent to preach to them.

2. It is an indication, not of lesser, but of greater power to do something

---

[21]*John* 12, 20-5   [22]*In Joan.* LI, 9, on 12, 20. PL 35, 1766

facere aliquid per alios quam per seipsum. Et ideo in hoc maxime potestas divina in Christo monstrata est, quod discipulis suis tantam virtutem contulit in docendo, ut gentes, quæ nihil de Christo audierant, converterent ad ipsum.

Potestas autem Christi in docendo attenditur et quantum ad miracula, per quæ doctrinam suam confirmabat, et quantum ad efficaciam persuadendi, et quantum ad auctoritatem loquentis, quia loquebatur quasi dominium habens super legem, cum diceret, *Ego autem dico vobis;*[23] et etiam quantum ad virtutem rectitudinis, quam in sua conversatione monstrabat, sine peccato vivendo.

3. Ad tertium dicendum quod, sicut Christus non debuit a principio indifferenter gentilibus suam doctrinam communicare, ut Judæis tanquam primogenito populo deditus observaretur, ita etiam non debuit gentiles omnino repellere, ne spes salutis eis præcluderetur. Et propter hoc aliqui gentilium particulariter sunt admissi propter excellentiam fidei et devotionis eorum.

articulus 2. utrum Christus debuerit Judæis sine eorum offensione prædicare

AD SECUNDUM sic proceditur:[1] 1. Videtur quod Christus debuerit Judæis sine eorum offensione prædicare, quia, ut Augustinus dicit, *in homine Jesu Christo se nobis ad exemplum vitæ præbuit Filius Dei.*[2] Sed nos debemus vitare offensionem non solum fidelium, sed etiam infidelium, secundum illud 1 ad *Cor.*, *Sine offensione estote Judæis, et gentibus, et Ecclesiæ Dei.*[3] Ergo videtur quod etiam Christus in sua doctrina offensionem Judæorum vitare debuerit.

2. Præterea, nullus sapiens debet facere, unde effectum sui operis impediat. Sed per hoc quod sua doctrina Christus Judæos turbavit impediebatur effectus ejus doctrinæ: dicitur enim *Luc.* quod cum Dominus Pharisæos et Scribas reprehenderet, *cœperunt graviter insistere; et os ejus opprimere de multis, insidiantes ei, et quærentes aliquid capere ex ore ejus, ut accusarent eum.*[4] Non ergo videtur conveniens fuisse quod eos in sua doctrina offenderet.

3. Præterea, Apostolus dicit 1 *Tim.*, *Seniorem ne increpaveris, sed obsecra ut patrem.*[5] Sed sacerdotes et principes Judæorum erant illius populi seniores. Ergo videtur quod non fuerint duris increpationibus arguendi.

SED CONTRA est quod *Isa.* fuerat prophetizatum quod Christus esset in *lapidem offensionis, et in petram scandali duabus domibus Israel.*[6]

[23]Matthew 5, 22, 28, 32, 34, 39, 44
[1]cf 2a2æ. 43, 7. In Matt. 15
[3]1 Corinthians 10, 32
[2]De Agone Christiano 11. PL 40, 298
[4]Luke 11, 53-4

through others rather than by oneself. And so the divine power in Christ was made most manifest in this, that he bestowed on his disciples such a power for teaching that they converted the gentiles to Christ, although these had heard nothing regarding him.

Now, in considering the power of Christ's teaching we take into account the following: the miracles by which he confirmed his teaching; his persuasiveness; the authority with which he spoke, because he spoke as one who was above the Law when he said, *But I say to you*;[23] and also, the force of uprightness which he showed in his manner of life, living as he did sinlessly.

3. Just as, at the outset, Christ should not have presented his teaching to the gentiles indiscriminately, in order that he might be seen as one who was sent to the Jews, as to the first-born people, so likewise he should not have shunned the gentiles altogether, lest they should be denied access to the hope of salvation. For this reason a few individual gentiles were admitted, on account of the excellence of their faith and devotion.

article 2. whether Christ should have preached to the Jews without offending them

THE SECOND POINT:[1] 1. It would seem that Christ should have preached without offence. For, as Augustine says, *In the man Jesus Christ, the Son of God gives himself to us as a model of life.*[2] But we should avoid offending, not only those who have the faith, but also those who lack the faith: *Never do anything offensive to anyone—to Jews or Greeks or to the Church of God.*[3] Therefore it would seem that, in his teaching, Christ also should have avoided offending the Jews.

2. Furthermore, no wise man should do anything that will hinder the effectiveness of his work. But because, in his teaching, Christ stirred up the Jews, its effectiveness was hindered; for it is written that when our Lord reproved the Pharisees and Scribes, they *began a furious attack on him and tried to force answers from him on many matters, setting traps for him and plotting to seize upon something he might say, that they might accuse him.*[4] It would seem therefore unfitting for him in his teaching to offend them.

3. Furthermore, St Paul says, *Do not rebuke a man older than yourself, but advise him as you would your own father.*[5] But the priests and leaders of the Jews were the elders of that people. Therefore it would seem that they should not have been rebuked with harsh words.

ON THE OTHER HAND it was prophesied by Isaiah that Christ would be *a stumbling-stone and a rock to bring down the two Houses of Israel.*[6]

---

[5] *1 Timothy* 5, 1   [6] *Isaiah* 8, 14

RESPONSIO: Dicendum quod salus multitudinis est præferenda paci quorumcumque singularium hominum. Et ideo quando aliqui sua perversitate multitudinis salutem impediunt, non est timenda eorum offensio a prædicatore vel doctore ad hoc quod multitudinis saluti provideat. Scribæ autem, et Pharisæi, et principes Judæorum sua malitia plurimum impediebant populi salutem, tum quia repugnabant Christi doctrinæ, per quam solam poterat esse salus, tum etiam quia pravis suis moribus vitam populi corrumpebant. Et ideo Dominus, non obstante offensione eorum, publice veritatem docebat quam illi oderant, et eorum vitia arguebat. Et ideo dicitur *Matt.* quod discipulis Domino dicentibus, *Scis quia Judæi, audito hoc verbo, scandalizati sunt?* respondit, *Sinite illos, cæci sunt ducesque cæcorum: cæcus autem si cæco ducatum præstet, ambo in foveam cadunt.*[7]

1. Ad primum ergo dicendum quod homo sic debet esse sine offensione omnibus ut nulli det suo facto vel dicto minus recto occasionem ruinæ; sed *cum de veritate scandalum oritur, magis est sustinendum scandalum, quam veritas relinquatur,* ut Gregorius dicit.[8]

2. Ad secundum dicendum quod per hoc quod Christus publice Scribas et Pharisæos arguebat non impedivit, sed magis promovit effectum suæ doctrinæ, quia cum eorum vitia populo innotescebant, minus avertebatur a Christo propter verba Scribarum et Pharisæorum, qui semper doctrinæ Christi obsistebant.

3. Ad tertium dicendum quod illud verbum Apostoli est intelligendum de illis senioribus qui non solum ætate vel auctoritate, sed etiam honestate sunt senes, secundum illud *Num., Congrega mihi septuaginta viros, de senioribus Israel, quos tu nosti, quod senes populi sint.*[9] Si autem auctoritatem senectutis in instrumentum malitiæ vertant publice peccando, sunt manifeste et acriter arguendi; sicut et *Dan.* dixit, *Inveterate dierum malorum,* etc.[10]

articulus 3. utrum Christus omnia publice docere debuerit

AD TERTIUM sic proceditur: 1. Videtur quod Christus non omnia publice docere debuerit. Legitur enim multa seorsum discipulis dixisse, sicut patet in sermone cœnæ;[1] unde et *Matt.* dixit, *Quod in aure audistis in cubilibus, prædicabitur in tectis.*[2] Non ergo omnia publice docuit.

2. Præterea, profunda sapientiæ non sunt nisi perfectis exponenda, secundum illud I ad *Cor., Sapientiam loquimur inter perfectos.*[3] Sed doctrina

---

[7]*Matthew* 15, 12 & 14
[8]*In Ezechiel* VII, 5. PL 76, 842
[9]*Numbers* 11, 16
[10]*Daniel* 13, 52
[1]*John* 13, 1

REPLY: The salvation of the many is to be preferred to the tranquillity of any individual whatsoever. And so, when a few, by their perversity, hinder the salvation of the many, the preacher and the teacher should not fear to offend those, in order to offer salvation to the many. Now the Scribes and Pharisees and the leaders of the Jews were by their malice hindering as much as possible the salvation of the people, both because they themselves were opposed to Christ's teaching, alone through which there can be salvation, and because by their evil ways they corrupted the life of the people. Consequently, our Lord, undeterred by their taking offence, openly taught the truth which they hated, and denounced their vices. And so it is written that when the disciples of our Lord said, *Do you know that the Pharisees were shocked when they heard what you said?* he answered, *Leave them alone: they are blind men leading blind men; and if one blind man leads another, both fall into the pit.*[7]

Hence: 1. A man ought so to avoid giving offence, that he is not by improper word or deed the occasion of anyone's downfall. *But if scandal arise from the truth, the scandal should be sustained rather than the truth be relinquished*, as Gregory says.[8]

2. By openly denouncing the Scribes and Pharisees, Christ promoted rather than hindered the effectiveness of his teaching. Because when the people came to know the vices of these, they were less inclined to turn against Christ on account of what they heard from the Scribes and Pharisees, who continued to resist Christ's teaching.

3. This saying of St Paul is to be understood of those elders who are old not only by reason of age and authority, but also by reason of probity: *Gather seventy of the elders of Israel, men you know to be elders of the people.*[9] But if by sinning openly they turn the authority of their old age into an instrument for wrongdoing, they should be denounced openly and severely; thus *Daniel, You have grown old in wickedness*, etc.[10]

article 3. whether Christ should have taught everything openly

THE THIRD POINT: 1. It would seem not. For we read that he said many things to his disciples apart, as is seen clearly in his discourse at the Supper.[1] For which reason he said, *What you have heard whispered in hidden places will be proclaimed on the housetops.*[2] Therefore he did not teach everything openly.

2. Furthermore, the depths of wisdom should be explained only to the perfect: *We speak of wisdom among those who have reached perfection.*[3] Now

---

[2]*Matthew* 10, 27 & *Luke* 12, 3 combined
[3]1 *Corinthians* 2, 6

Christi continebat profundissimam sapientiam. Non ergo erat imperfectæ multitudini communicanda.

3. Præterea, idem est veritatem aliquam occultare silentio et obscuritate verborum. Sed Christus veritatem, quam prædicabat, occultabat turbis obscuritate verborum, quia *sine parabolis non loquebatur ad eos*, ut dicitur *Matt.*[4] Ergo pari ratione poterat occultare silentio.

SED CONTRA est quod ipse dicit *Joan.*, In occulto locutus sum nihil.[5]

RESPONSIO: Dicendum quod doctrina alicujus potest esse in occulto tripliciter. Uno modo quantum ad intentionem docentis, qui intendit suam doctrinam non manifestare multis, sed magis occultare. Quod quidem contingit dupliciter. Quandoque ex invidia docentis, qui vult per suam scientiam excellere, et ideo scientiam suam non vult aliis communicare;[6] quod in Christo locum non habuit, ex cujus persona dicitur *Sap.*, *Quam sine fictione didici, et sine invidia communico, et honestatem illius non abscondo.*[7] Quandoque vero hoc contingit propter inhonestatem eorum quæ docentur, sicut Augustinus dicit quod *quædam sunt mala quæ portare non potest qualiscumque pudor humanus.*[8] Unde de doctrina hæreticorum dicitur *Prov.*, *Aquæ furtivæ dulciores sunt.*[9] Doctrina autem Christi non est neque de errore, neque de immunditia.[10] Et ideo Dominus dicit *Marc.*, *Numquid venit lucerna*, idest vera et honesta doctrina, *ut sub modio ponatur?*[11]

Alio modo aliqua doctrina est in occulto quia paucis proponitur: et sic Christus etiam nihil docuit in occulto, quia Christus omnem doctrinam suam vel turbæ toti proposuit, vel omnibus suis discipulis in communi. Unde Augustinus dicit, *Quis in occulto loquitur, qui coram tot hominibus loquitur; præsertim si hoc loquitur paucis, quod per eos vult innotescere multis?*[12]

Tertio modo aliqua doctrina est in occulto quantum ad modum docendi. Et sic Christus quædam turbis loquebatur in occulto, parabolis utens ad annuntianda spiritualia mysteria, ad quæ capienda non erant idonei vel digni: et tamen melius erat eis, vel sic sub tegumento parabolarum spiritualium doctrinam audire quam omnino ea privari. Harum tamen parabolarum apertam et nudam veritatem Dominus discipulis exponebat,[13] per quos deveniret ad alios qui essent idonei, secundum illud 2 *Tim.*, *Quæ audisti a me per multos testes, hæc commenda fidelibus hominibus, qui idonei erunt et alios docere.*[14] Et hoc significatum est *Num.*, ubi

---

[4]*Matthew* 13, 34 [5]*John* 18, 20
[6]Gregory, *Moral.* XXXI, 45. PL 76, 621. cf 2a2æ. 34, 4 ad 1; 162, 8 ad 3
[7]*Wisdom* 7, 13 [8]*In Joan.* XCVI, on 16, 12. PL 35, 1877
[9]*Proverbs* 9, 17 [10]cf 1 *Thessalonians* 2, 3
[11]*Mark* 4, 21 [12]*In Joan.* CXIII, 3 on 18. PL 35, 1934

CHRIST'S TEACHING

Christ's teaching contained the most profound wisdom. Therefore it should not have been made known to the many who were imperfect.

3. Furthermore, it amounts to the same thing, to hide the truth by keeping silence or by speaking obscurely. Now Christ, by speaking to the crowds obscurely, hid from them the truth which he preached, since *he would not speak to them except in parables.*[4] In the same way, therefore, the truth could have been hidden from them by his keeping silence.

ON THE OTHER HAND he himself says, *I have said nothing in secret.*[5]

REPLY: Anyone's teaching may be hidden in three ways. In the first way, as it regards the intention of the teacher, who does not intend to make his teaching known to many, but rather to hide it. And this may happen in two ways. Sometimes, on account of the teacher who, out of envy, wishes to excel in his knowledge and is therefore unwilling to communicate it to others.[6] But this could not be the case with Christ, of whose person it is said, *What I have learned without self-interest, I communicate without envy; I do not intend to hide her riches.*[7] But sometimes this happens because of the baseness of what is taught. As Augustine says, *There are some things so bad that no sort of human modesty can endure them.*[8] For which reason, regarding what the heretics teach, it is written, *Stolen waters are sweeter.*[9] But there is nothing erroneous or immoral about what Christ taught.[10] And so our Lord says, *Would you bring in a lamp,* i.e. a teaching which is true and pure, *and put it under a bushel basket?*[11]

Secondly, someone's teaching may be hidden by reason of its being presented to a few. And thus, again, Christ taught nothing in a hidden way, because he presented his entire teaching either to the whole crowd or to all his disciples gathered together. For this reason, Augustine says, *Who will say that he spoke in a hidden way when he spoke in the presence of so many? especially if what he said to a few he wished through them to be made known to many?*[12]

Thirdly, someone's teaching may be hidden regarding the manner in which it is taught. And thus Christ spoke certain things in a hidden way to the crowds, by employing parables to proclaim spiritual mysteries which they were either unfit or unworthy to grasp. Even so, it was better for them to hear spiritual teaching, although veiled in parables, than to be deprived of it altogether. Nevertheless our Lord explained the pure and unveiled truth of these parables to his disciples,[13] so that through them it might reach those others who were fit to receive it, *You have heard what I taught you openly; hand it on to reliable people who are fit to teach others.*[14] And this

---

[13]cf *Matthew* 13, 10   [14]II *Timothy* 2, 2

mandatur, quod filii Aaron involverent vasa sanctuarii, quæ Levitæ involuta portarent.[15]

1. Ad primum ergo dicendum quod, sicut Hilarius dicit exponens illud verbum inductum, *non legimus Dominum solitum fuisse noctibus sermocinari, et doctrinam tradidisse in tenebris; sed hoc dicit, quia omnis sermo ejus carnalibus tenebræ sunt, et verbum ejus infidelibus nox est. Itaque quod a se dictum est, cum libertate fidei et confessionis vult esse loquendum.*[16]

Vel secundum Hieronymum, comparative loquitur, quia videlicet erudiebat eos in parvo Judææ loco respectu totius mundi, in quo erat per Apostolorum prædicationem doctrina Christi publicanda.[17]

2. Ad secundum dicendum quod Dominus non omnia profunda suæ sapientiæ sua doctrina manifestavit, non solum turbis, sed nec etiam discipulis, quibus dixit *Joan., Adhuc multa habeo vobis dicere, quæ non potestis portare modo.*[18] Sed tamen quodcumque dignum duxit aliis tradere de sua sapientia, non in occulto, sed palam proposuit, licet non ab omnibus intelligeretur. Unde Augustinus dicit, *Intelligendum est ita dixisse Dominum, Palam locutus sum mundo, ac si dixisset, Multi me audierunt. Et rursus non erat palam, quia non intelligebant.*[19]

3. Ad tertium dicendum quod turbis Dominus in parabolis loquebatur, sicut dictum est,[20] quia non erant digni, nec idonei nudam veritatem accipere, quam discipulis exponebat.

Quod autem dicitur, quod *sine parabolis non loquebatur eis*, secundum Chrysostomum, intelligendum est quantum ad illum sermonem; quamvis alias sine parabolis multa turbis locutus fuerit.[21] Vel secundum Augustinum hoc dicitur, *non quia nihil proprie locutus est, sed quia nullum fere sermonem explicavit ubi non per parabolam aliquid significaverit; quamvis in eo aliqua proprie dixerit.*[22]

articulus 4. utrum Christus debuerit doctrinam suam scripto tradere

AD QUARTUM sic proceditur: 1. Videtur quod Christus doctrinam suam debuerit scripto tradere. Scriptura enim inventa est ad hoc quod doctrina commendetur memoriæ in futurum. Sed doctrina Christi duratura erat in æternum, secundum illud *Luc., Cœlum et terra transibunt, verba autem mea non transibunt.*[1] Ergo videtur quod Christus debuerit suam doctrinam scripto mandare.

---

[15] *Numbers* 4, 5
[17] *In Matt.* I, on 10, 27. PL 26, 66
[19] *In Joan.* CXIII, 3, on 18, 13. PL 35, 1934
[21] *In Matt.* XLVII. PG 58, 481
[22] *De Quæst. Evang. in Matt.* XVII, on 13, 24. PL 35, 1373
[1] *Luke* 21, 33

[16] *In Matt.* 10, 17. PL 9, 972
[18] *John* 16, 12
[20] in the corpus

is the reason why the sons of Aaron are commanded to cover the sanctuary vessels which, having been covered, are carried by the Levites.[15a]

Hence: 1. As Hilary says, explaining the passage quoted, *we do not read that our Lord was wont to preach at night, and present his teaching in the dark: but he says this, because what he says is darkness to the worldly-minded, and his words are night to unbelievers. And so, everything said by him should be spoken freely with faith and conviction in the midst of unbelievers.*[16]

Or, according to Jerome, he is making a comparison, because he was instructing them in Judaea, which is a small place in relation to the whole world, where Christ's teaching would be disseminated by the preaching of the apostles.[17]

2. Our Lord did not, by his teaching, make known all the depths of his wisdom, either to the crowds, or even to his disciples, to whom he said, *I still have many things to say to you but they would be too much for you now.*[18] Nevertheless whatever things out of his wisdom he deemed right to hand on, he explained, not in a hidden way, but openly, even though he was not understood by all. For this reason Augustine says, *We must understand that when our Lord said, 'I have spoken openly to the world,' it is as if he had said, 'Many have heard me', and, on the other hand, it was not openly, because they did not understand.*[19]

3. As stated above,[20] our Lord spoke to the crowds in parables, because they were neither fit nor worthy to receive the unveiled truth, which he disclosed to his disciples.

However, when he said *he would not speak to them except in parables*, we are to understand, according to Chrysostom, that it was in reference to that particular discourse, since at other times he said many things to the crowds without parables.[21] Or, according to Augustine, this means, *not that he spoke nothing in its proper sense, but that he hardly ever delivered a discourse where he did not bring out his meaning by reference to a parable, although during the course of it he said some things in their proper sense.*[22]

article 4. whether Christ should have put his teaching into writing

THE FOURTH POINT: 1. It would seem so. For it is the purpose of writing to call one's teaching to mind in the future. Now Christ's teaching was to last for ever: *Heaven and earth will pass away, but my words will never pass away.*[1] Therefore it would seem that Christ should have put his teaching into writing.

---

[a]Speaking in parables: this was adopted as a means of teaching, which was not thereby through plain-speaking. Parables, however, were never intended to obscure or deceive, a judgment of reprobation on the wilful blindness of Christ's hearers.

2. Præterea, lex vetus in figura Christi præcessit, secundum illud *Heb.*, *Umbram habens lex futurorum bonorum.*[2] Sed lex vetus a Deo fuit descripta, secundum illud *Exod.*, *Dabo tibi duas tabulas lapideas, et legem ac mandata quæ scripsi.*[3] Ergo videtur quod etiam Christus doctrinam suam scribere debuerit.

3. Præterea, ad Christum, qui venerat *illuminare his qui in tenebris et umbra mortis sedent*, ut dicitur *Luc.*,[4] pertinebat erroris occasiones excludere et viam fidei aperire. Sed hoc fecisset doctrinam suam scribendo: dicit enim Augustinus quod *solet nonnullos movere, cur ipse Dominus nihil scripserit, ut aliis de illo scribentibus necesse sit credere; hoc enim illi, et maxime pagani quærunt, qui Christum culpare aut blasphemare non audent, eique tribuunt excellentissimam sapientiam, sed tamen tanquam homini; discipulos vero ejus dicunt magistro suo amplius tribuisse quam erat, ut eum Filium Dei dicerent, et Verbum Dei, per quod facta sunt omnia.*[5] Et postea subdit, *Videntur parati fuisse hoc de illo credere quod de seipso scripsisset, non quod alii de illo pro suo arbitrio prædicassent.*[6] Ergo videtur quod Christus ipse doctrinam suam scripto tradere debuerit.

SED CONTRA est quod nulli libri ab eo scripti habentur in canone Scripturæ.

RESPONSIO: Dicendum conveniens fuisse Christum doctrinam suam non scripsisse. Primo quidem propter dignitatem ipsius: excellentiori enim doctori excellentior modus doctrinæ debetur. Et ideo Christo, tanquam excellentissimo doctori, hic modus competebat ut doctrinam suam auditorum cordibus imprimeret. Propter quod dicitur *Matt.* quod *erat docens eos, sicut potestatem habens.*[7] Unde etiam apud gentiles Pythagoras et Socrates, qui fuerunt excellentissimi doctores, nihil scribere voluerunt. Scriptura enim ordinatur ad impressionem doctrinæ in cordibus auditorum sicut ad finem.

Secundo, propter excellentiam doctrinæ Christi, quæ litteris comprehendi non potest, secundum illud *Joan.*, *Sunt et alia multa, quæ fecit Jesus, quæ si scribantur per singula, nec ipsum arbitror mundum capere posse eos, qui scribendi sunt, libros:*[8] quos, sicut Augustinus dicit, *non spatio locorum credendum est mundum capere non fortasse posse, sed capacitate legentium comprehendi non posse.*[9] Si autem Christus scripto doctrinam suam mandasset, nihil altius de ejus doctrina homines æstimarent quam quod scriptura contineret.

---

[2]*Hebrews* 10, 1
[3]*Exodus* 24, 12
[4]*Luke* 1, 79
[5]*De Consensu Evang.* I, 7. PL 34, 1047
[6]ibid, 12. PL 34, 1047
[7]*Matthew* 7, 29
[8]*John* 21, 25

2. Furthermore, the Old Law was a foreshadowing of Christ: *The Law has only a shadowy reflection of the good things to come.*[2] But the Old Law was put into writing by God: *I will give you two stone tablets—the law and the commandments—which I have written.*[3] Therefore it would seem that Christ also should have put his teaching into writing.

3. Furthermore, to Christ, who came *to enlighten those who sit in darkness,*[4] it belonged to remove any inducement to error and make clear the way to faith. Now he would have accomplished this by putting his teaching into writing: for Augustine says that *there are some who wonder why our Lord wrote nothing himself, so that we must believe what others have written about him. This question is asked most especially by the pagans who dare not blame or blaspheme Christ, and who ascribe to him most excellent, but merely human, wisdom. These say that the disciples made out the Master to be more than he was, as when they said he was the Son of God and the Word of God, by whom all things were made.*[5] And farther on he adds, *It seems that they were prepared to believe regarding him whatever he might have written himself, but not what others at their own discretion preached about him.*[6] Therefore it would seem that Christ himself should have put his teaching into writing.

ON THE OTHER HAND no books written by him are to be found in the canon of Scripture.

REPLY: It was fitting for Christ not to put his teaching into writing. First of all, on account of his dignity. For the more excellent the teacher, the more excellent should be his manner of teaching. And therefore the manner of teaching proper to Christ as the most excellent of teachers was one which would impress his teaching upon the hearts of his hearers. For this reason it is written that *he taught them as one having authority.*[7] And so even among the gentiles, Pythagoras and Socrates chose to write nothing. For what is written has this for its end: to impress its teaching upon the hearts of its hearers.

Secondly, on account of the excellence of Christ's teaching which cannot be contained in a book: *There were many other things that Jesus did, which, if all were written down, the world itself, I think, would not contain all the books that would have to be written.*[8] Which means, according to Augustine: *We are not to believe that as regards physical space the world could not contain them; but that as regards the capacity of the readers they could not be comprehended.*[9] But if Christ had put his teaching into writing, men would judge his teaching to be of no greater profundity than that which the writing could contain.

---

[9]*In Joan.* CXXIV, on 21, 25. PL 35, 1976

Tertio, ut ordine quodam ab ipso doctrina ad omnes perveniret; dum ipse scilicet discipulos suos immediate docuit qui postmodum alios verbo et scripto docuerunt. Si autem ipsemet scripsisset, ejus doctrina immediate ad omnes pervenisset. Unde et de sapientia Dei dicitur *Prov.* quod *misit ancillas suas vocare ad arcem.*[10]

Sciendum tamen est, sicut Augustinus dicit, aliquos gentiles existimasse, Christum quosdam libros scripsisse continentes quædam magica, quibus miracula faciebat, quæ disciplina christiana condemnat. *Et illi tamen qui Christi libros tales se legisse affirmant, nulla talia faciunt, qualia illum libris talibus fecisse mirantur. Divino enim judicio sic errant, ut eosdem libros ad Petrum et Paulum dicant tanquam epistolari titulo prænotatos, eo quod in pluribus locis simul eos cum Christo pictos viderunt. Nec mirum si a pingentibus fingentes decepti sunt; toto enim tempore quo Christus in carne mortali cum suis discipulis vixit, nondum erat Paulus discipulus ejus.*[11]

1. Ad primum ergo dicendum quod, sicut Augustinus dicit, *omnibus discipulis suis tanquam membris sui corporis Christus caput est. Itaque cum illi scripserunt quæ ille ostendit et dixit, nequaquam dicendum est quod ipse non scripserit; quandoquidem membra ejus id operata sunt quod dictante capite cognoverunt; quidquid enim ille de suis factis et dictis nos legere voluit, hoc scribendum illis, tanquam suis manibus imperavit.*[12]

2. Ad secundum dicendum quod quia lex vetus in sensibilibus figuris dabatur, ideo etiam convenienter sensibilibus signis scripta fuit. Sed doctrina Christi, quæ est *lex spiritus vitæ,*[13] scribi debuit *non atramento, sed Spiritu Dei vivi, non in tabulis lapideis, sed in tabulis cordis carnalibus,* ut Apostolus dicit 2 *Cor.*[14]

3. Ad tertium dicendum quod illi qui scripturæ Apostolorum de Christo credere noluerunt, nec ipsi Christo scribenti credidissent, de quo opinabantur quod magicis artibus fecisset miracula.

---

[10]*Proverbs* 9, 3
[11]*De Consensu Evang.* I, 9. PL 34, 1049
[12]ibid I, 35, 54. PL 34, 1070
[13]*Romans* 8, 2

CHRIST'S TEACHING

Thirdly, so that his teaching might reach everyone in an orderly manner: namely, that he himself teach his disciples immediately, and that they subsequently teach others by speaking and writing. If, however, he himself had written, his teaching would have reached everyone immediately. For this reason also it is said of Wisdom that *she has despatched her maidservants with invitations to the city's heights*.[10]

It must be observed, however, that, as Augustine says, some of the gentiles thought that Christ wrote certain books treating of the magical arts by which he worked his miracles: which arts are condemned by Christian doctrine. *And yet those who claim to have read these books of Christ do none of the things which they marvel at his doing according to these same books. Moreover, it is by God's decree that they go so far as to assert erroneously that these same books were entitled as letters to Peter and Paul, because they saw the latter so often depicted in the company of Christ. No wonder that those who fabricate such notions are deceived by the painters. For during the entire time that Christ lived in the mortal flesh with his disciples, Paul was not a disciple of his*.[11]

Hence: 1. As Augustine says in the same book, *Christ is the head of all his disciples who are members of his body. Consequently, when they put into writing what he expressed and said, by no means should we say that he wrote nothing: since it was with him dictating to them as their head, that his members set forth what they knew. For at his command they, being his hands, as it were, wrote whatever he wished us to read concerning his deeds and words.*[12]

2. Since the Old Law was given under sensible forms, therefore it was also fittingly written with sensible signs. But Christ's teaching, which is *the law of the spirit of life*,[13] had to be *written, not with ink, but with the Spirit of the living God; not on stone tablets, but on the tablets of fleshly hearts*, as St Paul says.[14]

3. Those who refuse to believe what the apostles wrote of Christ would not have believed the writings of Christ himself, concerning whom they held the opinion that he worked miracles by means of the magical arts.

---

[14] II Corinthians 3, 3; cf 1a2æ. 106, 1; 107, 1 & 2

DEINDE CONSIDERANDUM est de miraculis a Christo factis;

et primo, in generali;
secundo, in speciali de singulis miraculorum generibus;
tertio, in particulari de transfiguratione ipsius.

Quæstio 43. de miraculis a Christo factis in generali

Circa primum quæruntur quatuor:
1. utrum Christus debuerit miracula facere;
2. utrum fecerit ea virtute divina;
3. quo tempore incœperit miracula facere;
4. utrum per miracula fuerit sufficienter ostensa ejus divinitas.

articulus 1. utrum Christus debuerit facere miracula

AD PRIMUM sic proceditur.[1] 1. Videtur quod Christus miracula facere non debuerit. Factum enim Christi verbo ipsius debuit concordare. Sed ipse dicit *Matt., Generatio mala et adultera signum quærit, et signum non dabitur ei, nisi signum Jonæ prophetæ*.[2] Non ergo debuit miracula facere.

2. Præterea, sicut Christus in secundo adventu venturus est *in virtute magna et majestate*, ut dicitur *Matt.*,[3] ita in primo adventu venit in infirmitate, secundum illud *Isa., Virum dolorum, et scientem infirmitatem*.[4] Sed operatio miraculorum magis pertinet ad virtutem quam ad infirmitatem. Ergo non fuit conveniens quod in primo adventu miracula faceret.

3. Præterea, Christus venit ad hoc ut homines salvaret per fidem, secundum illud *Heb., Aspicientes in auctorem fidei et consummatorem Jesum*.[5] Sed miracula diminuunt meritum fidei: unde Dominus dicit, *Nisi signa et prodigia videritis, non credetis*.[6] Ergo non videtur quod Christus debuerit miracula facere.

SED CONTRA est quod ex persona adversariorum Dei dicitur *Joan., Quid facimus, quia hic homo multa signa facit?*[7]

RESPONSIO: Dicendum quod divinitus conceditur homini miracula facere, propter duo. Primo quidem et principaliter ad confirmandam veritatem quam aliquis docet: quia enim ea quæ sunt fidei humanam rationem excedunt non possunt per rationes humanas probari, sed oportet quod

---
[1] cf *Contra Græcos* 7   [2] *Matthew* 16, 4; cf *Matthew* 12, 39
[3] *Matthew* 24, 30   [4] *Isaiah* 53, 3
[5] *Hebrews* 12, 2   [6] *John* 4, 48   [7] *John* 11, 47

CHRIST'S MIRACLES IN GENERAL

WE MUST NEXT CONSIDER the miracles worked by Christ;[a]

and first, in general (43);
second, specifically of each kind of miracle (44);
third, in particular, of his transfiguration (45).

Question 43. the miracles worked by Christ, in general

Here there are four points to be treated:
1. whether Christ should have worked miracles;
2. whether he worked them by divine power;
3. the time when he began to work miracles;
4. whether his divinity was sufficiently manifested through his miracles.

article 1. whether Christ should have worked miracles

THE FIRST POINT:[1] 1. It would seem not. For Christ's deeds should have been consistent with his words. For he himself said, *An evil and unfaithful generation asks for a sign; the only sign it will be given is the sign of Jonah the prophet.*[2] Therefore he should not have worked miracles.

2. Furthermore, just as Christ, at his second coming, is to come *in power and great majesty*, as is written,[3] so at his first coming he came in weakness: *A man of sorrows and acquainted with weakness.*[4] But the working of miracles belongs more to power than it does to weakness. Therefore it was not fitting for him to work miracles at his first coming.

3. Furthermore, Christ came for the purpose of saving men by faith: *We look on Jesus, who is the source of faith and who brings it to perfection.*[5] But miracles diminish the merit of faith: for which reason our Lord says: *Unless you see signs and wonders you will not believe.*[6] Therefore it would seem that Christ should not have worked miracles.

ON THE OTHER HAND his adversaries are quoted as saying, *What are we to do, since this man is working so many signs?*[7]

REPLY: A man is empowered by God to work miracles for two reasons. First of all, and principally, in order to confirm the truth of what he teaches. For since what is of faith surpasses human reason, it cannot be

---

[a] cf Appendix 5. On miracle, cf 1a. 105, 6–8

probentur per argumentum divinæ virtutis; ut dum aliquis facit opera quæ solus Deus facere potest, credantur ea quæ dicuntur esse a Deo; sicut cum aliquis defert litteras annulo regis signatas, creditur ex voluntate regis processisse quod in illis continetur.

Secundo, ad ostendendam præsentiam Dei in homine per gratiam Spiritus Sancti, ut dum scilicet homo facit opera Dei credatur Deus habitare in eo per gratiam: unde dicitur *Gal.*, *Qui tribuit vobis Spiritum Sanctum operatur virtutes in vobis.*[8]

Utrumque autem circa Christum erat hominibus manifestandum, scilicet quod Deus esset in eo per gratiam, non adoptionis sed unionis, et quod ejus supernaturalis doctrina esset a Deo. Et ideo convenientissimum fuit ut miracula faceret. Unde ipse dicit *Joan.*, *Si mihi non vultis credere, operibus credite:*[9] et, *Opera quæ dedit mihi Pater ut faciam, ipsa sunt quæ testimonium perhibent de me.*[10]

1. Ad primum ergo dicendum quod hoc quod dicit, *Signum non dabitur ei, nisi signum Jonæ prophetæ,* intelligendum est ut Chrysostomus dicit quod tunc *non acceperunt tale signum, quale petebant, scilicet de cœlo, non quod nullum signum eis dederit; vel quia signa faciebat non propter eos quos sciebat lapideos esse, sed ut alios emendaret:*[11] *et ideo non eis, sed aliis illa signa dabantur.*[11]

2. Ad secundum dicendum quod licet Christus venerit in infirmitate carnis, quod manifestatur per passiones: venit tamen *in virtute Dei*,[12] quod erat manifestandum per miracula.

3. Ad tertium dicendum quod miracula intantum diminuunt meritum fidei inquantum per hoc ostenditur duritia eorum qui nolunt credere ea quæ Scripturis divinis probantur, nisi per miracula. Et tamen melius est eis ut vel per miracula convertantur ad fidem quam quod omnino in infidelitate permaneant: dicitur enim 1 ad *Cor.* quod *signa data sunt infidelibus,*[13] ut scilicet convertantur ad fidem.

articulus 2. utrum Christus fecerit miracula divina virtute

AD SECUNDUM sic proceditur:[1] 1. Videtur quod Christus non fecerit miracula divina virtute. Virtus enim divina est omnipotens. Sed videtur quod non fuerit omnipotens in miraculis faciendis: dicitur enim *Marc.* quod *non poterat ibi*, scilicet in patria sua, *virtutem ullam facere.*[2] Ergo videtur quod non fecerit miracula virtute divina.

2. Præterea, Dei non est orare. Sed Christus aliquando in miraculis

---
[8]*Galatians* 3, 5   [9]*John* 10, 38   [10]*John* 5, 36
[11]*In Matt.* XLIII, 1. PG 57, 457   [12]cf II *Corinthians* 13, 4   [13]I *Corinthians* 14, 22
[1]cf 3a. 13, 2. III *Sent.* XVI, 1, 3; IV, V, 1, 1 ad 3; *Respons. ad lector. Venet.* ad 17. *In Joan.* 2, 1

proved by human reasoning, but must be proved by the argument of divine power: so that when a man does works that God alone can do, we may believe that what he says is from God: just as when a man delivers a letter sealed with the king's ring, we believe that what it contains expresses the king's will.

Secondly, in order to make known God's presence in a man by the grace of the Holy Spirit: so that when a man does the works of God we may believe that God dwells in him by his grace. For which reason it is written: *He who gives you the Spirit and works miracles among you.*[8]

Now both of these things had to be made manifest to men concerning Christ—namely, that God was in him by grace, not of adoption, but of union;[a] and that his supernatural teaching was from God. And therefore it was most fitting for him to work miracles. For which reason he himself says, *Even if you refuse to believe in me, believe in my works.*[9] And, *The works my Father has given me to carry out, these same works give testimony concerning me.*[10]

Hence: 1. The words, *the only sign it will be given is the sign of Jonah the prophet*, mean, as Chrysostom says, that *they did not receive a sign such as they sought*, namely, *from heaven*: and not that he gave them no sign at all. Or, that *he worked signs not for the sake of those whom he knew were hardened, but to amend others.*[11] And so those signs were given, not to them, but to others.

2. Although Christ came *in the weakness* of the flesh, which is manifested in the passions, yet he came *in the power of God*,[12] and this had to be made manifest by miracles.

3. Miracles diminish the merit of faith in so far as they thereby reveal the obduracy of those who refuse to believe what is proved from the Scriptures, except through miracles. Nevertheless it is better for them to be converted to the faith even by miracles than for them to remain completely lacking in faith. For it is written that signs are given *to those who lack faith*, evidently so that they may be converted to the faith.[13]

article 2. whether Christ worked miracles by divine power

THE SECOND POINT:[1] 1. It would seem not. For divine power is almighty. But it seems that Christ was not almighty in working miracles; for it is written that *he could work no miracle there*, i.e. in his own country.[2] Therefore it would seem that he did not work miracles by divine power.

2. Furthermore, praying is not an activity proper to God. But Christ

---

[2]*Mark* 6, 5
[a]cf 3a. 2, 10; 6, 6; 7, 11

faciendis orabat, ut patet in suscitatione Lazari, *Joan*.,³ et in multiplicatione panum, ut patet *Matt*.⁴ Ergo videtur quod non fecit miracula virtute divina.

3. Præterea, ea quæ virtute divina fiunt, non possunt virtute alicujus creaturæ fieri. Sed ea quæ Christus faciebat poterant etiam fieri virtute alicujus creaturæ: unde et Pharisæi ei dicebant quod *in Beelzebub, principe dæmoniorum, ejiciebat dæmonia*.⁵ Ergo videtur quod Christus non fecerit miracula virtute divina.

SED CONTRA est quod Dominus dicit *Joan*., *Pater in me manens ipse facit opera*.⁶

RESPONSIO: Dicendum quod, sicut in prima parte habitum est,⁷ vera miracula sola virtute divina fieri possunt, quia solus Deus potest mutare naturæ ordinem, quod pertinet ad rationem miraculi. Unde Leo papa dicit quod in Christo sunt duæ naturæ; *una*, scilicet divina, *quæ fulget miraculis; alteras*, scilicet humana, *quæ succumbit injuriis*. Et tamen una earum agit *cum communicatione alterius*,⁸ inquantum scilicet humana natura est instrumentum divinæ actionis, et actio humana virtutem accipit a natura divina, sicut supra habitum est.⁹

1. Ad primum ergo dicendum quod hoc quod dicitur, *Non poterat ibi ullam virtutem facere*, non est referendum ad potentiam absolutam, sed ad id quod potest fieri congruenter. Non enim congruum erat ut inter incredulos operaretur miracula, unde subditur, *Et mirabatur propter incredulitatem eorum*.¹⁰ Secundum quem modum dicitur *Gen*., *Num celare potero Abraham quæ gesturus sum?*¹¹ et, *Non potero facere quidquam, donec ingrediaris illuc*.¹²

2. Ad secundum dicendum quod, sicut Chrysostomus dicit super illud *Matt*., *Acceptis quinque panibus, et duobus piscibus, aspiciens in cœlum benedixit, et fregit, oportebat credi de Christo quoniam a Patre est, et quod et æqualis est. Et ideo ut utrumque ostendat, nunc quidem cum potestate, nunc autem orans miracula facit: et in minoribus quidem respicit in cœlum*, puta in multiplicatione panum; *in majoribus autem quæ sunt solius Dei, cum potestate a se ipso agit*, puta quando peccata dimisit, mortuos suscitavit.¹³

Quod autem dicitur *Joan*. quod in suscitatione Lazari oculos sursum levavit,¹⁴ non propter necessitatem suffragii, sed propter exemplum hoc fecit; unde dicit, *propter populum, qui circumstat, dixi, ut credant quia tu me misisti*.

3. Ad tertium dicendum quod Christus alio modo expellebat dæmones

---

³*John* 11, 41-2 ⁴*Matthew* 14, 19 ⁵*Luke* 11, 15
⁶*John* 14, 10 ⁷1a. 110, 4 ⁸*Epist. ad Flavianum* XXVIII. PL 54, 767

CHRIST'S MIRACLES IN GENERAL

sometimes prayed when he was working miracles; as may be seen in the raising of Lazarus,[3] and in the multiplication of the loaves.[4] Therefore it would seem that he did not work miracles by divine power.

3. Furthermore, whatever is done by divine power cannot be done by the power of any creature. But what Christ did could be done also by the power of a creature: for which reason the Pharisees said that *it is by Beelzebub the prince of devils that he casts out devils.*[5] Therefore it would seem that Christ did not work miracles by divine power.

ON THE OTHER HAND our Lord said, *It is the Father, living in me, who does these works.*[6]

REPLY: As stated in the first part,[7] genuine miracles can be worked only by divine power; because God alone can change the order of nature, which is what is meant by a miracle. For this reason Pope Leo says[8] that, while there are two natures in Christ, there is *one* of them, namely, the divine, *which shines forth in miracles;* the other, namely, the human, *which submits to insults;* and yet *each of them communicates its actions to the other*: in so far as the human nature is the instrument of the divine action, and the human action receives power from the divine nature, as stated above.[9]

Hence: 1. When it is said that *he could work no miracle there*, it must not be in reference to absolute power, but to that which can be done fittingly: for it was unfitting for him to work miracles among the unbelieving. For this reason it is said later on, *He was amazed at their unbelief.*[10] In the same way it is written, *Can I conceal from Abraham what I am about to do?*[11] and, *I can do nothing until you reach it.*[12]

2. As Chrysostom says on, *He took the five loaves and the two fishes, and, looking up to heaven, he blessed and broke: It must be believed concerning Christ, both that he is from the Father and that he is equal to him. And so, in order to demonstrate both, he works miracles now with power, now with prayer. In the lesser things, certainly, he looks up to heaven*—for instance, in the multiplication of the loaves—*but in the greater, which are proper to God alone, he acts with power; for instance, when he forgave sins and raised the dead.*[13]

When it is said that in raising Lazarus *he lifted up his eyes,*[14] this was not because he needed assistance, but because he wished to give us an example. For this reason Chrysostom goes on, *For the sake of these who stand round me I speak, so that they may believe it was you who sent me.*

3. Christ cast out devils in a way other than by the power of devils. For

---

[9]3a. 19, 1   [10]Mark 6, 6   [11]Genesis 18, 17
[12]Genesis 19, 22   [13]*In Matt.* XLIX, on 14, 19. PG 58, 497   [14]John 11, 41

quam virtute dæmonum expellantur. Nam virtute superiorum dæmonum ita dæmones a corporibus hominum expelluntur, quod tamen remanet dominium eorum quantum ad animam; non enim contra regnum suum diabolus agit. Sed Christus dæmones expellebat non solum a corpore, sed multo magis ab anima. Et ideo Dominus blasphemiam Pharisæorum dicentium eum in virtute dæmoniorum dæmonia ejicere reprobavit:[15] primo quidem per hoc quod Satanas contra seipsum non dividitur; secundo, exemplo aliorum qui dæmonia ejiciebant per Spiritum Dei; tertio, quia dæmonium expellere non posset, nisi ipsum vicisset virtute divina; quarto, quia nulla convenientia in operibus, nec in effectu erat sibi et Satanæ; cum Satanas dispergere cuperet quos Christus colligebat.

articulus 3. utrum Christus incœperit facere miracula in nuptiis

AD TERTIUM sic proceditur:[1] 1. Videtur quod Christus non incœperit miracula facere in nuptiis, mutando aquam in vinum.[2] Legitur enim in libro *de Infantia Salvatoris*,[3] quod Christus in sua pueritia multa miracula fecit. Sed miraculum de conversione aquæ in vinum fecit in nuptiis trigesimo vel trigesimo primo anno suæ ætatis. Ergo videtur quod non incœperit tunc miracula facere.

2. Præterea, Christus faciebat miracula secundum virtutem divinam. Sed virtus divina in eo a principio suæ conceptionis erat: ex tunc enim fuit Deus et homo. Ergo videtur quod a principio miracula fecerit.

3. Præterea, Christus post baptismum et tentationem cœpit discipulos congregare, ut legitur *Matt.* et *Joan.*[4] Sed discipuli præcipue congregati sunt ad ipsum propter miracula; sicut dicitur *Luc.* quod Petrum vocavit obstupescentem propter miraculum quod fecerat in captura piscium.[5] Ergo videtur quod ante miraculum quod fecit in nuptiis, fecerit alia miracula.

SED CONTRA est quod dicitur *Joan.*, *Hoc fecit initium signorum Jesus in Cana Galilææ*.[6]

RESPONSIO: Dicendum quod miracula facta sunt a Christo propter confirmationem doctrinæ ejus, et ad ostendendam virtutem divinam in ipso. Et ideo quantum ad primum non debuit ante miracula facere quam docere inciperet: non autem debuit incipere docere ante perfectam ætatem, ut supra habitum est cum de baptismo ejus ageretur.[7]

[15]*Matthew* 12, 24; *Mark* 3, 22; *Luke* 11, 15
[1]cf 3a. 36, 4 ad 3. *In Joan.* 2, 1; 15, 5   [2]*John* 2, 11
[3]chaps. 26–41: ed. C. de Tischendorf, Leipzig 1876, pp. 93–110. cf 3a. 36, 4
[4]*Matthew* 4, 18; *John* 1, 35   [5]*Luke* 5, 4

devils are cast out from bodies by the power of higher devils in such a way as to keep their dominion over the soul: since the devil does not work against his own kingdom. But Christ cast out devils, not only from the body, but even more so from the soul. And so our Lord rebuked the blasphemy of the Jews who were saying he cast out devils by the power of the devils:[15] first of all, by saying that Satan is not divided against himself; secondly, by referring to the example of others who cast out devils by the Spirit of God; thirdly, because he could not have cast out a devil unless he had overcome him by divine power; fourthly, because his works and their effects do not accord in any way with those of Satan: since Satan's desire was to scatter those whom Christ had gathered together.

article 3. whether Christ began to work miracles at the wedding feast when he changed water into wine

THE THIRD POINT:[1] 1. It would seem that Christ did not begin to work miracles at the wedding feast when he changed water into wine.[2] For we read in the book on *the Saviour's Infancy*[3] that Christ worked many miracles in his childhood. But the miracle of changing water into wine was worked by him when he was thirty or thirty-one years old. Therefore it would seem that he did not begin to work miracles at that time.

2. Furthermore, Christ worked miracles by divine power. But divine power was his from the first moment of his conception; for from that time on he was both God and man. Therefore it would seem that he worked miracles from the very beginning.

3. Furthermore, Christ began to gather his disciples after his baptism and temptation.[4] But the disciples were gathered around him principally on account of his miracles: thus it is written that he called Peter, who was astonished on account of the miracle that he had worked in catching the fish.[5] Therefore it would seem that he worked other miracles before the miracle that he worked at the wedding feast.

ON THE OTHER HAND it is written, *This was the first of the signs worked by Jesus at Cana in Galilee.*[6]

REPLY: Christ wrought miracles in order to confirm his teaching, and in order to demonstrate the divine power that was his. And so, as regards the first, it was not proper for him to work miracles before he began to teach. For it was not proper for him to begin to teach before he had come of age, as stated above, when we discussed his baptism.[7]

---

[6]*John* 2, 11   [7]3a. 39, 3

Quantum autem ad secundum sic debuit per miracula deitatem ostendere, ut crederetur veritas humanitatis ipsius. Et ideo, sicut dicit Chrysostomus, *decenter non incœpit signa facere in prima ætate: existimassent enim phantasma* esse incarnationem; et ante opportunum tempus cruci eum tradidissent.*[8]

1. Ad primum ergo dicendum quod, sicut Chrysostomus dicit super *Joan.* ex verbo Joannis Baptistæ dicentis, *Ut manifestetur in Israel, propterea veni ego in aqua baptizare,*[9] manifestum est quod *illa signa quæ quidam dicunt in pueritia a Christo facta, mendacia et fictiones sunt. Si enim a prima ætate miracula fecisset Christus, neque Joannes eum ignorasset, neque reliqua multitudo indiguisset magistro ad manifestandum eum.*[10]

2. Ad secundum dicendum quod Dei virtus operabatur in Christo secundum quod erat necessarium ad salutem humanam, propter quam carnem assumpserat. Et ideo sic miracula fecit virtute divina ut fidei de veritate carnis ejus præjudicium non fieret.

3. Ad tertium dicendum quod hoc ipsum ad laudem discipulorum pertinet quod Christum secuti sunt, cum nulla eum miracula facere vidissent; sicut Gregorius dicit.[11] Et Chrysostomus dicit, *Tunc signa maxime necessarium erat facere quando discipuli jam congregati erant, et devoti, et attendentes his quæ fiebant;* unde subditur, *Joan., Et crediderunt in eum discipuli ejus,*[12] non quia tunc primum crediderunt, sed quia *tunc diligentius et perfectius crediderunt.*[13] Vel discipulos vocat eos qui futuri erant discipuli, sicut exponit Augustinus.[14]

articulus 4. utrum miracula per Christum facta sufficienter ejus divinitatem ostenderint

AD QUARTUM sic proceditur:[1] 1. Videtur quod miracula quæ Christus fecit non fuerint sufficientia ad ostendendam divinitatem ipsius. Esse enim Deum et hominem proprium est Christo. Sed miracula quæ Christus fecit etiam ab aliis sunt facta. Ergo videtur quod non fuerint sufficientia ad ostendendam divinitatem ipsius.

2. Præterea, virtute divina nihil est majus. Sed aliqui fecerunt majora miracula quam Christus: dicitur enim *Joan., Que credit in me, opera quæ ego facio, et ipse faciet, et majora horum faciet.*[2] Ergo videtur quod miracula quæ Christus fecit, non fuerint sufficientia ad ostendendam divinitatem ipsius.

---

* Leonine: *phantasiam*

[8]*In Joan.* XXI. PG 59, 130
[9]*John* I, 31
[10]*In Joan.* XVII. PG 59, 110
[11]*In Evang.* v, 1. PL 76, 1093
[12]*John* 2, 11
[13]*In Joan.* XXIII. PG 59, 139
[14]*De Consensu Evangelistarum* II, 17. PL 34, 1096

But as regards the second, it was proper that he should so demonstrate his divinity by miracles that men would believe in the reality of his humanity. And so, as Chrysostom says, *it was fitting that he should not begin to work wonders from an early age: for men would have judged the Incarnation to be imaginary, and would have handed him over to be crucified before the proper time.*[8]

Hence: 1. As Chrysostom says concerning John the Baptist's declaration, *It was to reveal him to Israel that I came baptizing with water,*[9] that it is clear that *the wonders which some assert were worked by Christ in his childhood are false and fictitious. For if Christ had worked miracles from an early age, John would by no means have been unacquainted with him, nor would the rest of the people have stood in need of a teacher to point him out to them.*[10]

2. Divine power was operative in Christ to the degree that it was necessary for the salvation of men, for which purpose he became flesh. Consequently he worked miracles by divine power in such a way as not to prejudice our belief in the reality of his flesh.

3. Praise is due to the disciples precisely because they followed Christ although *they had not seen him work any miracles,* as Gregory says in one of his homilies.[11] And, as Chrysostom says, *it was then that it was most necessary for him to work wonders, when the disciples were already gathered around and attached to him, and attentive to what was taking place. For this reason it is said further, And his disciples believed in him,*[12] not because they now believed in him for the first time, but because they now believed in him *with greater discernment and perfection.*[13] Or they are called disciples because *they were to be his future disciples,* as Augustine explains.[14]

article 4. whether the miracles which Christ worked were sufficient to demonstrate his divinity

THE FOURTH POINT:[1] 1. It would seem that they were not enough. For it is proper to Christ to be both God and man. But the miracles which Christ worked have been worked by others also. Therefore it would seem that they were not enough to demonstrate his divinity.

2. Furthermore, there is nothing greater than the divine power. But some have worked greater miracles than Christ, for it is written, *Whoever believes in me, the works I do he also shall do, and he shall do works even greater than these.*[2] Therefore it would seem that the miracles which Christ worked were not sufficient to demonstrate his divinity.

---

[1]cf III *Sent.* XVI, 1, 3. *CG*, I, 6; IV, 55. *Quodl.* II, 4, 1 ad 4. *In Joan.* 5, 6; 15, 5
[2]*John* 14, 12

3. Præterea, ex particulari non sufficienter ostenditur universale. Sed quodlibet miraculorum Christi fuit quoddam particulare opus. Ergo ex nullo eorum potuit manifestari sufficienter divinitas Christi, ad quam pertinet universalem virtutem habere de omnibus.

SED CONTRA est quod Dominus dicit *Joan.*, *Opera quæ dedit mihi Pater ut faciam, ipsa testimonium perhibent de me.*³

RESPONSIO: Dicendum quod miracula, quæ Christus fecit, sufficientia erant ad manifestandam divinitatem ipsius, secundum tria. Primo quidem secundum ipsam speciem operum, quæ transcendebant omnem potestatem creatæ virtutis: et ideo non poterant fieri nisi virtute divina. Et propter hoc cæcus illuminatus dicebat, *A seculo non est auditum, quia aperuit quis oculos cæci nati: nisi esset hic a Deo, non poterat facere quidquam.*⁴

Secundo propter modum miracula faciendi, quia scilicet quasi ex propria potestate miracula faciebat, non autem orando, sicut alii: unde dicitur *Luc.*, quod *virtus de illo exibat, et sanabat omnes;*⁵ per quod ostenditur, sicut Cyrillus dicit, *Non accipiebat alienam virtutem, sed cum esset naturaliter Deus, propriam virtutem super infirmos ostendebat; et propter hoc innumerabilia miracula faciebat.*⁶ Unde super illud *Matt., Ejiciebat spiritus verbo, et omnes male habentes curavit,*⁷ dicit Chrysostomus, *Intende quantam multitudinem hominum curatam transcurrunt Evangelistæ, non unumquemque curatum ennarrantes, sed uno verbo pelagus ineffabile miraculorum inducentes.*⁸ Et ex hoc ostendebatur quod haberet virtutem coæqualem Deo Patri, secundum illud *Joan.*, *Quæcumque Pater facit, hæc et Filius similiter facit;*⁹ et ibidem, *Sicut Pater suscitat mortuos, et vivificat, sic et Filius hominis quos vult vivificat.*¹⁰

Tertio, ex ipsa doctrina, qua se Deum dicebat, quæ nisi vera esset, non confirmaretur miraculis divina virtute factis: et ideo dicitur *Marc., Quænam doctrina hæc nova, quia in potestate spiritibus immundis imperat, et obediunt ei?*¹¹

1. Ad primum ergo dicendum quod hæc erat objectio gentilium. Unde Augustinus dicit, *Nullis, inquiunt, competentibus signis tantæ majestatis indicia claruerunt, quia larvalis illa purgatio, qua scilicet dæmones effugabat; debilium cura, reddita vita defunctis, si et alia considerentur, Deo parva sunt.*¹² Et ad hoc respondet Augustinus, *Fatemur et nos talia quædam fecisse prophetas; sed et ipse Moyses, et cæteri prophetæ Dominum Jesum prophetaverunt,*

---

³*John* 5, 36
⁶*In Luc.*, on 6, 19. PG 72, 588
⁸*In Matt.* XXVII. PG 57, 345
¹⁰*John* 5, 21
¹²*Epist. ad Volusianum* CXXXVII. PL 33, 521
⁴*John* 9, 32
⁷*Matthew* 8, 16
⁹*John* 5, 19
¹¹*Mark* 1, 27
⁵*Luke* 6, 19

3. Furthermore, the universal cannot be sufficiently demonstrated by appealing to the particular. But any one of Christ's miracles was a certain particular work. Therefore none of them is sufficient to demonstrate the divinity of Christ, which pertains to the universal power held over all things.

ON THE OTHER HAND our Lord said, *The works my Father has given me to perform, these same works give testimony concerning me.*[3]

REPLY: The miracles which Christ worked were sufficient to demonstrate his divinity, in three ways. First of all, according to the very nature of the works, which surpass totally the capability of any created power, and therefore could not be worked except by divine power. And for this reason the blind man, having been given his sight, said, *Ever since the world began it is unheard of that any man opened the eyes of one born blind. Unless this man were from God, he could not do a thing.*[4]

Secondly, on account of the way he worked miracles—because he evidently worked miracles as though by his own power, and not by praying, as others did. Accordingly it is written that *power came out from him that cured them all.*[5] By which it is demonstrated, as Cyril says, that *he did not receive power from another, but that since he was God by nature he demonstrated his own power over the sick. And because of this he worked countless miracles.*[6] For this reason, on the text, *He cast out the spirits with a word and cured all who were sick,*[7] Chrysostom comments, *Mark how the Evangelists pass quickly over a great number of persons healed, not mentioning them one by one, but in one single word traversing an ineffable sea of miracles.*[8] From this it is shown that he was equally as powerful as God the Father: *Whatever the Father does the Son does too;*[9] and, *As the Father raises the dead and gives them life, so the Son also gives life to whom he wills.*[10]

Thirdly, from his teaching by which he said he was God; which teaching, unless it were true, would not be confirmed by miracles worked by divine power. For this reason it is written, *What is this new teaching? For with power he gives orders to unclean spirits, and they obey him.*[11]

Hence: 1. This was the objection posed by the gentiles.[a] For which reason Augustine says, *No suitable wonders, they say, point clearly to so great a majesty, for the ghostly cleansing, by which he cast out demons, the cure of the sick, the restoration of life to the dead, if other miracles be taken into account, are small things before God.*[12] To this Augustine replies, *We admit that the prophets did as much. But even Moses himself and the other prophets made our Lord Jesus the object of their prophecy, and gave him great*

---

[a] e.g. Celsus

et ei gloriam magnam dederunt. Qui propterea talia et ipse facere voluit, ne esset absurdum, quæ per illos fecerat, si ipse etiam non faceret. Sed tamen et aliquid proprium facere debuit, nasci de virgine, resurgere a mortuis, cœlum ascendere. Hoc Deo qui parum putat, quid plus expectet ignoro. Num homine assumpto alium mundum facere debuit, ut eum esse crederemus, per quem factus est mundus? Sed nec major mundus, nec isti æqualis in hoc mundo fieri posset. Si autem minorem faceret infra istum, similiter hoc quoque parum putaretur.[13]

Quæ tamen alii fecerunt Christus excellentius fecit. Unde super illud *Joan., Si opera non fecissem in eis quæ nemo alius fecit*, etc.,[14] dicit Augustinus, *Nulla in operibus Christi videntur esse majora quam suscitatio mortuorum; quod scimus etiam antiquos fecisse Prophetas. Fecit tamen aliqua Christus quæ nemo alius fecit. Sed respondetur nobis, et alios fecisse quæ nec ipse, nec alius fecit. Sed qui tam multa vitia, et malas valetudines, vexationesque mortalium tanta potestate sanaret, nullus omnino legitur antiquorum. Ut enim taceam, quos jubendo, sicut occurrebat, salvos singulos fecit, Marcus dicit quod quocumque loco introibat in vicos, aut in villas, aut in civitates, 'in plateis ponebant infirmos, et deprecabantur eum ut vel fimbriam vestimenti ejus tangerent'; et quotquot tangebant eum, salvi fiebant.*[15] *Hæc nemo alius fecit in eis. Sic enim intelligendum est quod ait in eis, non inter eos, aut coram eis, sed prorsus in eis, quia sanavit eos. Nec tamen alius quicumque in eis talia opera fecit: quoniam quisquis alius homo aliquid eorum fecit, ipso faciente fecit; hoc autem ipse non illis facientibus fecit.*[16]

2. Ad secundum dicendum quod Augustinus, exponens illud verbum Joannis, inquit quæ sint ista opera majora, quæ credentes in eum erant facturi, *An forte quod ægros ipsis transeuntibus etiam eorum umbra sanabat? Majus est enim quod sanet umbra quam fimbria. Verumtamen quando ista Christus dicebat, verborum suorum facta et opera commendabat. Cum enim dixit, 'Pater in me manens ipse facit opera',*[17] *quæ opera tunc dicebat, nisi verba quæ loquebatur? Et eorumdem verborum fructus erat fides illorum. Verumtamen evangelizantibus discipulis, non tam pauci quam illi erant; sed gentes etiam crediderunt.*[18] *Quæ sequuntur, Nonne ab ore ipsius dives ille tristis abscessit, qui ab eo vitæ æternæ consilium quæsivit? et tamen postea quod ab illo auditum non fecit unus, fecerunt multi, cum per discipulos loqueretur. Ecce majora fecit, prædicatus a credentibus quam locutus audientibus.*[19]

Verum hoc adhuc movet quod hæc majora per Apostolos fecit. Non autem

---

[13]ibid, 13-14. PL 33, 521
[14]*John* 15, 24
[15]*Mark* 6, 56
[16]*In Joan.* XCI, 2, on 15, 24. PL 35, 1860
[17]*John* 14, 10
[18]*In Joan.* LXXI, on 14, 10. PL 35, 1821
[19]ibid, on 14, 12. PL 35, 1822

glory. He, therefore, chose to do similar things lest he fall into the inconsistency of failing to do himself what he had done through others. Nevertheless, it was also necessary for him to do something which no one else had done: to be born of a virgin, to rise from the dead, to ascend into heaven. If anyone consider this a small thing for God to do, I do not know what more he expects. Having become man, should he have made another world, that we might believe he was the one by whom the world was made? But in this world neither a greater world could be made nor one equal to it: and if he had made a lesser world in comparison with this one, that too would have been considered a small thing.[13]

Whatever miracles others may have worked, the ones which Christ did surpassed them. For this reason, on the text, *If I had not performed such works among them which no one else had done*, etc.,[14] Augustine says, *Among the works of Christ none would seem to be greater than the raising of the dead: which thing we know the ancient prophets did. Yet Christ did some works which no one else had ever done.* But we are told in response that others did works which he did not, and which no one else did. But to heal with such great power so many defects and infirmities and ailments of mortal men, this we read concerning none of those men of old. Not to mention those who, by his bidding, as they came his way, he made whole, as Mark says, 'Wherever he went, to village, or town, or farm, they laid the sick in the open spaces, and begged him to let them touch even the hem of his cloak; and as many as touched him were made whole.'[15] These works no other man ever did in them: for when he said 'in them', it is not to be understood to mean 'among them', or 'in their presence', but precisely 'in them', because he healed them. Therefore he who performed works of this sort in them performed works which no one else had ever done: since when any other man performed any of these works, he performed them together with Christ; whereas when Christ performed works, he performed them by himself.[16]

2. Augustine, while explaining upon this passage from *John*, inquires, *What are these greater works, which believers in him would do? That, as they passed by, their very shadow healed the sick? For it is greater that a shadow should heal than the hem of a cloak. However, when Christ uttered these words, the deeds and works he was referring to were his very words: for when he said,* 'It is the Father, living in me, who performs these works,'[17] *what works was he referring to, then, if not the words he was speaking? And the fruits of those same words was their faith. However, when the disciples preached the Gospel, it was not just a few like them who came to believe, but the very nations.*[18] *Did not that rich man leave his presence sorrowing? And yet afterwards, what one individual who heard him speak would not do, many did when he spoke through his disciples. Behold, he did greater works when spoken of by men who believed in him than when speaking to men who heard him.*[19]

Yet there remains this disturbing fact: that he did these greater works *ipsos tantum significans ait,* '*Qui credit in me, opera quæ ego facio, et ipse faciet.*' *Audi ergo, et intellige,* '*Qui credit in me, opera quæ ego facio, et ipse faciet.*' *Prius ego facio, deinde et ipse faciet, quia facio ut faciat. Quæ opera? nisi ut ex impio justus fiat? quod utique in illo, sed non sine illo Christus operatur. Prorsus majus hoc esse dixerim quam creare cœlum et terram. Cœlum enim et terra transibunt; prædestinatorum autem salus et justificatio permanebit. Sed et in cœlis angeli sunt opera Christi. Numquid etiam his operibus majora facit qui cooperatur Christo ad suam justificationem? Judicet qui potest utrum majus sit justos creare quam impios justificare. Certe si æqualis est utrumque potentiæ, hoc majoris est misericordiæ.*

Sed omnia opera Christi intelligere, ubi ait, '*Majora horum faciet*', *nulla nos necessitas cogit. Horum enim forsitan dixit quæ hora faciebat. Tunc autem verba fidei faciebat. Et utique minus est verba justitiæ prædicare, quod fecit præter nos, quam impios justificare, quod ita facit in nobis ut faciamus et nos.*[20]

3. Ad tertium dicendum quod quando aliquod particulare opus proprium est alicujus agentis, tunc per illud particulare opus probatur tota virtus agentis; sicut cum ratiocinari sit proprium hominis, ostenditur aliquis esse homo ex hoc ipso quod ratiocinatur circa quodcumque particulare propositum. Et similiter cum propria virtute miracula facere sit solius Dei, sufficienter ostensum est Christum esse Deum, ex quocumque miraculo quod propria virtute fecit.

---

[20]loc cit

through the apostles. But he was not alluding to them only when he said, 'Whoever believes in me.' Listen therefore: 'Whoever believes in me, the works I do he also shall do.' First, 'I do', then, 'he also shall do', because I do that he may do. What works, but that he who is ungodly should be made righteous? Which thing Christ worked in him, certainly, but not without him. I say that this is altogether greater than to create heaven and earth; for 'heaven and earth will pass away'; but the salvation and justification of those predestined shall remain.—But also in the heavens, the angels are the works of Christ. And does he who co-operates with Christ for his justification do greater works than these? Let him, who can, judge whether it is better to create a righteous man than to justify an ungodly one. Certainly, if both are of equal power, the latter is of greater mercy.

But there is no need for us to understand all the works of Christ, where he says, 'He shall do works even greater than these.' For by 'these' he meant to say, perhaps, those he was doing at that hour; now at that time he was uttering words of faith: and certainly it is a lesser work to preach words of righteousness, which he did without us, than to justify the ungodly, which he does in us in order that we also may do it.[20]

3. Whenever some particular work is proper to some agent, then the entire power of that agent is demonstrated by that particular work. Just as, since reasoning is proper to man, from the mere fact that someone reasons about any particular proposition it can be shown that he is a man. And in the same way, since the power to work miracles is proper to God alone, from any single miracle worked by Christ by his own power it is sufficiently shown that he is God.

Quæstio 44. de singulis miraculorum speciebus

DEINDE CONSIDERANDUM est de singulis miraculorum speciebus: et

1. de miraculis quæ fecit circa spirituales substantias;
2. de miraculis quæ fecit circa cœlestia corpora;
3. de miraculis quæ fecit circa homines;
4. de miraculis quæ fecit circa creaturas irrationales.

articulus 1. utrum miracula facta per Christum circa spirituales substantias fuerint convenientia

AD PRIMUM sic proceditur: 1. Videtur quod miracula quæ fecit Christus circa spirituales substantias non fuerint convenientia. Inter spirituales enim substantias sancti angeli præpollent dæmonibus: quia, ut Augustinus dicit, *Spiritus vitæ rationalis desertor atque peccator regitur per spiritum vitæ rationalem pium et justum.*[1] Sed Christus non legitur aliqua miracula fecisse circa angelos bonos. Ergo nec etiam circa dæmones aliqua miracula facere debuit.

2. Præterea, miracula Christi ordinabantur ad manifestandam divinitatem ipsius. Sed divinitas Christi non erat dæmonibus manifestanda, quia per hoc impeditum fuisset mysterium passionis ejus, secundum illud 1 *Cor.*, *Si cognovissent, nunquam Dominum gloriæ crucifixissent.*[2] Ergo non debuit circa dæmones aliqua miracula facere.

3. Præterea, miracula Christi ad gloriam Dei ordinabantur: unde dicitur *Matt.* quod videntes turbæ paralyticum sanatum a Christo, *timuerunt, et glorificaverunt Deum qui dedit potestatem talem hominibus.*[3] Sed ad dæmones non pertinet glorificare Deum, *quia non est speciosa laus in ore peccatoris*, ut dicitur *Eccl.*:[4] unde et sicut dicitur *Marc.* et *Luc.*[5] non sinebat dæmonia loqui ea quæ ad gloriam ipsius pertinebant. Ergo videtur non fuisse conveniens quod circa dæmones aliqua miracula faceret.

4. Præterea, miracula a Christo facta ad salutem hominum ordinantur. Sed quædam dæmonia ab hominibus ejecta fuerunt cum hominum detrimento quandoque quidem corporali, sicut dicitur *Marc.* quod dæmon ad præceptum Christi *exclamans, et multum discerpens hominem, exiit ab eo; et factus est sicut mortuus, ita ut multi dicerent, quia mortuus est;*[6] quandoque etiam cum damno rerum, sicut quando dæmones ad eorum preces misit in porcos quos præcipitaverunt in mare: unde cives illius regionis rogaverunt eum ut transiret a finibus eorum, ut legitur *Matt.*[7] Ergo videtur inconvenienter fecisse hujusmodi miracula.

---

[1] *De Trinitate* III, 4. PL 42, 873   [2] 1 *Corinthians* 2, 8   [3] *Matthew* 9, 8
[4] *Sirach* 15, 9   [5] *Mark* 1, 34; *Luke* 4, 41   [6] *Mark* 9, 24–6   [7] *Matthew* 8, 34

Question 44. the different kinds of miracles

WE MUST NEXT CONSIDER the miracles specifically:[a]
1. the miracles which he worked concerning spiritual substances;
2. concerning heavenly bodies;
3. the miracles which he worked concerning men;
4. concerning non-rational creatures.

article 1. whether the miracles were fitting which Christ worked concerning spiritual substances

THE FIRST POINT: 1. It would seem that the miracles were unfitting which Christ worked concerning spiritual substances. For among spiritual substances the holy angels rank above the evil spirits; for, as Augustine says, *The conscientious and upright rational spirit of life rules over the unfaithful and sinful rational spirit of life*.[1] But we do not read that Christ worked any miracles concerning the good angels. Therefore he also should not have worked any miracles concerning the bad spirits.

2. Furthermore, the miracles of Christ were ordered toward displaying his divinity. But the divinity of Christ was not displayed to the evil spirits, because this would have impeded the mystery of his passion: *If they had known, they would not have crucified the Lord of Glory*.[2] Therefore he should not have worked any miracles concerning evil spirits.

3. Furthermore, the miracles of Christ were ordered toward glorifying God. For this reason it is written, that *when the crowd saw* the paralytic healed by Christ, *they feared, and glorified God for giving such power to men*.[3] But the evil spirits have no part in glorifying God; since *praise is unseemly in a sinner's mouth*.[4] For which reason also *he would not allow them to speak*[5] those things which would give him glory. Therefore it would seem that he should not have worked any miracles concerning evil spirits.

4. Furthermore, the miracles worked by Christ are ordered toward the salvation of mankind. But sometimes the casting out of evil spirits from men was detrimental to man, in some cases to his body: thus it is written, that the evil spirit at Christ's command, *came out* from the man, *crying out and throwing the man into convulsions, leaving him so like a corpse that many of them said, He is dead*.[6] In some cases also to things: as when he sent the evil spirits, at their own request, into the herd of pigs, which they cast headlong into the sea: for which reason the inhabitants of that region *implored him to leave the neighbourhood*.[7] Therefore it would seem to be unfitting for him to have worked miracles of this sort.

---

[a] cf Appendix 5

SED CONTRA est quod *Zach.* hoc prænuntiatum fuerat; ubi dicitur, *Spiritum immundum auferam de terra.*[8]

RESPONSIO: Dicendum quod miracula quæ Christus fecit, argumenta quædam fuerunt fidei quam ipse docebat. Futurum autem erat ut per virtutem Divinitatis ejus excluderet dæmonum potestatem ab hominibus credituris in eum, secundum illud *Joan.*, *Nunc princeps hujus mundi ejicietur foras.*[9] Et ideo conveniens fuit quod inter alia miracula etiam obsessos a dæmonibus liberaret.

1. Ad primum ergo dicendum quod homines sicut per Christum erant a potestate dæmonum liberandi, ita per eum erant angelis consociandi, secundum illud *Col.*, *Pacificans per sanguinem crucis ejus, quæ in cœlis, et quæ in terris sunt.*[10] Et ideo circa angelos alia miracula hominibus demonstrare non conveniebat, nisi ut angeli hominibus apparerent: quod quidem factum est in nativitate ipsius,[11] et in resurrectione[12] et ascensione ejus.[13]

2. Ad secundum dicendum quod, sicut Augustinus dicit, *Christus tantum innotuit dæmonibus quantum voluit; tantum autem voluit quantum oportuit; sed innotuit eis, non sicut angelis sanctis per id quod est vita æterna, sed per quædam temporalia suæ virtutis effecta.*[14] Et primo quidem videntes Christum esurire post jejunium æstimaverunt eum non esse Filium Dei. Unde super illud *Luc.*, *Si Filius Dei es*, etc.,[15] dicit Ambrosius, *Quid sibi vult talis sermonis exorsus, nisi quia cognoverat Dei Filium esse venturum, sed venisse per infirmitatem corporis non putavit?*[16] Sed postmodum visis miraculis,[17] ex quadam suspicatione conjecturavit eum esse Filium Dei. Unde super illud *Marc.*, *Scio quod sis sanctus Dei,*[18] dicit Chrysostomus quod *non certam aut firmam adventus Dei habebat notitiam,*[19] sciebat tamen ipsum esse Christum in lege promissum;[20] unde dicitur *Luc.*, *Quia sciebant ipsum esse Christum.*[21] Quod autem ipsum confitebantur esse Filium Dei, magis erat ex quadam suspicione quam ex certitudine. Unde Beda dicit, *Et dæmonia Filium Dei confitebantur.* Et sicut postea dicit, *Sciebant eum esse Christum quia cum jejunio fatigatum eum diabolus videret, verum hominem intellexit; sed quia tentando non prævaluit, utrum Filius Dei esset, dubitabat. Nunc autem per signorum potentiam vel intellexit, vel potius suspicatus est esse Filium Dei.* Non ideo igitur Judæis eum crucifigere persuasit, quia Christum Dei Filium non esse putavit, sed quia se morte illius non prævidit esse damnandum: de hoc enim mysterio a seculis abscondito dicit Apostolus, 'Quod

---

[8]*Zechariah* 13, 2
[9]*John* 12, 31; cf below, 3a. 49, 2
[10]*Colossians* 1, 20
[11]*Luke* 2, 9
[12]*Matthew* 28; *Mark* 16; *Luke* 24; *John* 20, 12-13 [13]*Acts* 1, 10-11
[14]*De Civitate Dei* IX, 21. PL 41, 273. cf above, 3a. 41, 1 ad 1
[15]*Luke* 4, 3 [16]*In Luc.* IV, 18, on 4, 3. PL 15, 1617
[17]cf below, 3a. 47, 5 [18]*Mark* 1, 24

THE DIFFERENT KINDS OF MIRACLES

ON THE OTHER HAND this was foretold in *Zechariah*, where it is written, *I will rid the country of the spirit of impurity*.[8]

REPLY: The miracles which Christ worked were a kind of argument for the faith which he taught. Now it would come to pass that he would, by the power of his divinity, deprive the evil spirits of their power over those who would believe in him: *Now the prince of this world is to be cast out*.[9] Consequently it was fitting that, among other miracles, he should also deliver those who were possessed by evil spirits.

Hence: 1. Just as men would be delivered by Christ from the power of the evil spirits, so they would be brought by him into the company of the angels: *Whether on the earth or in the heavens, making peace through the blood of his cross*.[10] Therefore it was not fitting to present to men other miracles as regards the angels, except in so far as the angels appeared to men, as happened at his birth,[11] his resurrection[12] and his ascension.[13]

2. As Augustine says, *Christ was known to the evil spirits only so far as he willed; and he willed it only so far as was needed. But he was known to them, not as he was to the holy angels, as the source of eternal life, but as the cause of certain temporal effects*.[14] At first, when they saw that Christ was hungry after fasting they deemed him not to be the Son of God. And so, on the text, *If you are the Son of God*, etc.,[15] Ambrose writes, *Why did he address him in this way, unless it were because although he knew that the Son of God was to come, yet he did not think that he had come in the weakness of the flesh?*[16] But afterwards, having seen his miracles,[17] his suspicions aroused somewhat, he formed the conjecture that he was the Son of God. And so, on the text, *I know who you are, the Holy One of God*,[18] Chrysostom says that *he had no certain or firm knowledge of God's coming*.[19] However, he knew that he was *the Christ promised in the Law*,[20] and so it is written, *Because they knew he was the Christ*.[21] But it was more out of suspicion than from certitude that they confessed him to be the Son of God. For this reason Bede says, *The evil spirits confess him to be the Son of God, and, as stated farther on, 'they knew he was the Christ'. Because, when the devil saw him weakened by his fast, he knew he was a real man: but when he was not able to overcome him by temptation, he began to wonder whether he was the Son of God. And so now from the power of his miracles he either knew, or rather suspected, that he was the Son of God. Therefore his reason for persuading the Jews to crucify him was not that he considered him not to be Christ or the Son of God, but because he did not foresee that he would be the loser by his death.* For the Apostle says

---

[19]Victor of Antioch, *Cat. in Marc.* on 1, 23: found in I. A. Cramer, *Catenæ Græcorum Patrum in N.T.*, Oxford 1844, I, 275, 23; cf also St Thomas, *Catena aurea*, on *Mark* 1, 9
[20]cf *Quæst. Vet. et N. Test.* 66. PL 35, 2261   [21]*Luke* 4, 41

nemo principum hujus seculi cognovit: si enim cognovissent, nunquam Dominum gloriæ crucifixissent'.[22]

3. Ad tertium dicendum quod miracula in expulsione dæmonum non fecit Christus propter utilitatem dæmonum, sed propter utilitatem hominum, ut ipsi eum glorificarent. Et ideo prohibuit eos loqui ea quæ ad laudem ipsius pertinebant. Primo quidem propter exemplum, quia, ut dicit Athanasius, *Compescebat diaboli sermonem, quamvis vera fateretur, ut nos etiam assuefaciat, ne curemus de talibus, etiamsi vera loqui videantur; nefas est enim ut cum adsit nobis Scriptura divina, instruamur a diabolo;*[23] Est enim hoc periculosum, quia veritati frequenter dæmones immiscent mendacia. Secundo, quia sicut Chrysostomus dicit, *Non oportebat eos surripere officii Apostolici gloriam; nec decebat Christi mysterium lingua fœtida publicari, quia non est speciosa laus in ore peccatorum.*[24] Tertio, quia ut Beda dicit, *nolebat ex hoc invidiam accendere Judæorum.*[25] Unde etiam ipsi Apostoli jubentur reticere de ipso, ne divina majestate prædicata, passionis dispensatio differatur.[26]

4. Ad quartum dicendum quod Christus specialiter venerat docere et miracula facere propter utilitatem hominum principaliter quantum ad animæ salutem: et ideo permisit dæmones quos ejiciebat hominibus aliquod nocumentum inferre vel in corpore vel in rebus, propter animæ humanæ salutem, ad hominum scilicet instructionem. Unde Chrysostomus dicit quod Christus *permisit dæmonibus in porcos ire, non quasi a dæmonibus persuasus; sed primo quidem ut instruat magnitudinem nocumenti dæmonum, qui hominibus insidiantur; secundo, ut omnes discerent quoniam nec adversus porcos audeant aliquid facere, nisi ipse consenserit; tertio, ut ostenderet quod graviora in illos homines operati essent quam in illos porcos, nisi essent divina providentia adjuti.*[27]

Et propter easdem etiam causas permisit eum qui a dæmonibus liberabatur ad horam gravius affligi; a qua tamen afflictione eum continuo liberavit. Per hoc etiam ostenditur, ut Beda dicit, quod *sæpe, dum converti ad Deum post peccata conamur, majoribus novisque antiqui hostis pulsamur insidiis: quod facit, vel ut odium virtutis incutiat, vel expulsionis suæ vindicet injuriam.*[28] Factus est etiam homo sanatus *velut mortuus,* ut Hieronymus dicit, *quia sanatis dicitur Coloss.,* Mortui estis, et vita vestra abscondita est cum Christo in Deo.[29]

---

[22]1 *Corinthians* 2, 8. *In Luc.* II, on 4, 41. PL 92, 381; cf also *In Marc.* I, on 1, 34. PL 92, 143
[23]*Fragm. in Luc.* on 4, 33. PG 27, 1397. cf *Cat. aur. in Luc.* on 4, 34
[24]*Sirach* 15, 9; Cyril of Alexandria, *Comment. in Luc.* on 4, 41. PG 72, 552
[25]cf *Cat. aur. in Luc.* on 4, 41, under the name of Theophylactus; cf Theophylactus, *In Luc.* on 4, 41. PG 123, 756
[26]Bede, *In Luc.* II, on 4, 41. PL 92, 381

concerning this mystery which is hidden from the beginning, that 'none of the princes of this world knew it, for if they had known it they would not have crucified the Lord of Glory.'[22]

3. The miracles which Christ worked in expelling evil spirits were for the benefit, not of the evil spirits, but of men, that they might glorify him. And so he forbade them to speak those things which would be in praise of him. First, as an example to us. Because, as Athanasius says, *He checked his speech, although he was confessing the truth; to teach us not to care about such things, although what is said may seem to be true. For it is wrong to seek instruction from the devil when we have the divine Scriptures.*[23] Further, it is dangerous, since the evil spirits frequently mix falsehood with truth. Or, as Chrysostom says, *It was not right for them to usurp the glory of the apostolic office. Nor was it fitting for the mystery of Christ to be proclaimed by a foul tongue, because 'praise is unseemly in a sinner's mouth'.*[24] Thirdly, because, as Bede says, *He did not wish to arouse the envy of the Jews by reason of this.*[25] And so, even *the apostles are commanded to remain silent about him, lest, if his divine majesty were proclaimed, the gift of his Passion should be deferred.*[26]

4. Christ came specially to teach and to work miracles for the benefit of man, and principally as it regards the salvation of his soul. And so he permitted the evil spirits, which he cast out, to do man some harm, either in his body or in his property, for the salvation of man's soul—namely, for man's instruction. For this reason Chrysostom says that Christ *permitted the evil spirits to enter into the pigs, not as though he were persuaded by the evil spirits, but, first of all, in order to show what great harm evil spirits can do when they attack men; secondly, that all might learn that the evil spirits did not dare to harm even the pigs, without his permission; thirdly, to show how much more grievously they would have treated the men than the pigs, unless they had been protected by divine providence.*[27]

And for these same reasons he permitted the man, who was being delivered from the evil spirits, to be grievously afflicted for the moment; although he proceeded immediately to deliver him from this affliction. By this it is also shown, as Bede says, that *often, when after falling into sin we strive to return to God, we experience new and more grievous attacks from the ancient enemy. This he does either to inspire us with a hatred for virtue, or that he may avenge the affront he suffered when he was cast out.*[28] For the man who was healed became *like a corpse*, says Jerome, *because to those who are healed it is said, 'You have died, and now the life you have is hidden with Christ in God.'*[29]

---

[27]*In Matt.* XXVIII, on 8, 32. PG 57, 354 [28]*In Marc.* III, on 9, 18. PL 92, 221
[29]*Colossians* 3, 3; *In Marc.*, on 9, 25. PL 30, 616

articulus 2. *utrum convenienter facta fuerint miracula per Christum circa cœlestia corpora*

AD SECUNDUM sic proceditur:[1] 1. Videtur quod inconvenienter fuerint a Christo facta miracula circa cœlestia corpora. Ut enim Dionysius dicit, *Divinæ providentiæ non est naturam corrumpere, sed salvare*.[2] Corpora autem cœlestia secundum suam naturam sunt incorruptibilia et inalterabilia, ut probatur in I *de Cœlo*.[3] Ergo non fuit conveniens ut per Christum fieret aliqua immutatio circa ordinem cœlestium corporum.

2. Præterea, secundum motum cœlestium corporum temporum cursus designatur, secundum illud *Gen.*, *Fiant luminaria in firmamento cœli, et sint in signa, et tempora, et dies, et annos*.[4] Sic ergo mutato cursu cœlestium corporum, mutatur temporum distinctio et ordo. Sed non legitur hoc esse perceptum ab astrologis, qui *contemplantur sidera, et computant menses*, ut dicitur *Isa*.[5] Ergo videtur quod per Christum non fuerit aliqua mutatio facta circa cursum cœlestium corporum.

3. Præterea, magis competebat Christo ut faceret miracula vivens et docens quam moriens: tum quia, ut dicitur 2 ad *Cor.*, *Crucifixus est ex infirmitate, sed vivit ex virtute Dei*,[6] secundum quam miracula faciebat: tum etiam quia ejus miracula confirmativa erant doctrinæ ipsius. Sed in vita sua non legitur Christus aliquod miraculum circa cœlestia corpora fecisse; quinimo Pharisæis petentibus ab eo signum de cœlo, dare renuit, ut habetur *Matt*.[7] Ergo videtur quod nec in morte circa cœlestia corpora aliquod miraculum facere debuerit.

SED CONTRA est quod dicitur *Luc.*, *Tenebræ factæ sunt in universa terra usque ad horam nonam, et obscuratus est sol*.[8]

RESPONSIO: Dicendum quod, sicut supra dictum est,[9] miracula Christi talia esse debebant ut sufficienter eum esse Deum ostenderent. Hoc autem non ita evidenter ostenditur per transmutationes corporum inferiorum, quæ etiam ab aliis causis moveri possunt, sicut per transmutationem cursus cœlestium corporum, quæ a solo Deo sunt immobiliter ordinata: et hoc est quod Dionysius dicit, *Cognoscere oportet non aliter aliquando posse aliquid perverti cœlestis ordinationis et motus, nisi causam haberet ad hoc moventem, quæ facit omnia, et mutat secundum suum sermonem*.[10] Et ideo conveniens fuit ut Christus miracula faceret etiam circa cœlestia corpora.

1. Ad primum ergo dicendum quod, sicut inferioribus corporibus

---

[1] cf *In Matt.* 27   [2] *Div. Nom.* IV, 33. PG 3, 733. St Thomas, *lect.* 23
[3] *De Cœlo* I, 3. 270a12. St Thomas, *lect.* 6   [4] *Genesis* I, 44
[5] *Isaiah* 47, 13   [6] II *Corinthians* 13, 4
[7] *Matthew* 12, 38-9; 16, 1-4   [8] *Luke* 23, 44-5

THE DIFFERENT KINDS OF MIRACLES

article 2. whether it was fitting for Christ to work miracles concerning the heavenly bodies

THE SECOND POINT:[1] 1. Unfitting, it would seem. As Dionysius says, *It befits divine providence not to destroy, but to preserve, nature.*[2] Now, the heavenly bodies are by nature indestructible and unchangeable, as is proved in *De Cœlo*.[3] Therefore it was not fitting that Christ should effect any change in the order of the heavenly bodies.

2. Furthermore, the course of the seasons is marked out by the movement of the heavenly bodies: *Let there be lights in the vault of heaven as signs to indicate seasons, days and years.*[4] Therefore, if the movement of the heavenly bodies undergoes change, the distinction and order of the seasons is changed. But we do not read that this was perceived by the astronomers, *who study the stars and compute the months*, as it is written.[5] Therefore it would seem that Christ did not effect any change in the movement of the heavenly bodies.

3. Furthermore, it was more fitting for Christ to work miracles while living and teaching than while dying; both because, as it is written, *He was crucified through weakness, and yet he lives through the power of God*,[6] according to which he worked miracles; and also because his miracles were in confirmation of his teaching. But we do not read that Christ ever worked any miracles concerning the heavenly bodies during his lifetime: rather, on the contrary, when they asked him for *a sign from heaven* he refused.[7] Therefore it seems that neither in death should he have worked any miracles concerning the heavenly bodies.

ON THE OTHER HAND, it is written, *There was darkness over the whole land until the ninth hour; and the sun was darkened.*[8]

REPLY: As stated above,[9] it was necessary for Christ's miracles to be such as to manifest his divinity. Now this is not manifested so evidently by changes effected in the lower bodies, which changes can be brought about by other causes, as by changes effected in the movement of the heavenly bodies, which have been set by God alone in an unchangeable order. This is what Dionysius says in his letter to Polycarp, *We must realize that no change can take place in the order and movement of the heavens that is not caused by him who made all and changes all by his word.*[10] And so it was fitting for Christ to work miracles even concerning the heavenly bodies.

Hence: 1. As it is natural for the lower bodies to be moved by the

---

[9]3a. 43, 4
[10]*Epist. ad Polycarpum* VII, 2. PG 3, 1080

naturale est moveri a cœlestibus corporibus, quæ sunt superiora secundum naturæ ordinem; ita etiam naturale est cuilibet creaturæ ut transmutetur a Deo secundum ejus voluntatem. Unde Augustinus dicit, super illud, *Contra naturam insertus es*, etc.,[11] *Deus creator et conditor omnium naturarum nihil contra naturam facit, quia idest cuique rei natura, quod facit;*[12] et ita non corrumpitur natura cœlestium corporum, cum eorum cursus immutatur a Deo; corrumperetur autem, si ab aliqua alia causa immutaretur.

2. Ad secundum dicendum quod per miraculum a Christo factum non est perversus ordo temporum. Nam secundum quosdam,[13] illæ tenebræ vel solis obscuratio, quæ in passione Christi accidit, fuit propter hoc quod sol suos radios retraxit, nulla immutatione facta circa motum cœlestium corporum, secundum quem tempora mensurantur. Unde Hieronymus dicit, *Videtur luminare majus retraxisse radios suos, ne aut pendentem videret Dominum, aut impii blasphemantes sua luce fruerentur.*[14] Talis autem retractio radiorum non est sic intelligenda quasi sol in sua potestate habeat radios emittere vel retrahere: non enim ex electione, sed ex natura radios emittit, ut dicit Dionysius;[15] sed sol dicitur retraxisse radios, inquantum divina virtute factum est ut solis radii ad terram non pervenirent.

Origenes autem dicit hoc accidisse per interpositionem nubium. Unde super *Matt.* dicit, *Conveniens est intelligere quasdam tenebrosissimas nubes multas et magnas concurrisse super Jerusalem et terram Judææ: et ideo factæ sunt tenebræ profundæ a sexta hora usque ad nonam. Arbitror enim sicut cætera signa quæ facta sunt in passione, scilicet quod velum templi est scissum, quod terra tremuit, etc., in Jerusalem tantummodo facta sunt, ita et hoc. Aut si latius voluerit quis extendere ad terram Judææ, propter hoc quod dicitur, Tenebræ factæ sunt in universa terra*, quod intelligitur de terra Judææ: sicut dixit Abdias ad Eliam, *Vivit Dominus Deus suus, quia non est gens aut regnum, ubi non miserit dominus meus quærere te,*[16] ostendens quod eum quæsierat in gentibus quæ sunt circa Judæam.[17]

Sed circa hoc magis credendum est Dionysio, qui oculata fide inspexit hoc accidisse per interpositionem lunæ inter nos et solem: dicit enim, *Inopinabiliter soli lunam incidentem videbamus*, in Ægypto scilicet existentes, ut ibidem dicitur: et designat ibi quatuor miracula.[18] Quorum primum est quod naturalis eclipsis solis per interpositionem lunæ nunquam accidit,

---

[11] *Contra Faustum* XXVI, 3. PL 42, 480
[12] *Glossa ordin.*, on *Romans* 11, 24. PL 114, 508
[13] cf *Cat. aur. in Matt.*, on 27, 45, under the name of Chrysostom; cf John Chrysostom, *In Matt.*, LXXXVIII, 1. PG 58, 775
[14] *In Matt.* IV, on 27, 45. PL 26, 212
[15] *Div. Nom.* IV, 1. PG 3, 693. St Thomas, *lect.* 1
[16] 1 *Kings* 18, 10
[17] *Comment.*, on *Matthew* 27, 45. PG 13, 1784; cf *Cat. aur. in Matt.*, on 27, 45

heavenly bodies, their superiors in the order of nature, so it is natural for any creature whatsoever to be changed by God, according to his will. For which reason Augustine says,[11] *God, the Creator and Maker of all natures, does nothing contrary to nature; for whatever he does in each thing, that is its nature.*[12] And so the nature of a heavenly body is not destroyed when God changes its movement, though it would be impaired if any other cause effected the change.

2.[a] The order of the seasons was not destroyed by the miracle which Christ worked. For, according to some,[13] this darkening or obscuring of the sun, which occurred at the time of Christ's passion, was caused by the sun withdrawing its rays, without any change in the movement of the heavenly bodies according to which the seasons are measured. For which reason Jerome says, *It would seem as though the greater light withdrew its rays, lest it should look down upon our Lord hanging on the Cross, or provide light for the godless blasphemers.*[14] But this withdrawal of rays is not to be understood as though it were in the sun's power to send forth or withdraw its rays; for it sends forth its rays, not by choice, but by nature, as Dionysius says.[15] But the sun is said to withdraw its rays in so far as its rays were kept from reaching the earth by divine power.

Origen, however, says this was brought about by the interposition of clouds. For which reason he says, *We are led to suppose that many large and very dark clouds were massed together over Jerusalem and the land of Judaea; so that it was extremely dark from the sixth to the ninth hour. Therefore I am of the opinion that, just as the other signs which took place at the time of the Passion—namely, that the veil was rent, that the earth quaked,* etc., *took place in Jerusalem only, so this also. Although, if anyone prefer, it may be extended more widely to include the land of Judaea,* since it is said that '*there was darkness over the whole land*', which is understood as referring to the land of Judaea, as in 1 Kings,[16] when Obadiah says to Elijah, '*As your God lives, there is no nation or kingdom where my master has not sent in search of you,*' showing that they were searching for him among the nations round about Judaea.[17]

Regarding this, however, we ought rather to believe Dionysius who, having witnessed it with the eyes of faith, says that it occurred by the interposition of the moon between us and the sun. For he says, *Without doubt we saw the moon encroaching upon the sun,* while they were in Egypt, as he says in the same letter.[18] And in this regard he points out four miracles. The first of these is that the natural eclipse of the sun by the interposition of the moon never takes place except when the sun and the

---

[18]*Epistola ad Polycarpum* VII, 2. PG 3, 1081
[a]Even a curious student of theology may skip the following reply.

nisi tempore conjunctionis solis et lunæ. Tunc autem erat luna in oppositione ad solem quintadecima existens, quia erat Pascha Judæorum. Unde dicit, *Non enim erat conjunctionis tempus.*[19] Secundum miraculum est quod cum circa horam sextam luna visa fuisset simul cum sole in medio cœli, in vesperis apparuit suo loco, idest in oriente opposita soli. Unde dicit, *Rursus ipsam vidimus,*[20] scilicet lunam, *a nona hora,* in qua scilicet recessit a sole cessantibus tenebris, *usque ad vesperam supernaturaliter constitutam ad diametrum solis,* idest ut diametraliter esset soli opposita. Et sic patet quod non est turbatus consuetus temporum cursus, quia divina virtute factum est et quod ad solem supernaturaliter accederet præter tempus debitum, et quod a sole recedens in locum proprium restitueretur tempore debito. Tertium miraculum est quod naturalis eclipsis semper incipit ab occidentali parte solis, et pervenit usque ad orientalem: et hoc ideo, quia luna secundum proprium motum, quo movetur ab occidente in orientem, est velocior sole in suo proprio motu: et ideo luna ab occidente veniens attingit solem, et pertransit ipsum, ad orientem tendens. Sed tunc luna jam pertransiverat solem, et distabat ab eo quasi per medietatem circuli, in oppositione existens: unde oportuit quod reverteretur ad orientem versus solem et attingeret ipsum primo ex parte orientali, procedens versus occidentem. Et hoc est quod dicit, *Eclipsim etiam ipsam ex oriente vidimus inchoatam, et usque ad solarem terminum venientem* (quia totum solem eclipsavit) *postea regredientem.*[21] Quartum miraculum fuit, quod in naturali eclipsi ex eadem parte incipit sol prius reapparere, ex qua parte incœpit prius obscurari, quia scilicet luna se soli subjiciens, naturali suo motu solem pertransit versus orientem, et ita partem occidentalem solis, quam primo occupat, primo etiam derelinquit. Sed tunc luna miraculose ab oriente versus occidentem rediens, non pertransivit solem, ut esset eo occidentalior,* sed postquam pervenit ad terminum solis, reversa est versus orientem; et ita partem solis, quam ultimo occupavit, primo etiam dereliquit; et sic ex parte orientali inchoata fuit eclipsis, sed in parte occidentali prius incœpit claritas apparere. Et hoc est quod dicit, *Et rursus vidimus non ex eodem;* idest, non ex eadem parte solis, *et defectum, et purgationem, sed e converso secundum diametrum factam.*[22]

Quintum miraculum addit Chrysostomus dicens quod *tribus horis tunc tenebræ permanserunt, cum eclipsis solis in momento pertranseat: non enim habet moram, ut sciunt illi qui consideraverunt.*[23] Unde datur intelligi quod luna quieverit sub sole. Nisi forte velimus dicere quod tempus tenebrarum

---
*Piana: *orientalior,* more eastern
[19]*Epistola ad Polycarpum* VII, 2. PG 3, 1081
[20]ibid
[21]ibid
[22]ibid

moon are in conjunction. Yet at that time the sun and moon were in opposition, it being the fifteenth day, since it was the Jewish Passover. And so he says, *It was not the time of conjunction.*[19] The second miracle is that while at the sixth hour the moon was seen together with the sun in the middle of the heavens, in the evening it appeared in its place, that is, in the east, opposite the sun. For which reason he says, *And again we saw it,* that is, the moon, *returned supernaturally to its place opposite the sun,* so as to be diametrically opposed to the sun, having withdrawn from the sun *at the ninth hour,* when the darkness ceased, *until evening.*[20] Thus it is clear that the ordinary course of time was not disturbed, because by divine power the moon was made both to approach the sun supernaturally outside the appointed time, and then to withdraw from the sun and return to its proper place in accord with the time of year. The third miracle is that the eclipse of the sun naturally begins always on the western side of the sun and moves toward the east: and this is because the moon's proper movement from west to east is more rapid than the movement of the sun, and so the moon, coming up from the west, overtakes the sun and passes it, going toward the east. But in this case the moon had already passed the sun and was distant from it by half the circumference of the heavenly circle, being in opposition to the sun. Therefore it had to return eastward toward the sun, and come upon it from the east, and continue toward the west. This is why he says, *Moreover, we saw the eclipse begin to the east and move toward the western edge of the sun,* for it was a total eclipse of the sun, *and afterwards turn back.*[21] The fourth miracle was that, while in a natural eclipse the part of the sun which is first eclipsed is the first to reappear (because the moon, coming in front of the sun, by its natural movement passes the sun in an easterly direction, and so the western part of the sun which is occupied first, is also the first abandoned), in this case, however, the moon, returning miraculously from the east to the west, did not pass the sun so as to be west of it: but having reached the western edge of the sun turned back toward the east, so that the part of the sun which was occupied last was also the first abandoned. And thus the eclipse began to the east, but the reappearance of light began to the west. This is why he says, *Again we saw that the occultation and emersion of the sun did not begin at the same point,* that is, on the same side of the sun, *but rather on opposite sides.*[22]

Chrysostom adds a fifth miracle, saying that the darkness in this case lasted for three hours, while an eclipse of the sun *is over in a moment, for it does not linger, as those know who have observed one.*[23] So we are given to understand that the moon stood still in front of the sun, unless we prefer

---

[23]*In Matt.* LXXXVIII, 1. PG 58, 775

computetur ab instanti quo sol incœpit obscurari usque ad instans in quo totaliter fuit repurgatus.

Sed sicut Origenes dicit, *adversus hoc filii seculi hujus dicunt, Quomodo hoc factum tam mirabile nemo Græcorum aut barbarorum scripsit?*[24] Et dicit quod quidam, nomine *Phlegon, in Chronicis suis scripsit, hoc in principatu Tiberii Cæsaris factum;*[25] sed non signavit quod fuerit in luna plena. Potuit ergo hoc contingere, quia astrologi ubique terrarum tunc temporis existentes, non sollicitabantur de observanda eclipsi, quia tunc tempus non erat; sed illam obscuritatem ex aliqua passione aëris accidere putaverunt; sed in Ægypto, ubi raro nubes apparent propter aëris serenitatem, permotus est Dionysius et socii ejus ut prædicta circa illam obscurationem observarent.

3. Ad tertium dicendum quod tunc præcipue oportebat in Christo divinitatem per miracula ostendere, quando in eo maxime apparebat infirmitas secundum humanam naturam, et ideo in Christi nativitate stella nova in cœlo apparuit:[26] unde Maximus dicit, *Si præsepe despicis, erige parumper oculos, et novam in cœlo stellam protestantem mundo nativitatem dominicam contuere.*[27]

In passione autem adhuc major infirmitas circa humanitatem Christi apparuit; et ideo oportuit ut majora miracula ostenderentur circa principalia mundi luminaria: et, sicut Chrysostomus dicit, *hoc est signum quod petentibus promittebat dare dicens, 'Generatio prava et adultera signum quærit, et signum non dabitur ei nisi signum Jonæ prophetæ,' crucem significans et resurrectionem. Etenim multo mirabilius est in eo qui crucifixus erat, hoc fieri, quam ambulante eo super terram.*[28]

articulus 3. utrum convenienter Christus circa homines miracula fecerit

AD TERTIUM sic proceditur: 1. Videtur quod inconvenienter Christus circa homines miracula fecerit. In homine enim potior est anima quam corpus. Sed circa corpora multa miracula Christus fecit; circa animas vero nulla miracula legitur fecisse. Nam neque aliquos incredulos ad fidem virtuose convertit, sed admonendo et exteriora miracula ostendendo; neque etiam aliquos fatuos sapientes legitur fecisse. Ergo videtur quod non convenienter sit circa homines miracula operatus.

2. Præterea, sicut supra dictum est,[1] Christus faciebat miracula virtute divina, cujus proprium est subito operari, et perfecte absque adminiculo

---

[24]*Comment.*, on *Matthew*, 27, 45. PG 13, 1782
[25]ibid
[26]*Matthew* 2
[27]Homily XIII. PL 57, 251
[28]*In Matt.* LXXXVIII, 1. PG 58, 775

to say that the duration of darkness was measured from the first moment it began to be eclipsed to the moment when the sun had completely emerged from the eclipse.

But, as Origen says, *against this the children of this world say: How is it that such an extraordinary event is not recorded by any writer, either Greek or barbarian?*[24] And he says that someone named Phlegon *wrote in his chronicles that this took place during the reign of Tiberius Caesar, but he does not say that it took place at the full moon.*[25] Thus it could happen that, because it was not the time for an eclipse, the astronomers living then throughout the world were not inclined to look for one, and that they attributed this darkness to some disturbance of the atmosphere. In Egypt, however, where clouds rarely appear because of the stillness of the atmosphere, Dionysius and his companions were deeply moved to undertake the aforesaid observations about this darkness.

3. It was necessary for Christ to demonstrate his divinity by miracles at that time especially when the weakness of his human nature was most apparent. And so, at Christ's birth a new star appeared in the heavens.[26] For which reason Maximus says, *If you disdain the manger, raise your eyes a little and gaze on the new star in the heavens, proclaiming to the world the birth of our Lord.*[27]

But in his passion, the weakness of Christ's humanity was even more apparent. Consequently there was need for even greater miracles manifested in the most important lights of the world. And, as Chrysostom says, *This is the sign he promised to give to those who asked for one, saying, 'An evil and unfaithful generation asks for a sign; the only sign it will be given is the sign of Jonah the prophet,' referring to his cross and resurrection. For it was much more of a marvel that this should happen after he was crucified than when he was walking on earth.*[28]

article 3. whether the miracles were fitting which Christ worked concerning men

THE THIRD POINT: 1. It would seem not. For in man the soul is more important than the body. Now Christ worked many miracles affecting the body, but we do not read that he worked any miracles affecting the soul: for neither did he convert any unbelievers to the faith by employing force, but by persuading and convincing them with outward miracles, nor do we read that he made wise men out of fools. Therefore it would seem that he unfittingly worked miracles concerning men.

2. Furthermore, as stated above,[1] Christ worked miracles by divine power which has the characteristic mark of being exercised instantaneously,

---

[1] 3a. 43, 2

alicujus. Sed Christus non semper subito homines curavit quantum ad corpus; dicitur enim *Marc.* quod *apprehensa manu cæci eduxit eum extra vicum; et expuens in oculos ejus, impositis manibus, interrogavit eum si quid videret; et aspiciens ait, video homines velut arbores ambulantes. Deinde iterum imposuit manus super oculos ejus, et cœpit videre, et restitutus est ei visus, ut clare videret omnia.*[2] Et sic patet quod non subito eum curavit, sed primo quidem imperfecte et per sputum. Ergo videtur non convenienter circa homines miracula fecisse.

3. Præterea, quæ se invicem non consequuntur, non oportet quod simul tollantur. Sed ægritudo corporalis non semper ex peccato causatur, ut patet per illud quod Dominus dixit *Joan., Neque hic peccavit, neque parentes ejus, ut cæcus nasceretur.*[3] Non ergo oportuit ut hominibus corporum curationem quærentibus peccata dimitteret, sicut legitur fecisse circa paralyticum, *Matt.*;[4] præsertim quia sanatio corporalis, cum sit minus quam remissio peccatorum, non videtur esse sufficiens argumentum quod possit peccata dimittere.

4. Præterea, miracula Christi facta sunt ad confirmationem doctrinæ ipsius et testimonium divinitatis ejus, ut supra dictum est.[5] Sed nullus debet impedire finem operis sui. Ergo videtur inconvenienter Christus quibusdam miraculose curatis præcepisse ut nemini dicerent, ut patet *Matt.* et *Marc.*,[6] præsertim quia quibusdam aliis mandavit ut miracula circa se facta publicarent; sicut *Marc.* legitur quod dixit ei quem a dæmonibus liberaverat, *Vade in domum tuam ad tuos, et annuntia eis quanta tibi Dominus fecerit.*[7]

SED CONTRA est quod dicitur *Marc., Bene omnia fecit, et surdos fecit audire, et mutos loqui.*[8]

RESPONSIO: Dicendum quod ea quæ sunt ad finem debent fini esse proportionata. Christus autem ad hoc in mundum venerat et docebat ut homines salvos faceret, secundum illud *Joan., Non enim misit Deus Filium suum in mundum, ut judicet mundum, sed ut salvetur mundus per ipsum.*[9] Et ideo conveniens fuit ut Christus particulariter homines miraculose curando, ostenderet se esse universalem et spiritualem hominum salvatorem.

1. Ad primum ergo dicendum quod ea quæ sunt ad finem distinguuntur ab ipso fine. Miracula autem a Christo facta ordinabantur, sicut ad finem, ad rationalis partis salutem, quæ consistit in sapientiæ illustratione et hominum justificatione, quorum primum præsupponit secundum, quia, ut

---

[2]*Mark* 8, 22 [3]*John* 9, 3 [4]*Matthew* 9, 2
[5]3a. 43, 4 [6]*Matthew* 9, 30; *Mark* 8, 26 [7]*Mark* 5, 19

THE DIFFERENT KINDS OF MIRACLES

perfectly and without any assistance. But Christ did not always heal men instantaneously as regards their bodies: for it is written that, *taking the blind man by the hand, he led him out of the village; and, spitting upon his eyes and laying his hands on him, he asked him if he saw anything. And the man, who was beginning to see, replied, I see men like trees walking about. Then he laid his hands upon his eyes again, and he began to see, and he was healed so that he could see everything clearly.*[2] So it is clear from this that he did not heal him instantaneously, but only imperfectly at first, and by means of his spittle. Therefore it would seem that he unfittingly worked miracles concerning men.

3. Furthermore, there is no need to remove simultaneously things which do not follow from one another. Now bodily ailments are not always caused by sin, as is clear from what our Lord says, *Neither he nor his parents sinned, that he should be born blind.*[3] He should not, therefore, have forgiven the sins of those who asked to have their bodies healed, as we read that he did in the case of the paralytic:[4] especially since the healing of the body, being of less account than the remission of sins, does not seem to be a sufficient proof that he could forgive sins.

4. Furthermore, Christ's miracles were worked to confirm his teaching and give testimony to his divinity, as stated above.[5] Now no one should hinder the purpose of his own work. Therefore it would seem unfitting for Christ to have commanded those whom he had miraculously healed to tell no one,[6] especially since he commanded certain others to proclaim the miracles that he had worked for them; thus we read that he said to the man whom he had delivered from evil spirits, *Go home to your family and tell them all what great things the Lord has done for you.*[7]

ON THE OTHER HAND it is written, *He has done all things well: he has made the deaf hear and the dumb speak.*[8]

REPLY: Those things which are for an end should be proportionate to that end. Now Christ came into the world and taught in order to save men: *For God sent his Son into the world not to condemn the world but that through him the world might be saved.*[9] And so it was fitting for Christ to demonstrate that he was the universal and spiritual Saviour of all by working miracles of healing for particular men.

Hence: 1. Those things which are for an end are distinct from the end. Now the miracles worked by Christ have as their end that the rational part of man achieve salvation, which consists in the illumination of wisdom and the justification of men: the former of which presupposes the

---

[8] *Mark* 7, 37   [9] *John* 3, 17

dicitur *Sap.*, *In malevolam animam non introibit sapientia, nec habitabit in corpore subdito peccatis.*[10] Justificare autem homines non conveniebat nisi eis volentibus: hoc enim esset et contra rationem justitiæ, quæ rectitudinem voluntatis importat, et etiam contra rationem humanæ naturæ, quæ libero arbitrio ad bonum ducenda est, non autem per coactionem.[11] Christus ergo virtute divina interius homines justificavit, non tamen eis invitis: nec hoc ad miracula pertinet, sed ad miraculorum finem. Et similiter etiam virtute divina simplicibus discipulis divinam sapientiam infudit: unde dicit eis *Luc.*, *Ego dabo vobis os et sapientiam, cui non poterunt resistere et contradicere omnes adversarii vestri;*[12] quod quidem, quantum ad interiorem illuminationem, inter visibilia miracula non numeratur, sed solum quantum ad exteriorem actum, inquantum scilicet videbant homines, eos qui fuerant illitterati et simplices, tam sapienter et constanter loqui. Unde dicitur *Act.*, *Videntes* Judæi *Petri constantiam et Joannis, comperto quod homines essent sine litteris, et idiotæ, admirabantur.*[13] Et tamen hujusmodi spirituales effectus, etsi a miraculis visibilibus distinguantur, sunt tamen quædam testimonia doctrinæ et virtutis Christi, secundum illud *Heb.*, *Contestante Deo signis, et portentis, et variis virtutibus, et Spiritus Sancti distributionibus.*[14]

Sed tamen circa animas hominum, maxime quantum ad immutandas inferiores vires, Christus aliqua miracula fecit. Unde Hieronymus, super illud *Matt.*, *Surgens secutus est eum,*[15] dicit, *Fulgor ipse et majestas divinitatis occultæ, quæ etiam in facie relucebat humana videntes ad se trahere poterat ex primo aspectu.*[16] Et super illud *Matt.*, *Ejiciebat omnes vendentes et ementes,*[17] dicit idem Hieronymus, *Mihi inter omnia signa quæ fecit Dominus, hoc videtur esse mirabilius, quod unus homo, et illo tempore contemptibilis, potuerit ad unius flagelli verbera tantam ejicere multitudinem: igneum enim quiddam atque sidereum radiabat ex oculis ejus, et divinitatis majestas lucebat in facie ejus.*[18] Et Origenes dicit super *Joan.*, hoc esse majus miraculum eo quo aqua conversa est in vinum: eo quod *illic inanimata subsistit materia: hic vero tot millium hominum domantur ingenia.*[19] Et super illud *Joan.*, *Abierunt retrorsum, et ceciderunt in terram,*[20] dicit Augustinus, *Una vox tantam turbam odiis ferocem armisque terribilem sine telo ullo percussit, repulit, stravit: Deus enim latebat in carne.*[21] Et ad idem pertinet quod dicitur *Luc.* quod *Jesus transiens per medium illorum ibat:*[22] ubi dicit Chrysostomus quod *stare in medio insidiantium, et non apprehendi, divinitatis eminentiam ostendebat;*[23] et quod dicitur *Joan.*, *Jesus abscondit se, et exivit*

---

[10]*Wisdom* I, 4
[11]cf 1a2æ. 113, 3
[12]*Luke* 21, 15
[13]*Acts* 4, 13
[14]*Hebrews* 2, 4
[15]*Matthew* 9, 9
[16]*In Matt.* I, on 9, 9. PL 26, 56
[17]*Matthew* 21, 12
[18]*In Matt*, III, on 21, 15. PL 26, 152
[19]*In Joan.* x, 16. PG 14, 352
[20]*John* 18, 6
[21]*In Joan.* CXII, on 18, 4. PL 35, 1931
[22]*Luke* 4, 30

THE DIFFERENT KINDS OF MIRACLES

latter, since, as it is written, *Wisdom will not make its way into a crafty soul, nor dwell in a body which is subject to sin.*[10] Now it was unfitting for men to be justified unless they willed it: for this would be both against the nature of justice, which implies rectitude of the will, and against human nature itself, which must be led to good by free will, not by force.[11] Christ, therefore, justified man inwardly by divine power, but not against man's will. Nor did this pertain to his miracles, but to the end of his miracles. In like manner by divine power he also infused wisdom into his simple-minded disciples: for which reason he says to them, *I myself shall give you eloquence and wisdom that none of your opponents will be able to resist or contradict.*[12] And this, certainly, in so far as it is an inward illumination, is not to be reckoned among the visible miracles, but only in so far as it is an outward act—namely, in so far as men saw that those who had been uneducated and simple-minded spoke now with such wisdom and assurance. For which reason it is written, The Jews *were astonished at the assurance shown by Peter and John, considering they were uneducated laymen.*[13] Still, even though spiritual effects of this kind are distinct from visible miracles, they do, nevertheless, give testimony to the teaching and power of Christ: *God himself gave testimony with signs and marvels and miracles of all kinds, and by freely giving the gifts of the Holy Spirit.*[14]

Nevertheless Christ did work some miracles affecting the souls of men, especially by working changes which affected their lower powers. Thus Jerome, commenting on the text, *He got up and followed him,*[15] says, *The splendour and majesty of his hidden divinity which shone forth even in his human countenance was such that those who looked upon him were drawn to him at first sight.*[16] And on the text *He drove out all those who were selling and buying,*[17] the same Jerome says, *Of all the signs worked by our Lord, this one seems to me the most wondrous—that one man who was, at the time, considered contemptible, could, with the lashes of one whip, drive out such a multitude. A kind of heavenly fire flashed from his eyes, and the majesty of his divinity shone in his countenance.*[18] And Origen says that *this was a greater miracle than when he changed water into wine, for there he prevailed against inanimate matter, while here he tames the minds of thousands of men.*[19] And on the text, *They moved back and fell to the ground,*[20] Augustine says, *With one word, without a weapon, he attacked the crowd fierce in its hatred and terrible in its weapons, drove it back, and struck it down: for God lay hidden in his flesh.*[21] And to this must be referred what is written that Jesus *slipped through the crowd and went his way,*[22] on which Chrysostom observes, *That he stood in the midst of those lying in wait for him, and was not seized by them, demonstrates the superiority of his divinity.*[23] On the text,

---

[23] *In Joan.* XLVIII. PG 59, 269

de templo:[24] ubi Theophylactus dicit, *Non abscondit se in angulo templi quasi timens, vel post murum aut columnam divertens; sed divina potestate se invisibilem insidiantibus constituens, per medium illorum exivit.*[25]

Ex quibus omnibus patet quod Christus, quando voluit, virtute divina animas hominum immutavit, non solum justificando et sapientiam infundendo (quod pertinet ad miraculorum finem), sed etiam exterius allicendo, vel terrendo, vel stupefaciendo, quod pertinet ad ipsa miracula.

2. Ad secundum dicendum quod Christus venerat salvare mundum non solum virtute divina, sed per mysterium incarnationis ipsius. Et ideo frequenter in sanatione infirmorum non sola potestate divina utebatur, curando per modum imperii, sed etiam aliquid ad humanitatem ipsius pertinens apponendo. Unde super illud *Luc.*, *Singulis manus imponens, curabat omnes,*[26] dicit Cyrillus, super illud *Joan.*, *Nisi manducaveritis carnem*, etc., *Quamvis ut Deus potuisset omnes verbo pellere morbos, tangit tamen eos, ostendens propriam carnem efficacem ad præstanda remedia.*[27] Et super illud *Marc.*, *Expuens in oculos ejus, impositis manibus*, etc.,[28] dicit Chrysostomus, *Spuit quidem, et manus imponit cæco, volens ostendere quod verbum divinum operationi adjunctum miracula perficit: manus enim operationis est ostensiva, sputum sermonis ex ore prolati.*[29] Et super illud *Joan.*, *Fecit lutum ex sputo, et linivit lutum super oculos cæci*,[30] dicit Augustinus, *De saliva sua lutum fecit, quia Verbum caro factum est.*[31] Vel etiam ad significandum quod ipse erat, qui ex limo terræ hominem formaverat, ut Chrysostomus dicit.[32,33]

Est autem circa miracula Christi considerandum quod communiter perfectissima opera faciebat. Unde super illud *Joan.*, *Omnis homo primum bonum vinum ponit*,[34] dicit Chrysostomus, *Talia sunt Christi miracula, ut multo his quæ per naturam fiunt, speciosiora et utiliora fiant.*[35] Et similiter in instanti infirmis perfectam sanitatem conferebat: unde super illud *Matt.*, *Et surrexit, et ministrabat illis*,[36] dicit Hieronymus, *Sanitas quæ confertur a Domino, tota simul redit.*[37]

Specialiter autem in illo cæco contrarium fuit propter infidelitatem ipsius, ut Chrysostomus dicit.[38] Vel, sicut Beda dicit, *quem uno verbo totum simul curare poterat, paulatim curat, ut magnitudinem humanæ*

---

[24]*John* 8, 59
[25]*Catena aurea in Joannem*, on 8, 59, under the name of Augustine; cf Theophylactus, PG 124, 40
[26]*Luke* 4, 40
[27]*In Luc.*, on 4, 40. PG 72, 552
[28]*Mark* 8, 23
[29]*Cat. aur. in Marc.*, on 8, 23, under the name of Chrysostom; cf Victor of Antioch, *Cat. in Marc.*, found in I. A. Cramer, *Catenæ Græcorum Patrum in N.T.*, Oxford, 1844, I, 344
[30]*John* 9, 6

THE DIFFERENT KINDS OF MIRACLES

Jesus hid himself and left the Temple,[24] Augustine comments, *He did not hide himself in a corner of the Temple, as if afraid, or turn to hide behind a wall or pillar; but by his heavenly power, making himself invisible to those who lay in wait for him, he passed through their midst.*[25]

From all these cases it is clear that Christ when he willed, by divine power worked changes affecting the souls of men, not only by justifying them and infusing wisdom, which pertains to the end of miracles, but also by outwardly drawing them to himself, or by terrifying or stupefying them, which pertains to miracles themselves.

2. Christ came to save the world not only by divine power, but also through the mystery of his Incarnation. And so frequently in healing the sick he not only used divine power, healing by way of command, but also by applying something which belonged to his humanity. Thus, on the text, *Laying his hands on each one he healed them*,[26] Cyril says, *Although, as God, he could by one word have driven out all diseases, yet he touched them, showing them that his own flesh was capable of conferring the cure.*[27] And on the text, *Spitting upon his eyes and laying his hands on him*, etc.,[28] Chrysostom says, *He spat and laid his hands on the blind man, wishing to show that his divine word, accompanied by action, works wonders: for the hand signifies action; the spittle signifies the word which comes forth from the mouth.*[29] And on the text, *He made a paste with the spittle and spread the paste upon the eyes of the blind man*,[30] Augustine says, *From his spittle he made paste, because 'the Word was made flesh'.*[31] Or, as Chrysostom says,[32] also to signify that it was he who had formed man from *the slime of the earth.*[33]

Concerning the miracles of Christ it is also to be noted that generally what he did was most perfect. Thus, on *Every man sets forth the good wine first*,[34] Chrysostom says, *Christ's miracles are such that they are by far more splendid and useful than the works of nature.*[35] And likewise in an instant he conferred perfect health on the sick. Thus, on, *She arose and began to wait on him*,[36] Jerome says, *Health which is conferred by our Lord is restored all at once.*[37]

If, however, in the case of this blind man, he uncharacteristically went against his usual practice, it was because of the man's lack of faith, as Chrysostom says.[38] Or, as Bede says, *Whom he might have healed all at once by a single word, he heals little by little, to demonstrate the magnitude of human blindness which comes back to the light with difficulty and, as it were,*

---

[31]*In Joan.* XLIV, on 9, 6. PL 35, 1714
[32]*In Joan.* LVI. PG 59, 307
[33]*Genesis* 2, 7
[34]*John* 2, 10
[35]*In Joan.* XXII. PG 59, 136
[36]*Matthew* 8, 15
[37]*In Matt.* I, on 8, 14. PL 26, 52
[38]*Cat. aur. in Marc.*, on 8, 23, under the name of Chrysostom; cf Victor of Antioch, note 29

cæcitatis ostendat, quæ vix, et quasi per gradus ad lucem redeat, et gratiam suam nobis indicet, per quam singula perfectionis incrementa adjuvat.[39]

3. Ad tertium dicendum quod, sicut supra dictum est,[40] Christus miracula faciebat virtute divina. Dei autem *perfecta sunt opera*, ut dicitur *Deut.*[41] Non est autem aliquid perfectum, si finem non consequatur. Finis autem exterioris curationis per Christum factæ est curatio animæ. Et ideo non conveniebat Christo ut alicujus corpus curaret, nisi ejus curaret animam. Unde super illud *Joan.*, *Totum hominem sanum feci in sabbato*,[42] dicit Augustinus, quod *curatus est, ut sanus esset in corpore; et credidit, ut sanus esset in anima.*[43]

Specialiter autem paralytico dicitur, *Dimittuntur tibi peccata*, quia, ut Hieronymus dicit super *Matt.*, *Quid est facilius dicere? datur ex hoc nobis intelligentia, propter peccata plerisque evenire corporum debilitates: et ideo forsitan prius dimittuntur peccata, ut causis debilitatis ablatis, sanitas restituatur.*[44] Unde et *Joan.* dicitur, *Jam noli amplius peccare, ne deterius tibi aliquid contingat*,[45] ubi dicit Chrysostomus, *Discimus quod ex peccatis nata erat ei ægritudo.*[46]

Quamvis autem, ut Chrysostomus dicit, *quanto anima est potior corpore tanto peccatum dimittere majus sit quam corpus sanare; quia tamen illud non est manifestum, facit minus, quod est manifestius, ut demonstraret majus et non manifestum.*[47]

4. Ad quartum dicendum quod super illud *Matt.*, *Videte, ne quis sciat*,[48] dicit Chrysostomus, *Non est hoc contrarium quod hic dicitur ei quod alteri dicit, Vade et annuntia gloriam Dei: erudit enim nos prohibere eos qui volunt nos propter nos laudare; si autem ad Deum gloria refertur, non debemus prohibere, sed magis injungere ut hoc fiat.*[49]

---

articulus 4. utrum convenienter Christus fecerit miracula circa creaturas irrationales

AD QUARTUM sic proceditur: 1. Videtur quod inconvenienter fecerit Christus miracula circa creaturas irrationales. Bruta enim animalia sunt nobiliora plantis. Sed Christus fecit aliquod miraculum circa plantas, puta cum ad verbum ejus est siccata ficulnea, ut dicitur *Matt.*[1] Ergo videtur quod etiam circa animalia bruta miracula facere debuisset.

2. Præterea, pœna non juste infertur nisi pro culpa. Sed non fuit culpa ficulneæ quod in ea *Christus fructum non invenit*, quando *non erat tempus fructuum.*[2] Ergo videtur quod inconvenienter eam siccaverit.

---

[39]*In Marc.* II, on 8, 23. PL 92, 211
[41]*Deuteronomy* 32, 4
[43]*In Joan.* XXX, 5, on 7, 23. PL 35, 1635
[45]*John* 5, 14
[47]*In Matt.* XXIX, on 9, 5. PG 57, 360
[40]3a. 43, 2
[42]*John* 7, 23
[44]*In Matt.* I, on 9, 5 & 6. PL 26, 55
[46]*In Joan.* XXXVIII. PG 59, 211
[48]*Matthew* 9, 30

gradually: and to point out that it is by means of his grace that he helps us to grow in perfection.[39]

3. As stated above,[40] Christ worked miracles by divine power. Now it is written that *the works of God are perfect.*[41] But nothing is perfect unless it achieves its end. Now the end of the outward healing worked by Christ is the healing of the soul. And so it was not fitting for Christ to heal someone's body without healing his soul. For this reason, on the text, *I have healed the whole man on a Sabbath day*,[42] Augustine says, *Because he was healed, so as to be made sound in body; and he believed, so as to be made sound in soul.*[43]

However, in the case of the paralytic he says uncharacteristically, *Your sins are forgiven*, because, as Jerome says, *By this we are given to understand that most of our bodily ailments are due to sin: for which reason, perhaps, our sins are forgiven first, so that, when the cause of the ailment has been removed, we may be restored to health.*[44] For this reason also it is written, *Sin no more, or something worse may happen to you*,[45] from which, as Chrysostom says, *we learn that his sickness was the result of sin.*[46]

Nevertheless, as Chrysostom says, *To the extent that the soul is more important than the body, to this same extent is the forgiving of sins a greater work than healing the body; but because the one is not visible he does the lesser and more visible thing in order to prove the greater and invisible thing.*[47]

4. On, *Take care that no one learns about this*,[48] Chrysostom says, *What he says here is not contrary to what he says elsewhere, 'Go and proclaim the glory of God', for he teaches us to forbid those who would praise us for our own sakes; but if the glory be referred to God, then we must command rather than forbid that it be done.*[49]

article 4. whether the miracles were fitting which Christ worked concerning non-rational creatures

THE FOURTH POINT: 1. It would seem that the miracles were unfitting which Christ worked concerning non-rational creatures. For brute animals are more noble than plants. But Christ worked an occasional miracle concerning plants, as, for example, when at his command the fig-tree withered.[1] Therefore Christ should also have worked miracles concerning brute animals.

2. Furthermore, punishment is justly inflicted only for fault. But it was not the fault of the fig-tree that Christ found no fruit on it, since it was not the season for fruit.[2] Therefore it would seem unfitting that he withered it.

---

[49]*In Matt.* XXXII. PG 57, 378
[1]*Matthew* 21, 19   [2]*Mark* 11, 13

3. Præterea, aqua et aër sunt in medio cœli et terræ. Sed Christus aliqua miracula fecit in cœlo, sicut supra dictum est,[3] similiter etiam in terra, quando in ejus passione terra mota est.[4] Ergo videtur quod etiam in aëre et aqua aliqua miracula facere debuerit; ut mare dividere, sicut fecit Moyses,[5] vel etiam flumen, sicut fecerunt Josue,[6] et Elias:[7] et ut fierent in aëre tonitrua, sicut factum est in monte Sinai, quando lex dabatur,[8] et sicut Elias fecit.[9]

4. Præterea, opera miraculosa pertinent ad opus gubernationis mundi per divinam providentiam. Hoc autem opus præsupponit creationem. Inconveniens ergo videtur quod Christus in suis miraculis usus est creatione, quando scilicet multiplicavit panes.[10] Non ergo convenientia videntur fuisse ejus miracula circa irrationales creaturas.

SED CONTRA est quod Christus est Dei sapientia,[11] de qua dicitur *Sap.* quod *disponit omnia suaviter.*[12]

RESPONSIO: Dicendum quod, sicut supra dictum est,[13] miracula Christi ad hoc ordinabantur quod virtus divinitatis cognosceretur in ipso ad hominum salutem. Pertinet autem ad virtutem divinitatis ut omnis creatura sit ei subjecta. Et ideo in omnibus creaturarum generibus miracula eum facere oportuit, et non solum in hominibus, sed etiam in irrationabilibus creaturis.

1. Ad primum ergo dicendum quod animalia bruta propinque se habent secundum genus ad hominem: unde et in eodem die cum homine facta sunt.[14] Et quia circa corpora humana multa miracula fecerat, non oportebat quod circa corpora brutorum animalium aliqua miracula faceret; præsertim quia quantum ad naturam sensibilem et corporalem eadem ratio est de hominibus et de aliis animalibus, præcipue terrestribus. Pisces autem cum vivant in aqua magis a natura hominum differunt, unde et alio die sunt facti:[15] in quibus miraculum Christus fecit in copiosa piscium captura, ut legitur *Luc.* et *Joan.*,[16] et etiam in pisce quem Petrus cepit et in eo invenit staterem.[17] Quod autem porci in mare præcipitati sunt,[18] non fuit operatio divini miraculi, sed operatio dæmonum ex permissione divina.

2. Ad secundum dicendum quod, sicut Chrysostomus dicit, *cum in plantis vel brutis aliquid tale Dominus operatur, non quæras qualiter juste siccata est ficus, si tempus non erat: hoc enim quærere est ultimæ dementiæ, quia scilicet in talibus non invenitur culpa et pœna: sed miraculum inspice, et admirare miraculi factorem.*[19] Nec facit creator injuriam possidenti, si

---

[3]art. 2
[4]*Matthew* 27, 51
[5]*Exodus* 14, 21
[6]*Joshua* 3, 15 and 16
[7]*II Kings* 2, 8
[8]*Exodus* 19, 16
[9]*I Kings* 18, 45
[10]*Matthew* 14, 15; 15, 32
[11]*I Corinthians* 1, 24
[12]*Wisdom* 8, 1
[13]preceding art.
[14]*Genesis* 1, 24
[15]*Genesis* 1, 20
[16]*Luke* 5, 4; *John* 21, 6
[17]*Matthew* 17, 26

THE DIFFERENT KINDS OF MIRACLES

3. Furthermore, air and water are between heaven and earth. But Christ worked some miracles in the heavens, as stated above,[3] and, likewise, in the earth when at the time of his Passion he made the earth quake.[4] Therefore it would seem that he should also have worked miracles in the air and water, so as to divide the sea, as Moses did;[5] or even a river, as Joshua did,[6] and Elijah too;[7] and so as to make thunder break in the air, as occurred on Mount Sinai when the Law was given,[8] and as Elijah did.[9]

4. Furthermore, miraculous deeds belong to the work of divine providence in governing the world. But this work presupposes creation. Therefore it would seem unfitting that Christ in his miracles made use of creation: when, for example, he multiplied the loaves.[10] Therefore it would seem that the miracles which he worked concerning irrational creatures were unfitting.

ON THE OTHER HAND Christ is *the wisdom of God*,[11] of which it is written, *She orders all things for good.*[12]

REPLY: As stated above,[13] Christ's miracles were ordered to this end, that the divine power possessed by him for the salvation of men should be recognized. Now it pertains to the divine power to have every creature be subject to it. And so it was necessary for him to work miracles on every kind of creature, and not only on man, but also on non-rational creatures.

Hence: 1. Generically brute animals are closely related to man, and for this reason they were created on the same day as man.[14] And because he worked many miracles concerning human bodies, it was not necessary for him to work any miracles concerning the bodies of brute animals; and this is all the more so because, as regards their sensible and physical nature, the same reason applies to both men and animals, especially those which are terrestrial. Fish, however, since they live in water, are farther removed from human nature, and so for this reason were created on a different day.[15] On them Christ worked a miracle in the superabundant catch of fish;[16] and also in the fish that Peter caught and in which he found a stater.[17] However, the pigs cast headlong into the sea[18] was not a miraculous work of God, but the work of evil spirits, having received God's permission.

2. As Chrysostom says, *When our Lord performs any such work on plants or brute animals, seek not what makes it just to wither up the fig-tree if it was not the season for fruit; for to seek this is the ultimate in foolishness, because in such things there is no fault or punishment to be found. Look instead at the miracle and marvel at him who performed the miracle.*[19] Nor does the Creator

---

[18] *Matthew* 8, 32
[19] *In Matt.* LXVII. PG 58, 634

creatura sua suo arbitrio utatur ad aliorum salutem; sed magis, ut Hilarius dicit super *Matt., in hoc bonitatis dominicæ argumentum reperimus: nam ubi afferri voluit procuratæ per se salutis exemplum, virtutis suæ potestatem in humanis corporibus exercuit; ubi vero in contumaces formam severitatis constituebat, futuri speciem damno arboris indicavit*,[20] et præcipue, ut Chrysostomus dicit, in ficulnea, *quæ est humidissima, ut miraculum majus appareat*.[21]

3. Ad tertium dicendum quod Christus etiam in aqua et in aëre fecit miracula, quæ sibi conveniebant, quando scilicet, ut legitur *Matt., Imperavit ventis et mari; et facta est tranquillitas magna*.[22] Non autem conveniebat ei qui omnia in statum pacis et tranquillitatis revocare venerat, ut vel turbationem aëris vel divisionem aquarum faceret. Unde Apostolus dicit *Heb., Non accessistis ad tractabilem et accensibilem ignem, et turbinem, et caliginem, et procellam*.[23]

Circa passionem tamen *divisum est velum*, ad ostendendum reserationem mysteriorum legis: *aperta sunt monumenta*, ad ostendendum quod per ejus mortem mortuis vita daretur; *terra mota est, et petræ scissæ sunt*,[24] ad ostendendum quod lapidea hominum corda per ejus passionem emollirentur, et quod totus mundus virtute passionis ejus erat in melius commutandus.

4. Ad quartum dicendum quod multiplicatio panum non est facta per modum creationis, sed per additionem extraneæ materiæ in panes conversæ. Unde Augustinus dicit, *Unde multiplicat de paucis granis segetes, inde in manibus suis multiplicavit quinque panes*.[25] Manifestum est autem quod per conversionem grana multiplicantur in segetes.[26]

---

[20]*In Matt.* XXI, 6. PL 9, 1037
[21]*In Matt.* LXVII. PG 58, 634
[22]*Matthew* 8, 26
[23]*Hebrews* 12, 18

inflict any harm on the owner, if in accord with his will he uses his creatures for the salvation of others; as Hilary says, *We should perceive in this a proof of divine goodness. For when he wished to provide an example of the salvation he brought he exercised the fullness of his power on the human body; but when he wished to illustrate his severity toward the insolent, he indicated to them the manner of their future condemnation by condemning the tree.*[20] And most notably, as Chrysostom says, concerning a fig-tree, *which is full of moisture, so that the miracle seems all the greater.*[21]

3. When they were fitting for him he also worked miracles in the air and water; namely, as we read, when *he rebuked the winds and the sea, and there came a great calm.*[22] It was not, however, fitting for him, who came to restore all things to a state of peace and calm, either to create a disturbance in the air or to divide the waters. For this reason the apostle says, *What you have approached cannot be sensed: neither a blazing fire, nor a whirlwind, nor a gloomy darkness, nor a gale.*[23]

However, at the time of the Passion, *the veil was torn in two*, to indicate the unlocking of the mysteries of the Law; *the tombs opened*, to indicate that by his death life would be given to the dead; *the earth quaked and the rocks were split*,[24] to indicate that the stony hearts of men would be softened through his Passion, and that the whole world would be changed for the better in virtue of his Passion.

4. The multiplication of the loaves was not effected by way of creation, but by an addition of extraneous matter transformed into loaves. For which reason Augustine says, *As he multiplied the harvests from a few grains, so he multiplied the five loaves in his hands.*[25] But it is clearly by a process of transformation that grains are multiplied into harvests.[26]

---

[24] *Matthew* 27, 51–2
[25] *In Joan.* XXIV, 1, on 6, 1. PL 35, 1593
[26] cf 1a. 92, 3 ad 1

Quæstio 45. de transfiguratione Christi

DEINDE CONSIDERANDUM est de transfiguratione Christi, et circa hoc quæruntur quatuor:
1. utrum conveniens fuerit Christum transfigurari;
2. utrum claritas transfigurationis fuerit claritas gloriosa;
3. de testibus transfigurationis;
4. de testimonio paternæ vocis.

articulus 1. utrum fuerit conveniens Christum transfigurari

AD PRIMUM sic proceditur: 1. Videtur quod non fuerit conveniens Christum transfigurari.[1] Non enim competit vero corpori ut in diversas figuras mutetur, sed corpori phantastico. Corpus autem Christi non fuit phantasticum, sed verum, ut supra habitum est.[2] Ergo videtur quod transfigurari non debuerit.

2. Præterea, figura est in quarta specie qualitatis; claritas autem est in tertia, cum sit sensibilis qualitas.[3] Assumptio ergo claritatis a Christo transfiguratio dici non debet.

3. Præterea, corporis gloriosi sunt quatuor dotes, ut infra dicetur, scilicet *impassibilitas, agilitas, subtilitas et claritas*.[4] Non ergo debuit transfigurari magis secundum assumptionem claritatis, quam secundum assumptionem aliarum dotum.

SED CONTRA est quod dicitur *Matt.* quod *Jesus transfiguratus est* ante tres discipulorum suorum.[5]

RESPONSIO: Dicendum quod Dominus discipulis suis prænuntiata sua passione, induxerat eos ad suæ passionis sequelam.[6] Oportet autem, ad hoc quod aliquis directe procedat in via, quod finem aliqualiter præcognoscat; sicut sagittator non recte jaciet sagittam, nisi prius signum prospexerit in quod jaciendum est. Unde et Thomas dixit, *Joan., Domine, nescimus quo vadis: et quomodo possumus viam scire?*[7] Et hoc præcipue necessarium est, quando via est difficilis et aspera, et iter laboriosum, finis vero jucundus. Christus autem per suam passionem ad hoc pervenit ut gloriam obtineret non solum animæ, quam habuit a principio suæ conceptionis, sed etiam corporis, secundum illud *Luc., Hæc oportuit Christum pati, et ita intrare in gloriam suam*:[8] ad quam etiam perducit eos qui vestigia suæ passionis

---

[1]*Matthew* 17, 1–8; *Mark* 9, 1–7; *Luke* 9, 28
[2]3a. 5, 1
[3]cf 1a2æ. 49, 2
[4]cf *Supplement*, 82
[5]*Matthew* 17, 2
[6]*Matthew* 16, 21
[7]*John* 14, 5
[8]*Luke* 24, 26

Question 45. Christ's transfiguration

WE MUST NEXT CONSIDER Christ's transfiguration; regarding this there are four points of inquiry:[a]
1. whether it was fitting for Christ to be transfigured;
2. whether the splendour of the transfiguration was the splendour of glory;
3. the witnesses of the transfiguration;
4. the testimony of the Father's voice.

article 1. whether it was fitting for Christ to be transfigured

THE FIRST POINT: 1. It would seem that it was not.[1] For it is proper to an imaginary body, not to a real body, to be changed into divers figures. Now Christ's body was not imaginary, but real, as stated above.[2] Therefore it would seem that he should not have been transfigured.

2. Furthermore, figure is fourth among the species of quality,[b] whereas splendour is third, since it is a sensible quality.[3] Therefore Christ's assumption of splendour should not be called a transfiguration.

3. Furthermore, the glorified body has a fourfold endowment, as stated below,[4] namely, *impassibility, agility, subtlety and splendour.* Therefore his transfiguration should not have consisted in an assumption of splendour rather than the other endowments.

ON THE OTHER HAND it is written that Jesus was *transfigured* in the presence of three of his disciples.[5c]

REPLY: After having foretold his Passion to his disciples, our Lord had persuaded them to follow the path of his Passion.[6] Now in order for someone to go straight along the way, he must have some foreknowledge of the end; just as an archer will not shoot the arrow straight unless he has first seen the target he is aiming at. And for this reason Thomas said, *Lord, we do not know where you are going, so how can we know the way?*[7] And this is especially necessary when the way is rough and difficult, the journey wearisome, but the end delightful. Now Christ underwent the Passion in order to obtain glory, not only for his soul, which he had from the first moment of his conception, but also for his body; according to *Luke, Was it not necessary that Christ should suffer and so enter into his glory?*[8] To which glory he leads those who follow in the footsteps of his Passion;

---
[a] cf Appendix 6.
[b] Form and figure: a species of quality. See Aristotle, *Categories* 6.
[c] The Transfiguration appears in all three Synoptic Gospels.

sequuntur, secundum illud *Act.*, *Per multas tribulationes oportet nos intrare in regnum cœlorum.*⁹ Et ideo conveniens fuit ut discipulis suis gloriam suæ claritatis ostenderet, quod est ipsum transfigurari, cui suos configurabit, secundum illud *Philipp.*, *Reformabit corpus humilitatis nostræ configuratum corpori claritatis suæ.*¹⁰ Unde Beda dicit super *Marc.*, *Pia provisione factum est ut, contemplatione semper manentis gaudii ad breve tempus delibata, fortius adversa tolerarent.*¹¹

1. Ad primum ergo dicendum quod, sicut Hieronymus dicit super *Matt.*, *nemo putet Christum, per hoc quod transfiguratus dicitur, pristinam formam et faciem perdidisse, vel amisisse corporis veritatem, et assumpsisse corpus spirituale vel aëreum; sed quomodo transformatus sit, Evangelista demonstrat dicens, Resplenduit facies ejus sicut sol; vestimenta autem ejus facta sunt alba sicut nix. Ubi splendor faciei ostenditur et candor describitur vestium; non substantia tollitur, sed gloria commutatur.*¹²

2. Ad secundum dicendum quod figura circa extremitatem corporis consideratur: est enim *figura quæ termino vel terminis comprehenditur.*¹³ Et ideo omnia illa, quæ circa extremitatem corporis considerantur, ad figuram quodammodo pertinere videntur. Sicut autem color, ita et claritas corporis non transparentis in ejus superficie attenditur. Et ideo assumptio claritatis transfiguratio dicitur.

3. Ad tertium dicendum quod inter prædictas quatuor dotes sola claritas est qualitas ipsius personæ in seipsa; aliæ vero tres dotes non percipiuntur nisi in aliquo actu, vel motu, seu passione. Ostendit igitur Christus in seipso aliqua illarum trium dotium indicia, puta agilitatis, cum supra undas maris ambulavit;¹⁴ subtilitatis, quando de clauso utero virginis exivit;¹⁵ impassibilitatis, quando de manibus Judæorum vel præcipitare, vel lapidare eum volentium illæsus evasit.¹⁶ Nec tamen propter illas transfiguratus dicitur, sed propter solam claritatem, quæ pertinet ad aspectum personæ ipsius.

articulus 2. utrum claritas Christi in transfiguratione fuerit claritas gloriosa

AD SECUNDUM sic proceditur:¹ 1. Videtur quod illa claritas non fuerit claritas gloriosa.² Dicit enim quædam glossa Bedæ, supra illud *Matt.*, *Transfiguratus est coram eis,*³ *In corpore*, inquit, *mortali ostendit non immortalitatem, sed claritatem similem futuræ immortalitati.*⁴ Sed claritas gloriæ est claritas immortalitatis. Non ergo illa claritas quam Christus discipulis ostendit fuit claritas gloriæ.

---

⁹*Acts* 14, 21   ¹⁰*Philippians* 3, 21   ¹¹*In Marc.* III, on 8, 29. PL 92, 216
¹²*In Matt.* III, on 17, 2. PL 26, 122   ¹³Euclid, *Elements* I, 14
¹⁴*Matthew* 14, 25; *Mark* 6, 48; *John* 6, 19   ¹⁵cf 3a. 28, 2
¹⁶*Luke* 4, 29–30; *John* 8, 59; 10, 31 & 39   ¹cf III *Sent.* XVI, 2, 2. *In Matt.* 17

according to *Acts, We have to endure many hardships before we enter the kingdom of God.*[9] And so it was fitting for him to manifest his glorious splendour (which is to be transfigured), according to which he will configure those who belong to him; as it is written, *He will configure these wretched bodies of ours into copies of his glorious body.*[10] For this reason Bede says, *By his loving foresight he prepared them to endure adversity bravely by allowing them to taste for a short time the contemplation of everlasting joy.*[11]

Hence: 1. As Jerome says, *Let no one think that Christ, because it is said he was transfigured, thereby lost his original form and countenance, or laid aside his real body and took up a spiritual or ethereal body.* Now the Evangelist describes how he was transformed, when he says, *His face shone like the sun and his clothes became as white as snow. The brightness of countenance which is manifested, and the whiteness of clothes which is described, indicates not that his substance is taken away, but rather that his glory undergoes a change.*[12]

2. Figure has to do with the outline of a body, for a figure is *that which is encompassed by a boundary or boundaries.*[13] Therefore whatever has to do with the outline of a body seems to pertain somehow to the figure. Now the splendour, just as the colour, of a non-transparent body is perceived on its surface, and so the assumption of splendour is called transfiguration.

3. Among the aforementioned endowments, only splendour is a quality of the very person in himself; the other three qualities, however, cannot be perceived except in some action or movement, or in some passion. Christ, then, showed in himself certain signs of possessing these three qualities—of agility, for example, when he walked on the waves of the sea;[14] of subtlety, when he came forth from the closed womb of the Virgin;[15] of impassibility, when he escaped unhurt from the hands of the Jews who wished to hurl him down or to stone him.[16] Nevertheless, it is not said, on account of these, that he was transfigured, but only on account of his splendour, which pertains to his personal appearance.

article 2. whether his splendour was the splendour of glory

THE SECOND POINT:[1] 1. It would seem not.[2] [a] For as Bede says, *He was transfigured in their presence*[3] means that *in his mortal body he manifests not the state of immortality, but splendour similar to that of future immortality.*[4] But the splendour of glory is the splendour of immortality. Therefore the splendour which Christ manifested to his disciples was not the splendour of glory.

---

[2]*Matthew* 17, 1-8; *Mark* 9, 1-7; *Luke* 9, 28   [3]*Matthew* 17, 2
[4]*Glossa ordin.*, on *Matthew* 17, 2. PL 114, 143. cf Bede, *In Matt.* III, on 17, 2. PL 92, 80
[a]Not a quality residing in Christ, but rather a heavenly limelight thrown on him.

2. Præterea, super illud *Luc.*, *Non gustabunt mortem, donec videant regnum Dei*,[5] dicit glossa, *Idest glorificationem corporis in imaginaria repræsentatione futuræ beatitudinis.*[6] Sed imago alicujus rei non est ipsa res. Ergo claritas illa non fuit claritas beatitudinis.

3. Præterea, claritas gloriæ non est nisi in corpore humano. Sed claritas illa transfigurationis apparuit non solum in corpore Christi, sed etiam in vestimentis ejus, et in nube lucida quæ discipulos obumbravit. Ergo videtur quod illa claritas non fuerit claritas gloriæ.

SED CONTRA est quod super illud *Matt.*, *Transfiguratus est ante eos*,[7] dicit Hieronymus, *Qualis futurus est tempore judicii, talis Apostolis apparuit.*[8] Et super illud *Matt.*, *Donec videant filium hominis venientem in regno suo*,[9] dicit Chrysostomus, *Volens monstrare quid est illa gloria in qua postea venturus est, eis in præsenti vita revelavit, sicut possibile erat eos discere, ut neque in Domini morte jam doleant.*[10]

RESPONSIO: Dicendum quod claritas illa quam Christus in transfiguratione assumpsit fuit claritas gloriæ quantum ad essentiam, non tamen quantum ad modum essendi. Claritas enim corporis gloriosi derivatur ab animæ claritate, sicut Augustinus dicit.[11] Et similiter claritas corporis Christi in transfiguratione derivata est et a divinitate ipsius, ut Damascenus dicit,[12] et a gloria animæ ejus. Quod enim a principio conceptionis Christi gloria animæ non redundaret ad corpus ex quadam dispensatione divina factum est, ut in corpore passibili nostræ redemptionis expleret mysteria, sicut supra dictum est.[13] Non tamen per hoc adempta est Christo potestas derivandi gloriam animæ ad corpus. Et hoc quidem fecit quantum ad gloriæ claritatem in transfiguratione; aliter tamen quam in corpore glorificato. Nam ad corpus glorificatum redundat claritas ab anima, sicut qualitas quædam permanens corpus afficiens; unde fulgere corporaliter non est miraculosum in corpore glorioso. Sed ad corpus Christi in transfiguratione derivata est claritas a divinitate et anima ejus, non per modum qualitatis immanentis et afficientis ipsum corpus, sed magis per modum passionis transeuntis, sicut cum aër illuminatur a sole; unde ille fulgor tunc in corpore Christi apparens miraculosus fuit, sicut et hoc ipsum quod ambulavit super undas maris.[14] Unde Dionysus dicit, *Super hominem operabatur Christus ea quæ sunt hominis: et hoc monstrat Virgo super-*

---

[5]*Luke* 9, 27
[6]cf Alexander of Hales, *Summa* III, 21, 2
[7]*Matthew* 17, 2
[8]*In Matt.* III, on 17, 2. PL 26, 121
[9]*Matthew* 16, 28
[10]*In Matt.* LVI. PG 58, 549
[11]*Epistola ad Dioscorum* CXVIII, 3. PL 33, 439
[12]*Orat. de Transfig.* 12. PG 96, 564   [13]3a. 14, 1 ad 2   [14]*Matthew* 14, 25
[b]Jerusalem Bible: *the Kingdom of God.*

2. Furthermore, on the text, *Who will not taste death* unless *they see the reign of God*,⁵ ᵇ Bede's gloss says, *That is, the glorification of the body in an imaginary representation of future beatitude.*⁶ But the image of a thing is not the same as the thing itself. Therefore his splendour was not the splendour of beatitude.

3. Furthermore, the splendour of glory resides only in a human body. But the splendour of the transfiguration was manifested not only in Christ's body, but also in his clothes, and in the bright cloud which overshadowed the disciples. Therefore it would seem that his splendour was not the splendour of glory.

ON THE OTHER HAND, on the text, *He was transfigured in their presence*,⁷ Jerome says, *He appeared to the apostles such as he will appear on the day of judgment.*⁸ And on the text, *Until they see the Son of Man coming with his kingdom*,⁹ Chrysostom says, *Wishing to show them with what kind of glory he would come afterwards, in so far as it was possible for them to learn from it, he manifested it to them in their present life, so that they might not grieve even over the death of their Lord.*¹⁰

REPLY: The splendour which Christ assumed in the transfiguration was the splendour of glory as to essence, but not as to mode of being.ᶜ For the splendour of the glorious body is derived from the splendour of the soul, as Augustine says.¹¹ And similarly, the splendour of Christ's body in the transfiguration was derived from his divinity, as Damascene says,¹² and from the glory of his soul. That the glory of his soul did not overflow into his body from the first moment of Christ's conception was a divine dispensation, that, as stated above,¹³ he might fulfil the mysteries of our redemption in a passible body. This did not, however, deprive Christ of the power to let the glory of his soul flow into his body. And as regards splendour, this is what he did in the transfiguration, but other than in a glorious body. For splendour flows from the soul into the glorified body, by way of a permanent quality affecting the body. And so bodily refulgence is not miraculous in a glorified body. But in Christ's transfiguration, splendour flowed from his divinity and from his soul into his body, not by way of an inherent quality of his body, but rather by way of a transient passion, as when the air is lit up by the sun. And so the refulgence, which appeared in Christ's body, was miraculous; just as the fact that he walked upon the waves of the sea.¹⁴ For this reason Dionysius says, *Christ excelled man in doing what is natural to man: this is shown both by the Virgin con-*

ᶜThe four qualities of a glorified body: *impassibilitas*, or invulnerability, *Suppl.* 82; *subtilitas*, or 'not-denseness', ibid 83; *agilitas*, or lissomeness, ibid 84; *claritas*, or splendour, ibid 85.

naturaliter concipiens, et aqua instabilis materialium et terrenorum pedum sustinens gravitatem.[15]

Unde non est dicendum, sicut Hugo de S. Victore dicit,[16] quod Christus assumpsit quatuor dotes: *claritatis* in transfiguratione; *agilitatis*, ambulando super mare; *subtilitatis*, egrediendo de clauso utero Virginis; et *impassibilitatis* in cœna, quando dedit corpus suum ad edendum, sine hoc quod divideretur.* Quia dos nominat quamdam qualitatem immanentem corpori glorioso. Sed miraculose habuit ea quæ pertinent ad dotes. Et est simile quantum ad animam de visione, qua Paulus vidit Deum in raptu, ut in secunda parte dictum est.[17]

1. Ad primum ergo dicendum quod ex illo verbo non ostenditur quod claritas Christi non fuerit claritas gloriæ, sed quod non fuerit claritas corporis gloriosi, quia corpus Christi nondum erat immortale: sicut enim dispensative factum est ut in Christo gloria animæ non redundaret ad corpus, ita fieri potuit dispensative, ut redundaret quantum ad dotem claritatis, et non quantum ad dotem impassibilitatis.

2. Ad secundum dicendum quod illa claritas dicitur imaginaria fuisse, non quia esset vera claritas gloriæ, sed quia erat quædam imago repræsentans illam gloriæ perfectionem, secundum quam corpus erit gloriosum.

3. Ad tertium dicendum quod sicut claritas quæ erat in corpore Christi, repræsentabat futuram claritatem corporis ejus, ita claritas vestimentorum ejus designabat futuram claritatem sanctorum, quæ superabitur a claritate Christi, sicut candor nivis superatur a splendore solis. Unde Gregorius dicit quod *vestimenta Christi facta sunt splendentia, quia in supernæ claritatis culmine sancti omnes ei luce justitiæ fulgentes adhærebunt.* Vestium enim nomine justos, quos sibi adjunget, significat, secundum illud *Isa., His omnibus velut ornamento vestieris.*[18]

Nubes autem lucida significat Spiritus Sancti gloriam vel *virtutem paternam,* ut Origenes dicit, per quam sancti in futura gloria protegentur.[19] Quamvis etiam convenienter significare possit claritatem mundi innovati quæ erit sanctorum tabernaculum: unde, Petro disponente tabernacula facere, *nubes lucida discipulos obumbravit.*

articulus 3. utrum testes transfigurationis convenienter fuerint inducti

AD TERTIUM sic proceditur:[1] 1. Videtur quod non convenienter inducti fuerint testes transfigurationis. Unusquisque enim maxime potest perhibere

---

*Leonine edition omits the phrase 'et impassibilitatis in cœna . . . divideretur'.
[15]*Epistola ad Caium* IV. PG 3, 1072
[16]cf Innocent III, *De sacro altaris mysterio* IV, 12. PL 217, 864. *Serm. de temp.* XIV. PL 217, 382. cf Hugh of St Victor, *De sacram.* II, 8. PL 176, 462
[17]2a2æ. 175, 3 ad 2   [18]*Moral.* XXXII, 6. PL 76, 640. *Isaiah* 49, 18

ceiving him supernaturally, and by the unstable water sustaining the weight of material and earthly feet.[15]

For this reason it should not be maintained, as Hugh of St Victor said,[16] that Christ was endowed with the gift of splendour at his transfiguration, of agility when he walked upon the sea, of subtlety when he came forth from the Virgin's closed womb, and impassibility at the Supper when, without its being divided, he gave of his body to be eaten: because these gifts are inherent qualities of a glorified body. Rather, he was endowed miraculously with what pertained to these gifts. And so the explanation, as regards his soul, is similar to what is stated in the Second Part[17] concerning the vision in which Paul saw God in a rapture.

Hence: 1. These words do not prove that the splendour of Christ was not the splendour of glory, but that it was not the splendour of a glorious body, because Christ's body was not as yet immortal. For just as it was by dispensation that in Christ the glory of the soul did not overflow into the body, so likewise it was possible that by dispensation the glory might overflow as the gift of splendour but not as the gift of impassibility.

2. This splendour is said to have been imaginary, not as though it were not really the splendour of glory, but because it was a kind of image representing that perfection of glory according to which the body will be glorious.

3. Just as the splendour of Christ's body represented the future splendour of his body, so the splendour of his clothes signified the future splendour of the saints, which will be surpassed by the splendour of Christ, just as the brightness of the snow is surpassed by the brightness of the sun. For this reason Gregory says that Christ's clothes became resplendent, *because in the heights of heavenly splendour all the saints will cling to him as they shine brightly with the light of righteousness. For his clothes signify the righteous, whom he will unite to himself;* according to Isaiah, *You will be clothed with all these as with jewels.*[18]

The bright cloud, however, signifies the glory of the Holy Spirit or *the power of the Father,* as Origen says, by which the saints will be covered in their future state of glory.[19] Although it could also fittingly signify the splendour of the world made new, which splendour will cover the saints as a tent. And so, when Peter suggested that they make tents, *a bright cloud overshadowed* the disciples.

article 3. whether the witnesses of the transfiguration were fittingly chosen

THE THIRD POINT:[1] 1. It would seem not. For a man can best give witness regarding what he knows. But at the time of Christ's transfiguration no

---

[19] *In Matt.* XII. PG 13, 1082   [1] cf *In Matt.* 17

testimonium de notis. Sed qualis esset futura gloria tempore transfigurationis Christi nulli homini per experimentum erat adhuc notum, sed solis angelis. Ergo testes transfigurationis magis debuerunt esse angeli quam homines.

2. Præterea, testes veritatis non decet aliqua fictio, sed veritas. Moyses autem et Elias non ibi vere affuerunt, sed imaginarie: dicit enim quædam glossa super illud *Luc.*, *Erant autem Moyses, et Elias*, etc.,[2] *Sciendum est, non corpora, vel animas Moysi et Eliæ ibi apparuisse, sed in subjecta creatura illa corpora fuisse formata. Potest etiam credi, angelico ministerio hoc factum esse, ut angeli eorum personas assumerent.*[3] Non ergo videtur quod fuerint convenientes testes.

3. Præterea, *Act.* dicitur quod Christo *omnes prophetæ testimonium perhibent.*[4] Ergo non soli Moyses et Elias debuerunt adesse tanquam testes, sed etiam omnes prophetæ.

4. Præterea, gloria Christi omnibus Christi fidelibus repromittitur,[5] quos per suam transfigurationem ad illius gloriæ desiderium accendere voluit. Non ergo solos Petrum et Jacobum, et Joannem in testimonium suæ transfigurationis assumere debuit, sed omnes discipulos.

IN CONTRARIUM est Evangelicæ Scripturæ auctoritas, *Matt.*, et *Marc.*, et *Luc.*[6]

RESPONSIO: Dicendum quod Christus transfigurari voluit, ut gloriam suam hominibus ostenderet, et ad eam desiderandam homines provocaret, sicut supra dictum est.[7] Ad gloriam autem æternæ beatitudinis adducuntur homines per Christum, non solum qui post eum fuerunt, sed etiam qui eum præcesserunt. Unde, eo ad passionem properante, tam turbæ quæ sequebantur quam quæ præcedebant ei clamabant *Hosanna*, ut dicitur *Matt.*,[8] quasi salutem ab eo petentes. Et ideo conveniens fuit ut de præcedentibus ipsum testes adessent, scilicet Moyses et Elias; et de sequentibus ipsum, scilicet Petrus, et Jacobus, et Joannes, ut *in ore duorum vel trium testium staret hoc verbum.*[9]

1. Ad primum ergo dicendum quod Christus per suam transfigurationem manifestavit discipulis corporis gloriam, quæ ad solos homines pertinet. Et ideo convenienter non angeli, sed homines ad hoc pro testibus inducuntur.

2. Ad secundum dicendum quod glossa illa dicitur esse sumpta ex libro qui intitulatur *de mirabilibus sacræ Scripturæ*, qui non est liber authenticus, sed falso adscribitur Augustino.[10] Et ideo illi glossæ non est standum. Dicit enim expresse Hieronymus, super *Matt.*, *Et apparuerunt illis Moyses*, etc.,

---

[2]*Luke* 9, 30
[4]*Acts* 10, 43
[3]*Glossa ordin.* PL 114, 280
[5]II *Corinthians* 3, 18; *Philippians* 3, 21

man, but only angels, had as yet any knowledge from experience of the future state of glory. Therefore the witnesses of the transfiguration should have been angels rather than men.

2. Furthermore, truth, not deception, is becoming in a witness of the truth. Now, Moses and Elijah were not truly there, but only in an imaginary way; for there is a gloss on, *They were Moses and Elijah*, etc.,[2] which says, *It must be observed that neither the body nor the soul of either Moses or Elijah were actually there;* but those bodies *were supplied only with a form. It is also possible to believe that this was effected by angelic ministry, so that angels impersonated them.*[3] Therefore it does not seem that they were fitting witnesses.

3. Furthermore, it is written that *all the prophets give witness*[4] to Christ. Therefore, not only Moses and Elijah, but indeed all the prophets, should have been present as witnesses.

4. Furthermore, Christ's glory is promised to all the faithful[5] whom he wished through his transfiguration to enkindle with the desire for that glory. Therefore he should have taken up not only Peter, and James, and John, but all the disciples, to be witnesses of his transfiguration.

ON THE OTHER HAND there is the authority of the Gospels.[6]

REPLY: Christ wished to be transfigured in order to show men his glory, and to arouse men to a desire of it, as stated above.[7] Now men are led to the glory of eternal happiness by Christ—not only those who came after him, but also those who preceded him; and so, as the time of his Passion approached, both *the crowds who followed* and *who preceded him were all shouting, 'Hosanna,'*[8] begging him, as it were, to save them. And therefore it was fitting that there should be witnesses present from among those who preceded him—namely, Moses and Elijah—as well as from those who followed him—namely, Peter, James and John—so that *the evidence of two or three witnesses might sustain the assertion.*[9]

Hence: 1. By his transfiguration Christ manifested to his disciples the glory of his body, which is for men alone. And so, men rather than angels were fittingly chosen as witnesses to this.

2. This gloss is said to be taken from a book entitled *The Marvels of Holy Scripture*, which is not an authentic book, but wrongly ascribed to Augustine.[10] And so we should not stand by this gloss. For Jerome says it should be noted that *when the Scribes and Pharisees asked for a sign from*

---

[6]*Matthew* 17, 1–8; *Mark* 9, 1–7; *Luke* 9, 28
[7]art. 1   [8]*Matthew* 21, 9
[9]*Deuteronomy* 19, 15; *Matthew* 18, 16
[10]St Thomas considered it authentic when earlier he wrote *Quodl.* IX, iv, 1

Considerandum est quod Scribis et Pharisæis de cœlo signa poscentibus, dare noluit; hic vero, ut Apostolorum augeat fidem, dat signum de cœlo, Elia inde descendente, quo conscenderat, et Moyse ab inferis resurgente.[11] Quod non est sic intelligendum, quasi anima Moysi suum corpus resumpserit; sed quod anima ejus apparuit per aliquod corpus assumptum, sicut angeli apparent. Elias autem apparuit in proprio corpore, non quidem de cœlo empyreo allato, sed de aliquo eminenti loco, quo fuerat in curru igneo raptus.[12]

3. Ad tertium dicendum quod, sicut Chrysostomus dicit, Moyses et Elias in medium adducuntur propter multas rationes. Prima est hæc, *quia enim turbæ dicebant eum esse Eliam vel Jeremiam, aut unum ex prophetis, capita prophetarum secum ducit, ut saltem hinc appareat differentia servorum et Domini*. Secunda ratio est, *quia Moyses legem dedit, Elias pro gloria Domini æmulator fuit, unde per hoc quod simul cum Christo apparent, excluditur calumnia Judæorum accusantium Christum, tanquam transgressorem legis et blasphemum Dei sibi gloriam usurpantem*. Tertia ratio est, *ut ostendat se habere potestatem mortis et vitæ, et esse judicem mortuorum et vivorum, per hoc quod Moyses jam mortuum, et Eliam adhuc viventem secum ducit*. Quarta ratio est, quia, sicut *Lucas* dicit, *loquebantur cum eo de excessu, quem completurus erat in Jerusalem,*[13] idest de passione et morte sua. Et ideo ut supra hoc discipulorum animos confirmaret, *inducit eos in medium, qui se morti exposuerunt pro Deo: nam Moyses cum periculo mortis se obtulit Pharaoni, Elias vero regi Achab*. Quinta ratio est, quia volebat ut discipuli sui *æmularentur Moysi mansuetudinem, et zelum Eliæ*.[14] Sextam rationem addidit Hilarius, *ut ostenderet scilicet se per legem, quam dedit Moyses, et per prophetas, inter quos fuit Elias præcipuus, esse prædicatum.*[15]

4. Ad quartum dicendum quod alta mysteria non sunt omnibus exponenda immediate, sed per majores suo tempore ad alios debent devenire.[16] Et ideo, ut Chrysostomus dicit, *assumpsit tres tanquam potiores.*[17] Nam *Petrus excellens fuit in dilectione,* quam habuit ad Christum, et iterum in potestate sibi commissa;[18] Joannes vero in privilegio amoris, quo a Christo diligebatur propter suam virginitatem, et iterum propter prærogativam evangelicæ doctrinæ;[19] Jacobus autem propter prærogativam martyrii.[20] Et tamen hos ipsos noluit hoc quod viderant, aliis annuntiare ante resurrectionem, *ne*, ut Hieronymus dicit, *ei incredibile esset pro rei magnitudine; et post tantam gloriam apud rudes animos sequens crux*

---

[11] *In Matt.* III, on 17, 3. PL 26, 122
[12] II *Kings* 2, 11; cf below, 3a. 49, 5, 2
[13] *Luke* 9, 31   [14] *In Matt.* LVI, on 17, 3. PG 58, 550
[15] *In Matt.*, on 17, 2. PL 9, 1014
[16] cf 2a2æ. 1, 7; 2, 7
[17] *In Matt.* LVI. PG 58, 550
[18] *John* 21, 15; *Matthew* 16, 18–19

heaven, he refused to give them one; here, however, in order to increase the faith of the apostles, he gives a sign from heaven, *Elijah descending from the place to which he had ascended, and Moses arising from the lower regions.*[11] This must not be understood as though the soul of Moses reassumed his own body, but that his soul appeared through some assumed body, in the same way that angels appear. Elijah, however, appeared in his own body, having been brought down, not from the empyrean heaven, but from some high place to which he had been taken up in the fiery chariot.[12] [a]

3. As Chrysostom says, *Moses and Elijah are brought forward for many reasons. The first is this: Because the crowds said he was Elijah or Jeremiah or one of the prophets, he presented the chief prophets in his company, so that in this way, at least, the difference between the Lord and his servants might be apparent.* A second reason is *that Moses gave the Law and Elijah was jealous for the glory of the Lord.* Thus, their appearing together with Christ precludes the calumny of the Jews who *accused Christ of transgressing the Law and of blasphemously usurping the glory of God.* A third reason was *to show that he had power over life and death, and that he was judge of the living and the dead; by bringing with him Moses who had died, and Elijah who was still living.* A fourth reason was that, as Luke says, *they were speaking* with him *of his passing on which he was to accomplish in Jerusalem,*[13] that is, of his passion and death. So, *in order to encourage his disciples in view of this,* he brings before them those who had exposed themselves to death for God's sake: for, while risking death, Moses had set himself against Pharaoh, and Elijah against Achab the king. A fifth reason is *that he wished his disciples to imitate the meekness of Moses and the zeal of Elijah.*[14] Hilary adds a sixth reason, namely, *to show that he had been foretold by the Law, which Moses gave them, and by the prophets, among whom Elijah ranked first.*[15]

4. Sublime mysteries should not be explained to everyone immediately, but should be handed down through superiors to others in their proper turn.[16] And so, as Chrysostom says,[17] *he took up these three because they were superior to the rest. For Peter excelled in the love* he had for Christ and in the power entrusted to him;[18] John had the privilege of being loved by Christ on account of his virginity, and, again, he would have the privilege of being an Evangelist;[19] James would have the privilege of suffering martyrdom.[20] Nevertheless he did not wish them to proclaim what they had seen before the resurrection; *lest,* as Jerome says, *it seem incredible on account of its magnitude; and, lest, after such great glory, the cross which*

---

[19]Jerome, *Adv. Jovin.* I, 26. PL 23, 246. *Prol. in Matt.* PL 26, 18
[20]*Acts* 12, 2
[a]According to the then generally received opinion, not to theologically certain fact.

*scandalum faceret.*²¹ Vel etiam *ne totaliter impediretur a populo,*²² et *ut cum essent Spiritu Sancto repleti, tunc gestorum spiritualium testes essent.*²³

> articulus 4. utrum convenienter auditum fuerit testimonium paternæ vocis in transfiguratione

AD QUARTUM sic proceditur:¹ 1. Videtur quod inconvenienter auditum fuerit testimonium paternæ vocis, *Hic est filius meus dilectus*. Quia, ut dicitur *Job, Semel loquitur Deus, et secundo idipsum non repetit*.² Sed in baptismo hoc ipsum paterna vox fuerat protestata.³ Non ergo fuit conveniens quod hoc iterum protestaretur in transfiguratione.

2. Præterea, in baptismo simul cum voce paterna affuit Spiritus Sanctus in specie columbæ,⁴ quod in transfiguratione factum non fuit. Non ergo conveniens videtur fuisse Patris protestatio.

3. Præterea, Christus docere incœpit post baptismum;⁵ et tamen in baptismo vox Patris ad eum audiendum homines non induxerat. Ergo nec in transfiguratione inducere debuit.

4. Præterea, non debent aliquibus dici ea quæ ferre non possunt, secundum illud *Joan., Adhuc habeo vobis multa dicere, quæ non potestis portare modo*.⁶ Sed discipuli vocem Patris ferre non poterant: dicitur enim *Matt.* quod *audientes discipuli ceciderunt in faciem suam, et timuerunt valde*.⁷ Ergo non debuit vox paterna ad eos fieri.

IN CONTRARIUM est auctoritas evangelicæ Scripturæ, *Matt.* et *Marc.*⁸

RESPONSIO: Dicendum quod adoptio filiorum Dei est per quamdam conformitatem imaginis ad Filium Dei naturalem.⁹ Quod quidem fit dupliciter: primo quidem fit per gratiam viæ, quæ est conformitas imperfecta; secundo, per gloriam patriæ, quæ erit conformitas perfecta, secundum illud I *Joan., Nunc filii Dei sumus, et nondum apparuit quid erimus, scimus quoniam cum apparuerit, similes ei erimus, quoniam videbimus eum sicuti est.*¹⁰ Quia igitur gratiam per baptismum consequimur, in transfiguratione autem præmonstrata est claritas futuræ gloriæ, ideo tam in baptismo quam in transfiguratione conveniens fuit manifestari naturalem Christi

---

²¹*In Matt.* III, on 17, 9. PL 26, 123
²²Bede, XVIII, on Mark 9, 8. PL 94, 101
²³Hilary, *In Matt., on* 17, 3. PL 9, 1015
¹cf *In Matt.* 17   ²*Job* 33, 14
³*Matthew* 3, 17; *Mark* 1, 11; *Luke* 3, 22
⁴*Matthew* 3, 16; *Mark* 1, 10; *Luke* 3, 22
⁵*Matthew* 4, 17; *Mark* 1, 14; *Luke* 4, 15
⁶*John* 16, 12   ⁷*Matthew* 17, 6

would follow should cause *scandal*,²¹ or even be *completely hindered by the people*;²² and *so that, when they had been filled with the Holy Spirit, they might then give witness to these spiritual events.*²³

article 4. *whether the testimony of the Father's voice, saying, This is my beloved Son, was fittingly heard*

THE FOURTH POINT:¹ 1. It would seem not. For, as it is written, *God speaks once, and does not repeat the same thing a second time.*² But the Father's voice had already testified to this at the time of his baptism.³ Therefore it was not fitting for him to testify to it again at the time of his transfiguration.

2. Furthermore, at his baptism the Holy Spirit was present in the form of a dove at the same time that the Father's voice was heard.⁴ But this did not occur at the transfiguration. Therefore it would seem that the testimony of the Father was not fitting.

3. Furthermore, Christ began to teach after his baptism.⁵ Nevertheless, at his baptism the Father's voice did not urge men to hear him. Therefore, neither should he have urged them at the transfiguration.

4. Furthermore, things should not be said to those who cannot bear them: *I still have many things to say to you but they would be too much for you now.*⁶ But the disciples could not bear the Father's voice; for it is written that *when they heard this, the disciples fell on their faces and were overcome with fear.*⁷ Therefore the Father's voice should not have spoken to them.

ON THE OTHER HAND there is the authority of the Gospels.⁸

REPLY: Men become adopted sons of God by a certain conformity of image to the natural Son of God.⁹ ᵃ Now this is accomplished in two ways. First of all, by the grace of the wayfarer, which is an imperfect conformity; secondly, by glory, which is a perfect conformity: *We are already the children of God, and what we are to be has not yet been revealed; but we do know that when it is revealed we shall be like him, because we shall see him as he is.*¹⁰ Since it is by baptism that we acquire grace, while the splendour of our future glory was foreshadowed in the transfiguration, therefore it was fitting that at the time both of his baptism and of his transfiguration the natural sonship of Christ be made known by the testimony of the

---

⁸*Matthew* 17, 5; *Mark* 9, 6; *Luke* 9, 34
⁹cf above 3a. 3, 4 ad 3; 3, 5 ad 2; 3, 8; 39, 8 ad 3
¹⁰I *John* 3, 2
ᵃOn the Son as the Image of God, 1a. 35. On man as made to the image of God, 1a. 93.

filiationem testimonio Patris; quia solus est perfecte conscius illius perfectæ generationis simul cum Filio et Spiritu Sancto.

1. Ad primum ergo dicendum quod illud verbum referendum est ad æternam Dei locutionem, qua Deus Pater Verbum unicum protulit sibi coæternum. Et tamen potest dici quod licet idem corporali voce Deus protulerit, non tamen propter idem, sed ad ostendendum diversum modum quo homines participare possunt similitudinem filiationis æternæ.

2. Ad secundum dicendum quod sicut in baptismo, ubi declaratum fuit mysterium primæ regenerationis, ostensa est operatio totius Trinitatis, per hoc quod fuit ibi Filius incarnatus, apparuit Spiritus Sanctus in specie columbæ, et Pater fuit ibi declaratus in voce; ita etiam in transfiguratione, quæ est sacramentum secundæ regenerationis, tota Trinitas apparuit, Pater in voce, Filius in homine, Spiritus Sanctus in nube clara: quia sicut in baptismo dat innocentiam, quæ per simplicitatem columbæ designatur, ita in resurrectione dabit electis suis claritatem gloriæ et refrigerium ab omni malo quæ designantur in nube lucida.

3. Ad tertium dicendum quod Christus venerat gratiam actualiter dare, gloriam vero promittere verbo. Et ideo convenienter in transfiguratione inducuntur homines ut ipsum audiant, non autem in baptismo.

4. Ad quartum dicendum quod conveniens fuit discipulos voce paterna terreri et prosterni, ut ostenderetur quod excellentia illius gloriæ quæ tunc demonstrabatur, excedit omnem sensum et facultatem mortalium, secundum illud *Exod.*, *Non videbit me homo, et vivet.*[11] Et hoc est quod Hieronymus dicit quod *humana fragilitas conspectum majoris gloriæ ferre non sustinet.*[12] Ab hac autem fragilitate sanantur homines per Christum, eos in gloriam adducendo: quod significatur per hoc quod dixit eis, *Surgite, nolite timere.*[13]

---

[11]*Exodus* 33, 20
[12]*In Matt.* III, on 17, 6. PL 26, 123
[13]*Matthew* 17, 7

CHRIST'S TRANSFIGURATION

Father: since he alone together with the Son and the Holy Spirit is perfectly conscious of that perfect begetting.

Hence: 1. The words cited must be in reference to God's eternal utterance, by which God the Father expressed his single co-eternal Word.ᵇ Nevertheless, it may be said that God uttered the same thing a second time with bodily voice, although not for the same reason, but in order to show the different ways by which men can participate in the likeness of the eternal sonship.

2. Just as at the time of his baptism, when the mystery of the first regeneration was proclaimed, the operation of the entire Trinity was manifested, because the Incarnate Son was present there, the Holy Spirit appeared in the form of a dove, and the Father proclaimed his presence there in a voice; so also at the time of the transfiguration, which is a mystery of the second regeneration, the entire Trinity appears—the Father in the voice, the Son in the man, the Holy Spirit in the bright cloud; for just as in baptism he confers innocence, which is signified by the simplicity of the dove, so in the resurrection he will give his elect the splendour of glory and refreshment from every evil, which is signified by the bright cloud.

3. Christ came to give grace actually, but to give a verbal promise of glory. And so it was fitting that he urged men to hear him at the time of his transfiguration, but not at the time of his baptism.

4. Fittingly the disciples were terrified and made to fall by the voice of the Father, to show them that the magnificence of that glory which was then being manifested was beyond the capacity of every mortal sense and faculty; according to *Exodus*, *No man can see my face and live*.[11] And this is what Jerome says, *Such is human frailty that it cannot bear to gaze upon such great glory*.[12] But men are healed of this frailty by Christ when he brings them into glory.ᶜ And this is signified by his saying to them, *Stand up, and fear not*.[13]

ᵇThe Eternal *Logos*, cf 1a. 34
ᶜcf 1a. 13, 1. Vol. 3, ed H. McCabe. Introduction, T. Gilby.

Appendix 1
THE BAPTISM OF JOHN
(3a. 38)

BOTH THE Synoptic and Johannine traditions agree in placing the beginning of the public ministry of Jesus of Nazareth in the work of John the Baptist (*Mark* 1, 1-8. *Matt.* 3, 1-12. *Luke* 3, 1-20. *John* 1, 19-28). This is also attested in the kerygma of the primitive Church as recorded in the *Acts of the Apostles* (10, 37; 13, 24-5). For this reason Christian tradition would always be interested in the person and work of John. Yet from the available source-material, the Four Gospels and Josephus, very little can be gathered about his historical ministry. John's parents were both of priestly ancestry and well advanced in years when he was born (*Luke* 1, 7). He was named *John* meaning 'God is Gracious'—perhaps a reference to the fact that his parents had been childless for so many years (*Luke* 1, 57-63). The date of his birth is unknown, but it must have occurred during the latter part of the reign of Herod the Great (37-4 BC). His early years were spent in the desert (*Luke* 1, 80). What this means remains uncertain; it has been suggested that his priestly family had him educated by the priestly community at Qumran. How long this lasted cannot be determined, but it was brought to an end in the 15th year of the Emperor Tiberius (27/28 BC) when John began to preach and baptize. Indeed, his baptismal activity became so closely associated with him that he was surnamed the *Baptist* (*Mark* 6, 25; 8, 28. *Matt.* 3, 1; 11, 11 & 12; 14, 2 & 8; 16, 14; 17, 13. *Luke* 7, 20-33), or occasionally the *Baptizer* (*Mark* 1, 4; 6, 14-24). His public activity was concentrated in the Jordan Valley and perhaps in the adjacent wilderness area. This was north of the Dead Sea and within walking distance of the Qumran Community. The Johannine tradition states it was at Bethany on the Jordan, in the vicinity of the modern Jericho (*John* 1, 28). The Baptist began to attract considerable attention, and many Jews came to hear him. Jesus was one of those who came to him at the Jordan, and was baptized by him. Then Jesus began to assemble his own small band of disciples from the followers of John. After an indeterminate amount of time by the Jordan River and its valley, Jesus and his companions separated from the groups that followed John the Baptist. They went into Galilee, and there, after a short while, Jesus inaugurated his own mission.

There are other details concerning John the Baptist which emerge from the Synoptic tradition. He was the leader of his own band of disciples (*Mark* 2, 18. *Matt.* 9, 14. *Luke* 5, 33 and *Mark* 6, 29. *Matt.* 14, 12); he was revered by the common people as a prophetic figure (*Mark* 6, 14-16. *Luke* 9, 7-9); he was mistrusted and resented by the leaders of orthodox Judaism (*Matt.* 11, 7-19. *Luke* 7, 24-35 and *Mark* 11, 27-33. *Matt.* 21, 23-7. *Luke* 20, 1-8). Even more he voiced open opposition to the illegal marriage of Herod the Tetrarch to Herodias. Possibly this forced him to leave the Tetrarch's territory and establish himself at Ænon-by-Salim where he continued to preach and baptize (*John* 3, 22). How long this was to last cannot be determined. He was arrested by Herod, imprisoned and eventually executed (*Mark* 1, 14. *Matt.* 4, 12. *Luke* 3, 19–20 and *Mark* 6, 14–29. *Matt.* 14, 1–12. *Luke* 9, 7–9). The date of his death is unknown (c. 28). However, such material was only of secondary importance to Christian tradition. The Gospels are far more concerned with the significance of John the Baptist and his work. What was this?

Christian tradition was unanimous in seeing our Lord's mission as oriented first of all to Israel, the chosen people of God. It was Israel that had received God's grace and mercy, God's covenant law, and God's promise of salvation and judgment. Hence, in the divine plan of salvation Israel must be prepared for the advent of Jesus of Nazareth, God's unique and great representative in the salvation and judgment of men. This was the task of John the Baptist.

The Synoptic tradition introduces John as a prophetic figure, and it was in this light that he was to be seen. In the history of Israel the prophet had always been revered as one of God's great mediators in his divine direction of his people. But in the course of time the voice of prophecy began to die out, and by the 5th century BC it was almost extinct. Yet, there was always the hope that this would not be for ever (*Ps.* 74, 9). There was a very real expectation that in the future God would send his prophets to Israel once again (1 *Macc.* 4, 46; 9, 27; 14, 41)—in the future the sons and daughters of Israel would begin to prophesy once more (*Joel* 3, 1–2). This general expectation of the return and renewal of prophecy was quite active during the intertestamentary period. This common outlook began to crystallize in the expectation of one special prophet who would embrace the totality of the prophetic office in his person and message. This figure was described in eschatological terms: he would speak for God as his final end-time representative; he would prepare Israel and warn the nations of their impending judgment. There were various identifications made as to who this individual might be; the general tendency was to look to the past and discover in the religious history of Israel a prototype of the future prophet who was to come. In this process the most important figures were Moses and Elijah.

In Judaism, with its ever-growing emphasis on the Law as the supreme revelation of God, the role and person of Moses was greatly enhanced. Indeed, it seems that in some circles it was thought that a Moses-like figure—or perhaps even Moses himself—would return to speak for God as had been the case in the past. Thus, the Samaritans awaited such an individual, and they called him their *ta'eb* (cf. *John* 4, 19 & 25). The Qumran community appears to have described its own Teacher of Righteousness in terms suggesting that the prophet similar to Moses had appeared in their midst (1 *Qs.* 9, 10–11. 4 *Q. Test.* 5–8. cf 1 *Qh.* 2, 6–19). All this was based on the ancient promise given by Moses to the Israelites that God would continue to speak to them in the future through a prophet whom he would raise up from among them (*Deut.* 18, 15–18). It is extremely

APPENDIX I. THE BAPTISM OF JOHN

difficult to determine the extent of this hope, yet it was very much alive then.

Also current was perhaps an even greater expectation that the prophet Elijah would return. This was most likely based on the old story that he was taken up into heaven without ever having died (II *Kgs.* 2, 1-13). In the oldest form of the tradition he would appear before that great *Day* when God would judge the earth (*Mal.* 3, 1; 23 & 24). He was the precursor of God sent to prepare Israel for its final reckoning with God (*Sir.* 48, 10. cf *Isa.* 49, 6). But in a later form of the tradition of Elijah's return, he would be the forerunner of the Messiah, and perhaps even his associate. It remains uncertain how these traditions concerning the return of Moses and Elijah were interrelated during the intertestamentary period (cf *Mark* 9, 2-8. *Matt.* 17, 1-8. *Luke* 9, 28-36), but what does emerge is their anticipated appearance to usher in the eschatological events surrounding the judgment of God.

What has happened is that the Synoptic tradition has interpreted the appearance of John the Baptist in terms suggesting the advent of an eschatological prophet—indeed, of Elijah himself. Without hesitation John is described as a voice in the wilderness sent to prepare the way of the Lord—as a prophetic messenger commissioned to lead the people of God on their way to the possession of the promised land (*Mark* 1, 2-3. *Matt.* 3, 3. *Luke* 3, 4-6). His message was that salvation and judgment were at hand. John is placed in the desert adjacent to the Jordan River. It was in the desert of Sinai that Israel as a people first received the revelation and salvific help of its God, and it would be in the desert that God was to save his people once again (*Hos.* 2, 9-15. *Isa.* 40, 3-4; 41, 17-20; 43, 3 & 19-20; 48, 20-1; 49, 10-11 etc.). But it was also in the desert where Israel sinned against God, and it was to be there that God would appear in judgment against his people (*Num.* 14, 13-25. *Ezek.* 20, 34-8). So it is as a prophet that John the Baptist begins his work in the wilderness. He is clothed with a coat of camel's hair, and he wears a leather belt around his waist. For food he eats the wild vegetables and roots, locusts and honey of the desert region surrounding the Jordan (*Mark* 1, 6. *Matt.* 3, 4). His austerity of life was well known and highly honoured (*Mark* 2, 18-22. *Matt.* 9, 14-17. *Luke* 5, 33-9 and *Matt.* 11, 8 & 18. *Luke* 7, 25 & 33). Thus, John kept himself in close contact with the nomadic and prophetic ideal of Israel.

Indeed, his manner of life suggested the rigour of Elijah, and his fate was quite similar to that of the great prophet of old (I *Kgs.* 19, 1-10. II *Kgs.* 1, 8. cf *Zech.* 13, 8). He too would have to face the wrath of a royal family which he challenged (*Mark* 6, 17-29. *Matt.* 14, 3-12). Thus the Synoptic tradition associates John the Baptist with the person and work of Elijah—though with significant differences. The Lucan tradition speaks of John as a prophet of the Most High (*Luke* 1, 76), and it suggests that he will live in the spirit and power of Elijah (*Luke* 1, 17). Yet, the Baptist is still within the framework of the old covenant, though the greatest of its prophets (*Luke* 7, 24-8; 16, 16). The Markan tradition indicates that an Elijah-like figure has already appeared in Israel, but there is no clear identification of this individual with John the Baptist (*Mark* 9, 11-13). The Matthæan tradition offers the most pronounced association of John the Baptist with Elijah, whose eschatological role he fulfils in proclaiming the advent of the Kingdom of Heaven (*Matt.* 11, 7-15; 17, 10-13). Thus, though there are variations in attitude and stress, the Synoptics describe John the Baptist as an eschatological prophet, Elijah-like in character. His task is to prepare the way of God and the coming of this Anointed One.

John the Baptist also had a prophetic mission to fulfil, and one which was eschatological. He was to preach to those who would listen, warning them of the imminence of God's judgment and the necessity of preparedness for this event. In harmony with his religious tradition, he calls Israel to a recognition of its disobedience and sinfulness. He appeals to Israel in rebellion against God (cf *Isa.* 1, 2; 59, 2. *Jer.* 2, 9; 3, 13. *Ezek.* 36, 25. *Hos.* 14, 2-5) to acknowledge its need for conversion and its return to God (*Isa.* 30, 15; 55, 6-7. *Jer.* 18, 8; 23, 14 & 22; 25, 5; 35, 15; 36, 3 & 7. *Hos.* 2, 9; 3, 5. *Amos* 5, 6. *Joel* 2, 12-14). Even more he asks for a public declaration of sinfulness and the acceptance of a water purification in the River Jordan (*Mark* 1, 5. *Matt.* 3, 6). He proclaims the need of baptism of repentance for the forgiveness of sins (*Mark* 1, 4). Thus an awareness of sin and a determination to renounce sin and serve God was a necessary precondition of the Baptism of John. Indeed, his baptism of water was a sign of repentance, a symbol of God's cleansing action. John's baptism was the public expression of a repentant heart and a new attitude of service and submission to the will of God. Hence this baptism could also lead to the performance of appropriate good works befitting this changed or converted attitude (*Matt.* 3, 11). His social preaching, even granted its traditional Old Testament pattern and associations, still presumes a repentant and converted outlook in view of the impending judgment (*Luke* 3, 10-14).

His baptism of repentance is for the forgiveness of sins. God was prepared to forgive men their sins because he was merciful and understanding (*Isa.* 43, 25; 44, 22. *Jer.* 5, 1 & 7. *Amos* 7, 2. *Mic.* 5, 18. *Ps* 32, 1; 85, 3 etc.). Indeed, his divine forgiveness was also eschatological in character. In the future at the restoration of all things God would cleanse men of all their sins and iniquities and give them a new heart and spirit (*Jer.* 31, 33-4. *Ezek.* 36, 25-9. *Ps.* 51, 10). Repentance and the forgiveness of sins shared in the eschatological renewal of Israel. Hence, John's baptism did not forgive sins. It was the sign of a repentant heart and a renewed submission to the will of God who himself pardoned guilt and cleansed sin. His water baptism was a sign of conversion and an assurance of forgiveness. But it was also a very real warning and threat given to those who refused to repent. The Pharisees and Sadducees—indeed all those who depended on their own deeds as well as the great works of Abraham—were in imminent danger of condemnation. The judgment is at hand (*Matt.* 3, 7-10. *Luke* 3, 7-9), and baptism is imperative.

Yet, even granted the urgency of John's prophetic mission, his baptism

APPENDIX I. THE BAPTISM OF JOHN

was not a permanent rite. Rather, the Synoptic tradition interprets his work as a preparation for another baptism. This is the baptism of the *Mightier One*, one who is mightier than John, and even mightier than Satan himself (cf *Mark* 3, 27. *Matt.* 12, 29). He will be the great deliverer who is to render judgment and bring about salvation. Before him John the Baptist is but a lowly slave, unworthy to carry his sandals (*Mark* 1, 7-8. *Matt.* 3, 11-12. *Luke* 3, 15-18). He will appear as the bringer of an even greater purification—a baptism of the Holy Spirit and Fire.

This Spirit-baptism of the Mightier One is contrasted to the water-baptism of John. As with the forgiveness of sins, so too with the communication of the Spirit the eschatological context is preserved and heightened. In the last days God would send and pour out his Spirit to recreate, re-establish, reform, resanctify (*Isa.* 44, 3. *Ezek.* 36, 25-7. *Zech.* 12, 10; 13, 1. *Joel* 3, 1-2). Fire was also a sign of the last days and a symbol of judgment (*Isa.* 31, 9. *Amos* 7, 4. *Mal.* 3, 2. cf I *Cor*, 3, 13. II *Thess.* 1, 7-8). Fire would cleanse, purify and recast; fire would test and prove the mettle of all creatures. The spirit of judgment and the spirit of burning would signal the eschatological drama at the close of the present age (cf *Isa.* 4, 4-6). Could John the Baptist have perceived this contrast and spoken so clearly of the Spirit-baptism of the Mightier One? The Qumran literature suggests that this is so. For, the community viewed the gift of the Spirit and its presence as eschatological phenomena. And even more, the gift of the Spirit was closely linked to the water-cleansing of those candidates entering the Brotherhood. The Spirit purified him and prepared him for his new life in the sect (1 *Qs.* 3, 3-9; 4, 20-1. cf 1 *Qh.* 3, 28-32). It was perhaps possible that God's own Anointed would give to the members of the community a knowledge of the Spirit (*Cd.* 2, 12-13). Accordingly, granted John's earlier link to the Qumran foundation, he could have seen the Mightier One as the bringer of a new baptism of the spirit and fire. With his presence the eschatological judgment had begun.

The Gospel of St John reveals several points of contact with the material found in the Synoptic tradition, but it treats it in its own manner. Very little of the historical character of John the Baptist emerges in the Johannine tradition. Presumably more information was available and known in the Christian circles with which St John had dealings, but it is not reported. It is in the Prologue to the Fourth Gospel that the Johannine tradition manifests its own interpretation of the person and work of the Baptist. He was not the light, but he was to bear witness to the light so that all might believe through him (*John* 1, 6-8). Two important elements of the Johannine portrayal of the Baptist appear here.

John the Baptist is not the light and he is not the Messiah (*John* 1, 20 & 25; 3, 28). Why it is necessary to make this point is uncertain. Apparently some of John's contemporaries thought that he was the long-awaited Messiah, and so continued to follow him and revere his name (*Luke* 3, 15). However, Christian tradition goes to some length to deny that the Baptist had made any pretensions to be the Anointed One (cf *Luke* 3, 15-16.

Acts 13, 25 and *John* 1, 20 & 25). Thus, when he is interrogated by an official delegation from Jerusalem he reflects this negative attitude. Even more, the Johannine tradition presents the Baptist as disclaiming any relationship to the eschatological prophet Elijah (*John* 1, 19–28). This is quite unlike the Synoptic gospels, but it must be understood in its own context. The Johannine tradition wishes to preserve the unique and total role of Christ as God's mediator. Everything else is but a preparation for his life-giving work. But the Synoptic tradition reflects an attitude which at times places Elijah on the threshold of the inbreaking of the Kingdom of God (*Matt.* 11, 11–14. cf *Luke* 7, 25–8); it sees John the Baptist as an Elijah-like figure labouring for the conversion of the people of Israel, striving for their preparation to receive the revelation of God (*Luke* 1, 16–17); it sees John intimately involved in Elijah's task of the eschatological restoration of all things (*Mark* 9, 12–13). The Johannine tradition seeks to reserve all this to Christ alone. Hence it dissociates John the Baptist from any such eschatological role.

It is only as a *Witness* that John the Baptist appears in the Fourth Gospel. He is a voice crying in the wilderness (*John* 1, 23). But this is not the voice of the eschatological prophet and preacher of repentance, so familiar in the Synoptic gospels. Rather, the Baptist is a witness to the light (*John* 1, 7–8), a witness to the truth (*John* 5, 33). He is a precursor and herald of Christ— whose testimony is far greater than John's (*John* 1, 34; 5, 36). His task is to declare the presence of the Anointed One of God. This he does in proclaiming Jesus to be the Lamb of God (*John* 1, 29 & 36), and the Son of God (*John* 1, 34). The water-baptism of John is itself a witness to the Spirit-baptism of Jesus (*John* 1, 31–3). John's witness to Jesus is his supreme role according to the Fourth Gospel. He reveals Jesus to his own disciples, and then they begin to follow him and declare him to be the Messiah (*John* 1, 35–41). After this his mission is finished. He is the friend of the bridegroom who leaves once the marriage is concluded (*John* 3, 25–30); he is the lighted lamp which shines brightly until an even stronger light is present (*John* 5, 35). With the appearance of Jesus his witness is brought to its fulfilment.

The Johannine tradition places full stress on the Baptist's mission as a witness to Christ. He must prepare Israel for the revelation of Jesus (*John* 1, 31). John does not emerge as an eschatological figure or a baptist preacher of repentance. He heralds Jesus the light of the world and the bringer of the Spirit. The work of John the Baptist and Jesus with his disciples appears to have overlapped for a short while (*John* 3, 22–3; 4, 1–2). However, nothing is reported of this period. It only saw the end of John's mission. He still appears in the framework of the old Israel, and in spite of his recognition and witness of Jesus he seems not to have grasped the full mystery of Jesus' person and mission. Even from the Baptist it remained in part hidden—to be revealed fully at Jesus' death and exaltation (*John* 1, 31. cf *Matt.* 11, 2. *Luke* 7, 19). For this John was the great preparation.

Appendix 2
THE BAPTISM OF CHRIST
(3a 39)

JOHN THE BAPTIST appeared proclaiming the urgency of repentance and the necessity of baptism in view of the forthcoming eschatological judgment. He attracted the attention of the religious leaders of Judaism and the admiration of the crowds, for many went out to the Jordan River so as to hear him and be baptized by him. He was esteemed as a prophet and the purification he demanded was a very real sign of conversion. In this John the Baptist was within the religious traditions of Israel. Throughout the ancient Near East water—and especially flowing water—was thought to have a mysterious divine power to give and sustain life. God revealed his awesome greatness and his control of life and death through water. Hence, in the various religious experiences of the area, water rites always enjoyed a prominent role. Any approach to or withdrawal from God and the sphere of the sacred necessitated a ritual washing. In this way man was cleansed and renewed in his contact with God, particularly if he saw himself as separated from God and guilty of sin. Thus in the religious practice of Israel there were many ceremonial ablutions prescribed so as to preserve and restore a harmonious relationship with God, the master of life and death, the lord of his chosen people (e.g. *Exod.* 19, 10–14; 29, 4; 30, 17–21. *Lev.* 11, 24–8, 32 & 39–40; 15, 1–33 etc.). The people of God should always reflect and reverence the holiness of God.

Their awareness of the holiness of God, the origin and end of life, coupled with the ever-growing understanding of human sinfulness, could prompt the prophets to look to the future and see there a decisive cleansing of the people of God with water (*Ezek.* 36, 24–7. *Zech.* 13, 1). Before the final restoration at the end, there must be a final purification of Israel—and indeed, of all men. Such speculation was proto-eschatological in character and led to new religious insights in special circles of Jewish thought. One such circle was that which was to constitute the Essene Community at Qumran. The exact reasons which motivated the foundation of this settlement by the Dead Sea during the 2nd century BC are uncertain. Yet the eschatological orientation of the sect is clear. The end was already at hand; it was the time of the last generation, the time of struggle and conflict (1 *Qs.* 3, 23; 4, 18–19. 1 *QpHab.* 2, 7; 5, 3–5; 7, 1, 2 & 12; 8, 1; 9, 6. 1 *Qm.* passim). Light was already appearing in the darkness; it was the time of the new creation (1 *Qs.* 4, 25. 1 *Qh.* 11, 10–13; 13, 11–12); it was the time of the new covenant (*Cd.* 8, 15 & 37; 9, 28). The Qumran sectaries felt that they were sharing in the new creation and covenant of the Age to come. Hence, they dedicated themselves to a more fervent observance of the law of the new covenant as they understood and interpreted it. Their whole life was focused on study of

God's revealed word and on purity of character. At Qumran the Brotherhood already lived in the eschatological age to come.

For this reason entrance and admission into the community was a most important step. After a given period of probation the candidate was received into membership and expected to practise the full life of the community. In the context of the annual renewal of the covenant, the candidate was subjected to a special initiation rite, a cleansing by immersion in a pool of water. Having successfully passed through his period of probation, the aspirant to the Qumran Brotherhood was exhorted to renounce evil and, having confessed his sins, to turn to the faithful service of God and a life of dedication to moral and ritual purity. Then, if his dispositions proved acceptable he was allowed to descend into the waters of purification and cleanse himself (1 *Qs.* 1, 16–3; 12. cf Josephus *Bel. Jud.* II 8, 7 and 1 *Qs.* 6, 14–23). This ceremony marked the candidate's admission into the eschatological life of the community, and so it was eschatological in character. However, there is no indication that this rite effected or produced any state of purity or sanctity. Rather, it was an appropriate sign of the candidate's own conversion and dedication to God in this new way of life, and it was a sign that he had been purified and sanctified by the spirit of holiness, given him as a mark of divine favour (1 *Qs.* 3, 7–8; 4, 20–3). As in traditional Jewish thought, the ceremonial rite signified what had taken place in the mind and heart of the candidate—and what had found divine approval. This initiation rite expressed a renunciation of evil, and a renewed consecration to the life and law of the chosen people of God.

This religious notion of a renunciation of evil and a consecration to the life and law of the chosen people of God appears to be at the basis of giving a special ceremonial water-cleansing to those gentiles who were converted to Judaism and sought to become Jews. It came to be known as Jewish proselyte baptism. As a ceremonial rite it is attested from the 2nd century of the Christian era, and certain references to rabbinic disputes in this matter as well as other apparent allusions to this practice suggest that it was known and practised during the 1st century AD (cf *Epictetus Diss.* II, 9, 9–21. *Syb. Orac.* IV, 165). Prior to the year AD 50 there is no evidence that the Jews did so purify their gentile converts. Indeed, from what is attested of this rite, it seems to fit into the traditional pattern of orthodox Judaistic and rabbinic thought. It was a liturgical rite, expressive of the neophyte gentile's aversion of sin and adhesion to the chosen people and its law. The newly-baptized proselyte was compared to a child who had just been born and who was starting a new life. However, this was not eschatological; it was the ritual expression of a repentant attitude of mind and heart and a fresh way of life in Judaism.

Therefore, the baptismal message and practice of John do not appear as isolated phenomena; they express a complex attitude within intertestamentary Judaism focusing on an awareness of impending eschatological judgment and a renewed dedication to observance of the covenant-law of the people of God as it was variously understood and interpreted. Given this

APPENDIX 2. THE BAPTISM OF CHRIST

situation there appears ample reason why Jesus should have been associated with John and received his baptism. The Synoptic tradition gives a very forthright presentation of this event. In its expression in the Markan tradition—the most primitive form—Jesus is described as having come from Nazareth of Galilee and been baptized in the Jordan by John (*Mark* 1, 9). This account appears to characterize Jesus as but one more of the many Jews who went out to see and hear John and be baptized by him. It places Jesus among the ranks of John's following, and even suggests that he also submitted to a baptism of repentance for the forgiveness of sins along with the others who confessed their sins (*Mark* 1, 4–5. cf *Matt.* 3, 6). What it does not do is reveal Jesus' motives for being baptized by John.

This did not escape Christian thought, and the other evangelists reveal a development here. They seek to eliminate any suggestion that Jesus is subordinated to John and his work, and they try to clarify Jesus' motives for receiving the baptism of John. Thus in the Lucan tradition John the Baptist fulfils his appointed task preaching to Israel the imminent judgment of God and the need of baptism (*Luke* 3, 1–17). Then, having reproved the Tetrarch Herod for his illicit marriage, John is arrested, imprisoned and effectively removed from the scene of events (*Luke* 3, 18–20). Only then does Jesus appear at the Jordan; only then does he accept baptism (*Luke* 3, 21). Thus Jesus' baptism is separated—though in direct line with—the activity of John. The use of the passive form of the verb reflects a very old manner of pointing to the intervention of God and the expression of his will.

In the Matthæan tradition all doubt concerning Jesus' baptism is removed. Jesus leaves Galilee and travels to the Jordan with the full intention of being baptized by John. This was no chance happening; rather it was fully determined by the will of God (*Matt.* 3, 13). John the Baptist is portrayed as recognizing the uniqueness of this event. He protests his unworthiness and declares his own need to be baptized by Jesus. In this manner the person and mission of John are subordinated to Jesus of Nazareth. John's water-baptism is on a far lower level than the Spirit-baptism of the *Mightier One* (*Matt.* 3, 13–14). Why then does Jesus submit to the baptism of John? The reason given is so that he might fulfil all righteousness (*Matt.* 3, 15). Such an expression is rich in meaning and not without some obscurity. Yet the language of the text, when added to the Matthæan vocabulary, indicates that Jesus must obey God and that it is divine decree in this matter. Jesus must reveal by his own action that it was God's will that men be baptized by John in preparation for an even greater baptism. If Jesus is to be the key figure in this salvific process, then he must be identified with all those who needed to be cleansed and purified of their sins. John the Baptist was the greatest of the prophets; he was the Elijah who was to come (*Matt.* 11, 11–14; 17, 11–13). John's baptism was from heaven and decreed by God (*Matt.* 21, 23–7). Thus Jesus fulfils and manifests God's will in submitting to this rite. He reveals its ultimate meaning in God's plan of salvation (cf *Matt.* 5, 17–18).

The subordination of Jesus to God and the subordination of John to

Jesus becomes clear in the Fourth Gospel. John is but a witness to the person of Jesus and his baptism. His function is but to declare that he is the Lamb of God and the Son of God whose mission is to take away the sin of the world. The entire force of John's baptism is to prepare for Jesus' revelation to Israel. This is what takes place at his baptism according to the presentation of the Fourth Gospel. Jesus' baptism is the first public revelation to the world of his mysterious personality and mission. Thus in the Gospel tradition as it reflects the faith of the primitive Christian community, the baptism of Jesus was not a chance occurrence. Rather it was an event of decisive importance in salvation history. Indeed, it was seen as Jesus' public consecration and dedication to the salvific mission he was about to undertake in fulfilment of the will of God.

What this entailed is given in the theophany as recorded in the Synoptic tradition (*Mark* 1, 10–11. *Matt.* 3, 16–17. *Luke* 3, 21–2). When Jesus is baptized—unlike the many similar baptisms in the Jordan River—the heavens are opened, the Spirit descends upon Jesus in a dove-like appearance, and a heavenly voice speaks and reveals the significance of the event. Very clearly the Synoptic tradition sees here a divine communication to and about Jesus.

This is suggested immediately in the splitting or opening of the heavens, which was a favourite apocalyptic setting for a divine communication (cf *Apoc. Bar.* 22, 1. *Test. Levi* 2, 6; 5, 1. *Apoc.* 11, 19; 19, 11 and *Acts* 7, 56). But the theme is older than this, and has its roots in the prophetic experience of the initial vocation to become God's spokesman (*Isa.* 6, 1–13. *Ezek.* 1, 1). Even before this, God had revealed himself to Israel at Sinai and his glory came down from heaven and settled in the midst of the people (*Exod.* 19, 11; 24, 16). The opening of the heavens meant that God and his people were in direct contact. Thus it could be a prophetic prayer that as God had torn open the heavens in the past when he revealed himself during the Exodus and guided his people to their land of deliverance, so he would do the same again in the future (*Isa.* 63, 11–19; 64, 1–7). Now at this decisive event the heavens are opened again. But this time it is above Jesus, for he is to be the unique and supreme point of contact between God and man (cf *Mark* 15, 38. *John* 1, 51).

Closely connected to the opening of the heavens is the descent of the Spirit. The use of the term is highly complex both in Jewish as well as in Christian thought. Spirit was an analogical expression which described a relationship between subject and object of force and event. Spirit was a power to be and to do. Considered theologically, Spirit could designate God in action, whether in creation or in salvation. Thus when God created the heavens and the earth it was through the activity of the Spirit (*Gen.* 1, 2). So too when God guided the course of his chosen people, he gave his Spirit to the whole group, to Israel (*Isa.* 59, 21) or far more commonly to its chosen leaders, to the seventy elders of Israel (*Num.* 11, 25), to Moses the leader of Israel (*Num.* 11, 17) to David, the King of Israel (II *Sam.* 23, 2). All had various tasks to perform and so all had need of the Spirit in diverse

APPENDIX 2. THE BAPTISM OF CHRIST

ways. Even more, both the Messiah and Servant of God would be given the Spirit so that they too would be empowered to fulfil their particular missions in the salvation of the chosen people (*Isa.* 11, 1-2; 42, 1; 61, 1. cf *Æth. Hen.* 49, 3; 62, 2. *Test. Levi* 18; *Test. Judah* 24; *Ps.* 17, 42). Indeed in the future it would be the Spirit that would constitute a new covenant in the hearts of men as against the old covenant which was written in stone (*Jer.* 31, 31-4; 32, 38-40. *Ezek.* 36, 24-8). So the prophets could hope and pray for a return of the Spirit which would bring them to eternal life and salvation (*Isa.* 63, 10-14. *Joel* 3, 1-2). Thus at the baptism of Jesus, when the Spirit is described as descending upon him, it was not to give him life—because the Spirit was active in his very conception in the womb of the Virgin (*Matt.* 1, 18-21. *Luke* 1, 30-5). Rather, the Spirit was given to Jesus to assist him in the fulfilment of the mission which he was about to undertake. Jesus was anointed with the Spirit to begin his God-given salvific work (cf *Acts* 10, 38).

It was the power of God that was to constitute and govern Jesus' mission which began publicly at his baptism. Hence the Synoptic tradition can speak of the Spirit as descending like a dove (*Mark* 1, 10. *Matt.* 3, 16. *Luke* 3, 22). Indeed, to underscore the reality of this gift of the Spirit, the Lucan tradition specifies that this dove came upon Jesus in bodily form while he was praying. Truly the power of God was with Jesus in a special way at his baptism. The dove was a symbol of the new creation and the new covenant given to Noah by way of promise after the waters began to recede (*Gen.* 8, 8-12; 9, 8-17). Hence Jesus' baptism with water and the Spirit prepares and consecrates him to his mission in the inauguration of a new creation and a new covenant. The dove left Noah never to return. But now it finally did return and remained with Jesus (*Gen.* 8, 12. *John* 1, 32).

To strengthen the significance of this scene the Synoptic tradition indicates that a heavenly voice spoke to Jesus (*Mark* 1, 11. *Matt.* 3, 17. *Luke* 3, 22. cf *John* 1, 34). Here there is described a divine communication of God's mind and will. In the past God was said to have conversed with Moses (*Exod.* 20, 22), with the prophets (*Isa.* 6, 1-13. *Ezek.* 1, 1 & 28), with the kings of the earth (*Dan.* 4, 31). But now there is a simple declaration of what this event was to mean in the life of Jesus. The heavenly voice reveals something of the person and the mission of Jesus. Here there is found the high point of the entire episode.

The heavenly voice declares Jesus to be God's Son, the beloved one with whom he is well pleased. Here there is a combination of two Old Testament passages which reveal the significance of the baptism of Jesus (*Ps.* 2, 7 and *Isa.* 42, 1). The textual tradition is complex, and there are certain variant readings which attempt to assimilate the Greek to one or the other of the passages. However, it appears that this mixed citation was intentional. The reference to *Ps.* 2, 7 recalls the royal enthronement-ritual wherein the new monarch is proclaimed the vice-regent and adopted son of God who is to reign in his place. Israel always remembered the promise given to David that his line would endure for ever (II *Sam.* 7, 14 & 16. *Ps.* 89, 26-7)—and there was always the hope in the post-exilic Jewish community that God would raise up a new son of David to become God's adopted son. He would rule over a restored kingdom as God's great representative (cf *Isa.* 9, 6; 11, 1-9; 16, 5; 55, 3-4. *Jer.* 17, 25; 23, 5-6; 30, 10; 33, 17. *Ezek.* 17, 22-4; 34, 23-4; 37, 24-8 etc.). Jewish apocalyptic literature only tended to glorify this Davidic figure, one who would liberate Israel from its bondage (*Æth. Hen.* 46, 51-3. *Syb. Or.* 3, 653. IV *Ezra* 11, 46; 12, 34; 13, 5, 37 & 38), and who would subject its oppressors to the power of God and his peace (*Ps.* 17, 21-32. *Test. Judah* 24. *Jub.* 17, 32. *Syb. Or.* 5, 429). Thus Judaism always saw in its Davidic Messiah a Victor-King, one who would conquer the enemies of Israel and overcome the forces of evil. He was God's anointed representative, yet united with his people as their leader.

In this mixed citation from the Old Testament there is also a reference to *Isaiah* 42, 1. The figure of the servant has always been obscure. Other renowned characters have appeared in the footsteps of Moses, the great servant of God. But this prophetic figure is distinctive because of his mission. Whether he is described in national or individual terms he is clearly representative of both God and his chosen people (*Isa.* 42, 1-4; 49, 1-6; 50, 4-11; 52, 13-53, 12). His mission is to establish justice and obedience to the will of God (*Isa.* 42, 1-4; 53, 11), but this he is to do by atoning for the sins of others through his vicarious suffering. This will lead to his death, but ultimately God will exalt him for his steadfast devotion (*Isa.* 53, 42).

The baptism of Christ is given its significance in the Synoptic tradition by this combination of two important passages from the sacred writings of Israel. At his baptism Jesus is dedicated and consecrated to fulfil the mission of both the Messiah and the Servant of God. He must fulfil the will of God by leading the chosen people to a victory over Satan and the forces of evil, and he must restore for ever the Kingdom of God. However, this triumph is to be realized through his obedient service to God—his representative suffering for the sins and crimes of others. In the mission of Jesus of Nazareth, as inaugurated at his baptism, exaltation and victory are to be found through suffering and death. This is the role of the Messiah-Servant.

These same basic ideas emerge in the Johannine tradition and its description of the baptism of Jesus. It is the testimony of John which acts as a substitute for the heavenly voice. Yet, his witness is clearly in line with the Christology of the Synoptic tradition. Jesus is proclaimed the *Lamb of God* (*John* 1, 29 & 36). The introduction of this figure suggests at once the warrior lamb which would lead God's flock (*Apoc.* 7, 17), and judge in wrath (*Apoc.* 6, 16; 14, 1-5) and conquer and destroy the powers of evil who struggle against God (*Apoc.* 17, 14. cf *Test. Joseph* 19, 8). But besides this image of conquest, judgment and victory the lamb also suggests the suffering servant of God whose representative ordeal is compared to that of a sheep being led to the slaughter and a lamb to the shearers (*Isa.* 53, 7; cf *Matt.* 8, 17; 12, 18-21. *Acts* 8, 32. *Heb.* 9, 28). This lamb would make himself an offering for sin, and so take away the sin of the world (*Isa.* 53, 10. *John* 1, 29 & 36).

APPENDIX 2. THE BAPTISM OF CHRIST

Accordingly, Christian thought has uniformly seen Jesus' baptism as the beginning of his representative mission of Messiah–Servant. This does not eliminate other thematic associations, such as Jesus the new Adam, the new Moses, the new High Priest, but these two are paramount. The richness of the setting with the splitting of the heavens, the descent of the Spirit, the heavenly voice with its divine revelation—all serve to confirm God's involvement in this event, and to clothe it with a full soteriological and eschatological significance. Jesus' baptism was willed by God as that act of dedication to the salvation and judgment of men. His baptism was a representative action wherein Jesus associates himself with the sinful people of God—and all peoples—as Messiah and Servant. In accordance with the will of God, Jesus, God's dutiful Son will fulfil all righteousness of identifying himself with sinners, by cleansing himself in the waters of the Jordan as a sign of his future act of purifying and sanctifying them by his death and exaltation.

This certainly reflects the Christology of the primitive Church, but the question remains: does it reflect Jesus' own personal outlook? Did he approach John and receive baptism as a sign of his mission, which was to take upon himself the salvific roles of Messiah and Servant, to atone for all sinners by his suffering and death, and to conquer the power of sin by his new life and exaltation? Did he see that his baptism would be a sign of his death/life mission which would serve to constitute the beginning of a new creation and the foundation of a new covenant?

It is impossible to give any definitive answer to such questions because there is no way to measure Jesus' own thoughts in this respect. Certainly diverse positions have been maintained in this regard. It has been suggested that all this is the product of the primitive community living in the certitude of its post-resurrection faith and that Jesus received baptism as but another penitent, at the most only remotely aware of what his future mission would entail. On the other hand, it has also been suggested that Jesus could very really have seen in his own baptism a sign of his forthcoming work which would terminate in his death and exaltation. This is possible only if Jesus could see in the water into which he descended and from which he emerged a symbol of death and life. Thus his baptism would at once fulfil the baptism of John and promise an even greater baptism in the future, that of death, resurrection and gift of the Spirit.

Did water have such a death–life symbolism? There are some indications that it did in the Old Testament. Thus, in the Deluge, water was an instrument of judgment and death, and it was likewise an instrument of salvation and life. Sinners perished in the waters which covered the land, but Noah and his family were saved (*Gen.* 6–9). So too at the Exodus, when Israel crossed the Red Sea, the waters parted to save the people of God, but they closed to destroy the pursuing Egyptians (*Exod.* 14). These and other examples suggest that water could be viewed as a symbol of death or a symbol of life. Indeed, in subsequent Christian thought both the Deluge and the Exodus were to become important symbols of judgment and salvation, death and life. And both were expressly connected to the baptismal experience of the Christian (1 *Cor.* 10, 1–2. 1 *Pet.* 3, 20–1). Baptism was seen to suggest death and life, judgment and salvation.

The same associations were also possible in the Qumran Community. Water could purify and destroy (1 *Qh.* 3, 28–32. *Cd.* 2, 19–3, 1, 11 & 12. cf *Isa.* 4, 4; 30, 27–8). Water could also purify and recreate, as was the case in the baptism-like cleansing of those entering into full association with the eschatological community (1 *Qs.* 1, 16–3, 12; 5, 7–15; 6, 14–23; and 1 *Qh.* 11, 10–13; 13, 11–12). It cannot be demonstrated that the Qumran Brotherhood thought that its initial purification and sign of the Spirit was symbolic of death and life—nor can it be shown that such was the baptismal view of John the Baptist. Nevertheless all the elements were there and Jesus could have had his own special insight, and so symbolically linked his water-baptism in the Jordan to his mission which was to be brought to a close with his death and exaltation. Even more, Jesus' avoidance of baptizing any of his disciples (cf *John* 3, 22; 4, 1–2), and his restricted use of a baptismal terminology to suffering and death (*Mark* 10, 38. *Luke* 12, 49–50. cf *Mark* 14, 36) suggest that he might have had this particular insight linking baptism with his death and life—granted his special understanding of his mission as Messiah–Servant.

More cannot be said. Primitive tradition immediately connected the water-baptism of the Christian to the death and resurrection of Christ (*Rom.* 6, 1–11. *Col.* 2, 11–12). It is quite possible that this is based on the insight of Jesus himself. Certainly Christian tradition suggests that this was possible, and it does interpret this event as the consecration of Jesus to his mission and the gift of the Spirit as a means of fulfilling its demands. Jesus was baptized for the salvation and judgment of men as their representative. At this moment his work would begin.

Appendix 3
THE MISSION OF CHRIST
(3a. 40)

THE MISSION of Jesus of Nazareth was deeply rooted in the religious history of Israel. The disciples of Jesus, those who had followed him during the course of his public ministry and those who had believed in him as the supreme revelation of God, were all Jews and heirs to the ancient religious heritage of Israel. They believed that God revealed himself to Israel, choosing it as his special people; they believed that this revelation took place in the context of the events of their national history; they believed that God revealed himself for a purpose, their salvation and ultimately that of all peoples; they believed that God gave to Israel its covenant-law as an expression of his divine will for their salvation; they believed that God gave to his chosen people special mediators who would explain and interpret the meaning of this covenant relationship. Israel was a covenant people living in the expectation of salvation and judgment.

It was true that Israel had already experienced specific acts of salvation and judgment in its own history. Here God was seen to be revealing himself. However, this was not to continue indefinitely. In the future God would manifest himself in a final and complete way—a way which would have both national and cosmic proportions. Israel still awaited its full salvation and judgment. Before this would happen God's final representative would appear and would begin to prepare Israel for its ultimate encounter with God. The character of this mediating representative figure was described in a variety of ways, but his mission was to prepare for the final revelation of God himself. All that God had said and all that he had done for his chosen people in the past was seen to be a foreshadowing of what the future would be.

This was the atmosphere in which the life and mission of Jesus must be situated. He had a message to proclaim and he associated his own person with its realization. Jesus declared that the future was already present, revealing the imminence of the Kingdom of God and showing himself as God's representative in its revelation. He gathered a number of disciples about himself who were committed to him personally. Yet even they needed time to grasp something of the unique significance of his person and mission. It demanded the finality of his death and resurrection to enable them to see that both his person and mission were decisive for all salvation history. Indeed the entire history of God's revelation to Israel—and to all peoples—had been leading up to Jesus of Nazareth. He gave to those who believed in him a key to understand the total course of salvation history. This was a conviction of faith, but once that faith was had, it placed Jesus in the centre-point of time. Past, present and future had their meaning because of Jesus.

For this reason, not only the present and future were important to the

Christian community, but also the past. Jesus' disciples, living in the faith of the resurrection, believed that he was now gloriously alive, nevermore to die. He was at once with God in the new world which he had brought about and with his community in the old world which he would bring to an end at his second coming. Hence his disciples had a very real interest in the present and the future.

However, they also had a genuine involvement in the past. Through the eyes of faith they wished to see how God's revelation to Israel had been fulfilled in Jesus. The entire Old Testament had to be related to him. Even more, they wished to know what Jesus had done and what he had said while he laboured in Galilee and Judaea so that his revelation of God and the good news of salvation and judgment would still be with them. Although there was always a very real religious sense in their appreciation of the past, the disciples of Jesus, those who constituted his Church, never lost sight of the historical context in which the mission of Christ took place. Jesus was the dutiful Son of God who revealed his works and words. But he was also a man, living among men and dying at their hands. The Synoptic tradition especially shows how the Church preserved both an interest and reverence for Jesus' historical mission to the people of God. How was this expressed?

The two centuries preceding the life and mission of Jesus of Nazareth had witnessed a considerable growth in the Jewish expectation of the inbreaking of the Kingdom of God and the re-establishment of his sovereign rule over his chosen people. As God had governed his people through its anointed kings in the past, so he would rule over his people through his great Anointed One in the future. The apocalyptic literature, and especially the Book of Daniel, attest the intensity of this hope in the 2nd century BC. A basic reason for this was the change in the political situation of Israel. The independent kingdoms of Israel and Judah had been gradually absorbed into the various world empires of the period, the Assyrian, Babylonian, Persian and Greek. All the Jews had left was their religious faith and practices which became ever more important to them as time went on. These convictions were generally respected by the occupying powers, with only a few exceptions. The greatest challenge to that faith came in the 2nd century BC when the very practice of Judaism had been forbidden by the pagan Seleucids, the Greek-oriented masters of Syria and Palestine. Even the Temple at Jerusalem had been converted into a Greek shrine (165–163 BC). A long and costly struggle followed, and, if the Jews were ultimately successful in gaining some measure of political and religious autonomy under their Maccabean and Hasmonean princes, this was only due to the weakness of the Seleucid Empire, and not to an emerging tolerance on their part.

The Romans eventually determined to put a stop to the various political intrigues which were going on in Palestine, and so Jerusalem was taken and the country incorporated into the Roman provincial system (63 BC). The reign of Herod the Great did little to improve this situation (37–4 BC). He was always a client-king of the Roman state, and even worse, a half-Jew of Idumaean ancestry. After his death he was succeeded by some of his sons,

APPENDIX 3. THE MISSION OF CHRIST

and a series of Roman-appointed administrators who controlled various parts of Palestine. Their rule was always unpopular, and at the most tolerated for fear of worse. The heavy repressive measures of these officials coupled with their service to a pagan ruler made Jewish life in first-century Palestine extremely difficult. The Jews ardently sought the intervention of God and the appearance of his Messiah to bring this situation to an end and inaugurate his Kingdom.

This was the historical context in which Jesus was born. The Synoptic tradition has situated this event at Bethlehem while Herod the Great was still living (*Matt.* 2, 1-2. cf *Luke* 1, 5). The Lucan tradition also associates the birth of Jesus with a census administered by (P. Sulpicius) Quirinius, probably for taxation purposes (*Luke* 2, 1-5). The dating of this census is highly problematical, the only such event being placed by Josephus in the year AD 6! (*Ant. Jud.* XVII, 13, 5. XVIII, 1, 1; 2, 1. XX, 5, 2. *Bel. Jud.* II. 8, 1). However, references to the proximate death of Herod (4 BC) and the inception of the rule of Archelaus (4 BC–AD 6) suggest that Jesus was born about the year 6/5 BC (*Matt.* 2, 19-22).

Jesus grew up at Nazareth in Galilee, but nothing is known of this period of his life. His father was called Joseph the carpenter, and apparently Jesus followed him in this craft (*Mark* 6, 3. *Matt.* 13, 55). His mother was named Mary, and it was she who provided him with personal support. This was not forthcoming from his more distant relatives who lived in the area (*Mark* 3, 31-5; 6, 3. *Matt.* 12, 46-50; 13, 55-6. *Luke* 8, 19-21. *John* 2, 12; 7, 3-5; 19, 25). There is no indication that Jesus ever studied in any of the local rabbinical schools or that he left personal writings to his disciples. Yet he was able to read and write, and he certainly knew the sacred writings and traditions of his people (*Luke* 4, 16-20. *John* 7, 15. cf *John* 8, 6). These many years at Nazareth were subsequently seen to be a period of preparation for his mission.

It was at the Jordan that Jesus was baptized by John and from there he began his public mission. The sole source for any chronology from this period is the Lucan tradition which seeks to connect the important events of salvation history to contemporary world history (*Luke* 3, 1-2). Yet even here there are obscurities. The references are either unable to be dated (Lysanias), or are too vague—Pontius Pilate (26-36), Herod Antipas (4 BC–AD 39), Philip (4 BC–AD 34), Caiaphas (18-36). The most precise chronological reference is to the reign of the Emperor Tiberius (14-37). John began his work in the fifteenth year of his rule. It is difficult to be certain what calendar was used by St Luke (Roman, Syrian) and how the years were computed (regnal, civil). But a close approximation would be from October of the year 27 to September of the year 28 as being the 15th year of Tiberius. Accordingly, John the Baptist would have inaugurated his mission in late 27 or early 28. Since Jesus appears on the scene almost immediately this would have made him about 34 years old when he went to join John at the Jordan. This agrees well with another statement of the Lucan tradition which describes Jesus as about 30 years old when he began his mission (*Luke* 3, 23). Considering the general lack of interest in such precise data in the Gospel traditions, this is remarkably close reckoning.

According to the Synoptic tradition Jesus returned to Galilee where he began to proclaim the inbreaking of the Kingdom of God and the need for conversion and faith in the Gospel (*Mark* 1, 15. *Matt.* 4, 17). From this moment Jesus concentrates on the Jews of Galilee, and operates from the small town of Capharnaum on the Sea of Galilee. The Gospels do not relate any real sequence of events, but rather a selection of scenes. The Synoptic tradition presents the mission of Jesus in separate episodes loosely connected together according to various theological, Christological, ecclesiological, soteriological, eschatological and topological themes. The Johannine tradition is even more pronounced in this direction. Various events or incidents are reported, but really to provide a vehicle for further theological and Christological elaboration by way of developed discourses. In this manner the works and words of Jesus gently yield to the reflections of the Church. The meaning of the mission and person of Jesus is discovered by a more penetrating meditation on his works and words. Accordingly it is impossible to present any integrated exposition of the life and mission of Christ. Modern standards of historiography did not apply in the ancient world. What does emerge from the Gospel traditions is a pattern of events leading through Galilee to Judaea and the final days at Jerusalem, and a portrait of Jesus' activity and personality as transmitted through the profound faith of the Christian community.

The early weeks of the mission of Jesus are reflected in the typological setting of the day at Capharnaum (*Mark* 1, 21–34). He teaches in the synagogue, the local centre of learning, and provokes astonishment and admiration, for he speaks on his own authority, and not on that of tradition as did the scribes. He exercises his personal power and authority in breaking Satan's power over the minds and bodies of the sick. Soon not only all Capharnaum, but the whole region is speaking of Jesus of Nazareth. His fame spreads throughout Galilee (*Matt.* 4, 23–5. cf *Mark* 1, 39. *Luke* 4, 44). Thenceforth he travels throughout that area, in and out of its little villages and hamlets—always proclaiming the inbreaking of the Kingdom of God. During his mission in Galilee he was constantly on the move, without any permanent place of residence (*Matt.* 8, 20. *Luke* 9, 58). Yet, he was constantly involved in the lives and needs of others. He mixed freely with all types of people without scruple or hesitation; all needed to witness his revelation of God. The Gospel traditions speak with special emphasis on his eating and drinking with others as indicative of the universality of his appeal to conversion. Sometimes Jesus dined quietly with his friends or family (*Mark* 1, 29–31. *Matt.* 8, 14–15. *Luke* 4, 38–9; 10, 38–42. *John* 2, 1–11); sometimes he ate in the open air with travellers or pilgrims on their way to Jerusalem the Holy City (*Mark* 6, 30–44. *Matt.* 14, 13–21. *Luke* 9, 10–17. *John* 6, 1–13, and *Mark* 8, 1–10. *Matt.* 15, 32–9); sometimes he ate with those whom he met on his travels, whether disciples or chance acquaintances (*Mark* 8, 14. *John* 4, 8–31; 21, 12); sometimes he dined with distinguished

APPENDIX 3. THE MISSION OF CHRIST

Pharisees, those regarded as pillars of propriety and righteous under the Law (*Luke* 7, 36-50; 14, 1); sometimes he ate with those who were outcasts of society and held in contempt under the Law (*Mark* 2, 15-17. *Matt.* 9, 10-13. *Luke* 5, 29-32); sometimes he even dwelt with such public sinners (*Luke* 19, 1-10). Apparently this reached such a point that his adversaries could charge him with being a glutton and drunkard, the friend of tax-collectors and notorious evil-doers (*Matt.* 11, 16-19. *Luke* 7, 31-5). Nevertheless, this did not deter him from his course. Jesus sought out those who needed the mercy and forgiveness of God; he ate and drank with them to express his willingness to be associated and identified with them (*Luke* 15, 1-2). It was his mission to proclaim the coming of salvation to sinners.

It is during the course of his public activity that the full humanity of Jesus emerges. His mission to proclaim the gospel of the Kingdom was very demanding. Both the Synoptic and Johannine traditions describe with tenderness the ordeal that Jesus had to undergo in the fulfilment of his God-given task. He experienced hunger and thirst (*Matt.* 4, 2 = *Luke* 4, 2. *Mark* 11, 12 = *Matt.* 21, 18 and *John* 4, 7. cf *Matt.* 25, 35, 37, 42 & 44); he suffered fatigue and weariness in his work, and so he needed rest and sleep (*Mark* 4, 38. *Matt.* 8, 24. *Luke* 8, 23 and *John* 4, 6). In his work Jesus knew the full meaning of sorrow (*Mark* 14, 34. *Matt.* 26, 38. *John* 12, 27) and joy (*Luke* 10, 21. *John* 11, 15), anger (*Mark* 3, 5; 8, 12. *Matt.* 17, 16. *John* 2, 15-17) and love (*Mark* 10, 21. *John* 11, 5 & 35). Occasionally Jesus was able to find some moments of solitude when he would withdraw to an isolated or wilderness area—much as he did in the beginning of his public activity (*Mark* 1, 35 & 45. *John* 6, 15); and when possible he sought a few moments alone when he could pray to God (*Mark* 1, 35; 6, 46; 14, 32-42. cf *Mark* 9, 2). However, the crowds would soon be on their way to him (*Mark* 1, 37 & 45). His mission necessitated a constant response so as to help those who sought him. The months that Jesus spent in Galilee were given to the proclamation of the gospel of the Kingdom in works and words. This was his mission.

The mission of Jesus was not confined to Galilee at this time, and there are stories of his travels to the east of the Sea of Galilee (*Mark* 4, 35—5, 43) and to the more distant areas of Tyre, Sidon and the Decapolis (*Mark* 7, 24—8, 26. *Matt.* 15, 21—16, 12). Even more, the Johannine tradition speaks of several journeys taken to Jerusalem at this time. Thus Jesus was continually travelling about during much of his public ministry. But he was not alone. Jesus began to father a select group of followers from the very inception of his mission in Galilee. The historical situation is extremely difficult to determine, but it does appear certain that Jesus did have a small number of disciples who were committed to him and to his way of life. He had first called them, and they had answered his call (*Mark* 1, 16-20. *Matt* 4, 18-22. *Mark* 2, 13-17. *Matt.* 9, 9-13. *Luke* 5, 27-32 and 5, 1-11. cf *John* 1, 35-51; 2, 2, 12 & 22 etc.). The Synoptic tradition especially shows that his followers had a broad background with diverse social ties and attitudes (*Mark* 3, 13-19. *Matt.* 10, 1-4. *Luke* 6, 12-16). Their task as chosen disciples was to live eschatologically with Jesus, to follow him personally and to share in his mission (*Mark* 6, 7-13. *Matt.* 10, 1—11, 1. *Luke* 9, 1-6; 10, 1-12). They would eat and drink with him and those with whom he associated (*Mark* 2, 15-17. *Matt.* 9, 10-13. *Luke* 5, 29-32); they would withdraw with him into the desert for prayer and spiritual renewal (*Mark* 1, 35-6; 6, 31 & 32). His disciples participated in his soteriological and eschatological way of life.

Because of this mission and the very significance of the Kingdom of God, Jesus proclaimed and lived a life of poverty. His works and words revealed the inbreaking of God's dominion in human history, and so the need for conversion. But one of the greatest obstacles to repentance and return to the service of God was wealth. It was not that possessions and money were evil —for indeed, Jesus was supported in his mission by the help of wealthy friends such as Johanna and Susanna (*Luke* 8, 1-3), Lazarus, Martha and Mary (*Luke* 10, 38-42. *John* 11, 1-53), Zacchæus (*Luke* 19, 1-10), Nicodemus (*John* 3, 1-10; 7, 50-2; 19, 39) and Joseph of Arimathæa (*Mark* 15, 43. *Matt.* 27, 57. *Luke* 23, 51. *John* 19, 38). Jesus always accepted their assistance with gratitude, and they attended to him to the very end of his life. On the other hand, wealth was a most serious danger to salvation. Wealth was man's great deception since it encouraged him to trust himself and rely on the autonomous power given him by money—rather than depend on God (*Luke* 12, 22-34). Wealth and the cares it entailed provoked a divided allegiance (*Matt.* 6, 24. *Luke* 16, 13); wealth was an enticement to rebel against God and to serve self-interest (*Luke* 12, 16-21; 16, 1-13 & 19-31). This had long been recognized in the religious traditions of Israel where one current of thought saw the poor as the true servants of God (*Ps.* 86, 1-7), and conversely trusted in God and his Anointed as the true protectors of the poor (*Prov.* 22, 22-3. *Isa.* 11, 4. cf *Ps.* 72, 2, 4 & 12-14). Even more, some such as those who lived in the Qumran Community could see wealth as evil (1 *Qs.* 10, 19. 1 *Qh.* 15, 23. *Cd.* 8, 5) and poverty as a sign of the grace of salvation, and so a way of life pleasing to God (1 *Qh.* 2, 31-2; 5, 22. 1 *Qm.* 11, 7-9 & 13; 13, 14 and 1 *Qs.* 1, 11-12; 6, 20; 9, 7-8, 1 *QpHab.* 12, 2-10). In line with this tradition Jesus of Nazareth proclaimed the good news of salvation to the poor. They had been without wealth, and even more, they had been able to trust God in whatever situation they found themselves. At last, their trust would be finally answered and rewarded (*Luke* 4, 18. *Matt.* 11, 5. *Luke* 7, 22. cf *Luke* 6, 20 and *Matt* 5, 3 and 1 *Qm.* 14, 7). Jesus himself came from a carpenter's family and so he most likely had few possessions of his own. His mission involved constant journeying from place to place, and so, there was very little he could call his own (*Matt.* 8, 20. *Luke* 9, 58). Jesus was a poor man, dependent on God and his fellow men for help. So it was to be with his disciples. Those who followed Jesus were expected to trust God on earth and seek true wealth in heaven (*Matt.* 6, 19-21. cf *Luke* 12, 33-4); they were challenged to sell their possessions and become poor themselves (*Mark* 10, 17-31. *Matt.* 19, 16-30. *Luke* 18, 18-30); they were asked to carry on his missionary work but to do so in poverty as he did

APPENDIX 3. THE MISSION OF CHRIST

(*Mark* 6, 8-9. *Matt.* 10, 7-10. *Luke* 9, 2-3; 10, 4-9. cf *Luke* 22, 35-7). Again, his disciples shared fully in his way of life.

The work of Jesus was well received at first and he enjoyed a reputation beyond the confines of Galilee, both to the north and the south. But this situation began to change and Jesus lost much of the popular support he at one time had. The people and leaders of Israel could not see in him their picture of God's soteriological and eschatological representative. The turning-point in the Galilean ministry is symbolized in his rejection at Nazareth —by those who should have perceived who he was (*Mark* 6, 1-6. *Matt.* 13, 53-8. cf *Luke* 4, 16-30). Gradually Jesus expands his mission outside of Galilee and begins to concentrate more energetically on the formation of his closest followers. Conversely, his teaching takes on a much sharper tone, as he is brought more directly into controversy with his opponents (*Mark* 6, 30—7, 37. *Matt.* 14, 13—15, 31 and *Mark* 8, 1-26. *Matt* 15, 22—16, 12). The conclusion of his mission in Galilee is situated in the transfiguration by the Synoptic tradition (*Mark* 9, 2-8. *Matt* 17, 1-8. *Luke* 9, 28-36). After this he begins his fateful journey to Jerusalem, where he would come into final conflict with his adversaries who could not accept his understanding of the Kingdom of God and its soteriological and eschatological character. At the Holy City of God the mission of Christ comes to an end, and there the mission of the Church begins.

The length of his mission is very difficult to determine from the Synoptic tradition. Although there are many episodes from his ministry which offer a very real insight into his manner of life, there is no sequence of time. The Johannine tradition is at once more helpful and more complex. The Synoptic Gospels concentrate on Jesus' mission in Galilee, and then move to Jerusalem, where they locate all of Jesus' contacts with the city and its leadership in the last few days of his life. The Johannine tradition suggests more frequent contacts with Judaea and Jerusalem which are spread over a period of at least two years and some months. After his baptism and the subsequent inauguration of his mission in Galilee, Jesus leaves Capharnaum to go to Jerusalem to celebrate the Pasch (*John* 2, 12 & 23). He returns to Galilee through Samaria after the feast is over (*John* 4, 1-6). There while engaged in his ministry Jesus celebrates another Pasch (*John* 6, 4). Afterwards Jesus journeys to Jerusalem once again, but this time for the solemnities surrounding the Feast of Tabernacles (*John* 7, 2). Yet again he travels from Galilee to celebrate the winter feast of the Dedication of the Temple at the Holy City (*John* 10, 22). He returns to Galilee, and then decides to travel to Jerusalem for the forthcoming Pasch. It is at this feast that he is arrested and eventually executed (*John* 11, 55—12, 1). Thus if Jesus of Nazareth began his public mission in the year 27 or early 28, he would have been crucified in the year 30. This cannot be established with certitude and the present calculation is based on the text of the Fourth Gospel as it now stands; it presumed that the basic sequence of events is accurate and that the references are to three distinct paschal feasts at Jerusalem. However, if the Gospel text has been subjected to redactional emendations or dislocations, then this sequence may not be correct. As the Johannine tradition is the sole source for this chronology it offers the only real possibility of determining the length of the ministry. It appears that Jesus preached the inbreaking of the Kingdom of God for approximately two or two and a half years before he was crucified. His execution as a pretended King of the Jews brings the mission of Christ to its conclusion.

The faith of the Christian Community kept his memory ever alive, and saw in him the Risen Lord who reigned over his disciples in the present and in the future. That faith was able to re-evaluate and reinterpret the significance of his works and words in the light of the resurrection. That faith was prepared to see in him God's unique Son, his supreme Mediator in all creation and salvation (*John* 1, 3–4. I *Cor.* 8, 6. *Heb.* 1, 1–3. I *Tim.* 2, 5). That faith has directed the full presentation of his activity. But still, that faith is the reflection of the hidden events of a human life caught up in the momentum of the world in which that man lived. Faith formed by events; faith forms events. Through faith the labours of Jesus assume decisive importance and his mission emerges as that of a man who spent himself in the service of those to whom he brought the message and the reality of the Kingdom of God.

Appendix 4
THE TEMPTATION OF CHRIST
(3a. 41)

THE TEMPTATION of Jesus is closely connected to his baptism in the Synoptic tradition. There is no intervening event separating the two episodes. There is the declaration of the heavenly voice that Jesus is God's Son, and then he is driven or led out into the wilderness (*Mark* 1, 12. *Matt.* 4, 1). In the Lucan tradition there is a secondary expansion of the background of his sonship (*Luke* 3, 23–38). This proclaimed, the genealogy of Jesus is traced back through Joseph and the great leaders of the history of Israel, to its patriarchs and through them to Adam who was himself a son of God. All human history has been pointing to Jesus who now begins his mission as Son of God.

At once he is brought into the wilderness or desert to meet Satan (*Mark* 1, 12–13. *Matt.* 4, 1–11. *Luke* 4, 1–13). This setting serves as a close link to what has preceded. John the Baptist received his vocation in the desert (*Luke* 3, 2); he preached in the desert (*Matt.* 3, 1); he baptized in the Jordan River which was hemmed in by the desert (*Mark* 1,4. *Matt* 3,6). Indeed, John preached a return to the desert, as did the Qumran Brotherhood in its own desert foundation on the Dead Sea, a short distance from the Jordan. There in this parched area Jesus was baptized, and in a locale which cannot be determined Jesus spent many days and nights alone with God—and there in the isolation of this wilderness area adjacent to the Jordan River and the Dead Sea, Jesus encountered Satan.

In many ways the desert represented an ideal for Israel. It was in the wilderness that God first revealed himself to Israel as a nation. There in the desert God revealed his name and gave his covenant-law to his people. There in the desert of Sinai the people of God became aware of its election, and there it agreed to serve God and obey its covenant-responsibilities. There in the desert Israel became the people of God (*Exod.* 19, 1–6). There God revealed his special love for Israel; there God manifested his will to his people; there God acquired new and peculiar rights over his people, and they became subject to special duties and obligations. In the desert of Sinai God saved his people from the bondage of Egypt, and there he guided it to the land of promise. There in the desert Israel became the first-born Son of God—with all the rights and duties connected to the notion of sonship (*Exod.* 4, 22–3. *Deut.* 1, 31; 8, 5; 14, 1–2; 32, 6–10. cf *Isa.* 63, 15–16. *Jer.* 3, 4, 19 & 22. *Hos.* 11, 1–2. *Mal.* 1, 2 & 6; 2, 10). Thus, it was in the desert that Israel first became conscious of its own sonship and God's spiritual fatherhood. The wilderness was henceforth to symbolize that period of solicitude and affection when God and his people came to know and love one another. It was an ideal time which was to be long remembered in the religious consciousness of many of the prophets of Israel.

However, there was another more sombre aspect to the desert. It was also a place of restiveness and revolt against God. Certainly God was with his people in the wilderness; he was their leader and guide throughout the course of their wanderings. As a loving Father, God was always prepared to help his children in the desert. And yet, they must respond to his will as was expected of a dutiful child. Israel had to learn that it depended on God for its salvation and sustenance—that it must serve him faithfully as his son. God was prepared to test his people in their Exodus through the desert of Sinai so as to discover if they would acknowledge their constant need of his care and protection, and recognize how very much they depended on him for everything. God tried Israel so as to bring about this state of self-awareness (*Deut.* 4, 34; 7, 19; 8, 2, 3 & 16). But, Israel would not respond; it refused to respond. The people of God would not serve him. Indeed, they even sought to test him—demanding food and drink from him, and murmuring threats of open rebellion if their incessant requests were not met. As God's representative, Moses became a constant object of reproach (*Exod.* 15, 24; 16, 2; 17, 2. *Num.* 14, 2-3; 21, 5). Indeed, in a supreme act of infidelity and disobedience Israel defiantly worshipped a brazen calf instead of God its Lord and Father (*Exod.* 32. *Deut.* 9, 6-21). Thus the desert could recall not only a period of happiness when God led his chosen people to their promised land, but also a time of revolt and sin against God.

This view of the desert, with its good and bad sides, its fidelity and infidelity, is to be found well represented in the psalms and prophetic writings of the Old Testament. The desert was remembered as a place of God's involvement with his people, a place where he both punished and helped them (*Ps.* 29, 8; 66, 10-12; 78, 11-16 & 38-9; 80, 8; 81, 5-10; 99, 7; 106, 1-12 & 44-6; 107, 4-9). The desert was a place of joy where God called Israel his Son (*Jer.* 2, 2. *Hos.* 11. 1-2. *Amos* 2, 10. *Ezek.* 20, 5-7). Yet, as an understanding Father, God had to discipline his son (*Deut.* 8, 5). He had to test their loyalty. Then they revolted and sinned against him, challenging him and daring to tax him with their own demands (*Ps.* 78, 5-8, 17-20, 40-1 & 56-8; 95, 7-9; 106, 13-27 & 32-9). Even Moses, the great servant of God, was not without fault (*Ps.* 106, 32-3). In the desert Israel sought to be served by God instead of itself serving him.

There was hope for the future, however. The prophets looked to the past and saw in the Exodus a mirror of Israel's whole relationship to God. Indeed, Israel had revolted against God in the wilderness and had worshipped other gods; it had truly deserved the divine wrath and punishment. Yet, God would not fully abandon his chosen people (*Ezek.* 20, 5-26). In the future the people of God must return to that state of trust and dependence on God which was first evidenced in the desert. As Israel refused to serve God in the desert in the past, so it would have to serve him in the desert in the future. Israel must allow God to restore it to a state of filial obedience and lead it through the wilderness once again (*Hos.* 2, 14-15. *Ezek.* 20, 33-44), Israel must anticipate and prepare itself for a new Exodus through the desert (*Mic.* 2, 12-13; 7, 15. *Isa.* 40, 3-5; 41, 17-20; 43, 16-21; 49,

APPENDIX 4. THE TEMPTATION OF CHRIST

9–11). Then the desert will become like a new paradise with gardens abounding in riches and paths easy to follow (*Isa.* 35, 1–2 & 6–7; 48, 20–1; 51, 3; 52, 12). Then the desert ideal will be restored.

It was in this frame of mind that Judaistic eschatology always kept looking to the future. The primitive relationship of God and Israel, father and son, must be revived in the desert. This was the hope of the Qumran Community (1 *Qs.* 5, 8; 8, 12–16; 9, 19. 1 *Qm.* 1, 2. *Cd.* 20, 23); this was the challenge of the message of John the Baptist (*Mark* 1, 1–8. *Matt.* 3, 1–12. *Luke* 3, 1–20).

Israel's experience in the desert appears to have provided the context for the description of Jesus' withdrawal into the wilderness. It is in the desert that Jesus, the consecrated Son of God, remains totally submissive to the divine will and thereby remedies the rebellion of Israel, the first-born Son of God. The thematic elements of the Synoptic tradition connect the temptation of Christ in the desert to the Exodus of Israel through the wilderness of Sinai. Thus, it was the wind or Spirit of God that divided the waters of the Red Sea for the salvation of Israel (*Exod.* 14, 21–2), and it was the Spirit of God that guided the chosen people in their pilgrimage through the desert of Sinai (*Isa.* 44, 3; 63, 10–14. cf 32, 15). So also it was the Spirit of God which was given to Jesus at his baptism that led him out into the desert and gave him strength and guidance for the ordeal he would have to undergo there (*Mark* 1, 12. *Mark.* 4, 1. *Luke* 4, 1). For forty years Israel was in the desert, and it was a symbolic forty days that Jesus spent in the wilderness in his own personal trial. And as Moses the representative of Israel went without food and drink before he was to contact God in the desert, so too Jesus went without food and drink for forty days before beginning his mission as the representative of the new people of God (*Mark* 1, 13. *Matt.* 4, 2. *Luke* 4, 2. cf *Exod.* 24, 18; 34, 28. *Deut.* 9, 9, 18, 19 & 25–9; 10, 10).

The dangers which Israel experienced from deadly reptiles and insects during its exile in the desert are reflected in Jesus' own encounter with wild animals (*Mark* 1, 13). Serpents and scorpions attacked the chosen people in the wilderness (*Num.* 21, 6–9. *Deut.* 8, 15), and most certainly there were other wild beasts and reptiles in its wastes. Indeed, the desert was proverbially a land inhabited by ferocious animals. They even came to symbolize its desolation and emptiness, its isolation and abandonment by God (*Isa.* 30, 20–2; 34, 8–14; 35, 7. *Jer.* 10, 22. *Ezek.* 34, 5, 6, 8 & 25. cf *Ps.* 22, 12–21). So it was that God could promise his people protection and deliverance from the assaults of such creatures (*Ps.* 91, 11–13). And, in the future, when Israel passes through the desert in a new Exodus, there will be no threat from wild beasts (*Isa.* 35, 9; 43, 20). When the Anointed One of God appears to lead his people to their salvation, the primitive harmony of nature will be restored: men and animals will live together in peace (*Isa.* 11, 6–9; 65, 25). Thus Jesus, the leader and saviour of the new people of God, must encounter wild beasts in the desert—and perhaps as a new Adam he lives with them in tranquillity.

Israel was not bereft of God's help, however. In the desert the chosen people were also guided and protected by his heavenly ministers or angels (*Exod.* 14, 19; 23, 20–2 & 23; 32, 34; 33, 2). Their function was to be of service to God, and so to assist men. For this reason the angels could even be called sons of God because they dutifully carried out their divine commissions (*Deut.* 32, 8. *Ps.* 29, 1; 89, 7). They watched over men (*Ps.* 91, 11. *Dan.* 3, 49–50. *Tob.* 3, 17); they protected the people of God in time of danger and battle (*Dan.* 10, 13–21; 12, 1. cf *Test. Neph.* 8, 4. I *Qm.* 1, 10–11; 12, 8–9; 13, 10; 17, 6 and I *Qs.* 3, 24–5. I *Qh.* 5, 21). The angels of God would even protect men against wild beasts and the evil they symbolized (*Ps.* 91, 11–13). So it was only to be expected that Jesus would be given the assistance of the angels of God at the time of his ordeal in the desert (*Mark* 1, 13. *Matt.* 4, 11).

It is that situation in which Satan or the Devil appears and puts Jesus to the test. Jesus, the Son of God, must suffer the assaults of the Prince of Evil. He must be tempted or tested to see if he will remain loyal and submissive to the will of God the Father, or if he will revolt and rebel against the divine will. As Israel tried God in the desert, demanding special signs of his care, so Jesus is encouraged to do the same thing. According to the Markan tradition Jesus' trial takes place during his sojourn in the desert. There is no description of what it entailed; there is no report of its outcome. There remains only the simple fact that Satan put Jesus to the test. It is not the last time that Jesus would encounter the forces of evil. No, for in the Markan tradition, Jesus continues to be in combat against his adversary. However, there is never any doubt as to the results of their meeting. In all such situations Jesus, the revealer of the Kingdom of God and one endowed with divine power and authority, always triumphs. Does this happen because of his victory over Satan in the wilderness? The Markan tradition does not say.

Rather, it is in the tradition represented by Matthew and Luke that this question is answered. The Devil tries to tempt Jesus to abuse the very meaning of his sonship, but he does not succeed. Clearly Jesus emerges as the victor. The adversary leaves him; the Devil is vanquished, though in anticipation of the final and ultimate victory on the cross (*Matt* 4, 11. *Luke* 4, 13). Indeed, Jesus went into the desert prepared to be tempted; he must face the Devil (*Matt.* 4, 1). Even more, the content and the course of Jesus' ordeal is portrayed in graphic terms. He must endure a very real test to his own mission; he must prove the meaning of his own sonship; he must succeed where Israel, the first-born son of God, failed. Thus, the Devil is described as approaching Jesus and tempting him to change the stones of the desert into bread (*Matt.* 4, 3–4. *Luke* 4, 3–4). This test does not aim at discovering who Jesus is. His mysterious personality is already known by the adversary (*Mark* 1, 24; 3, 11 etc.). Its purpose is to find out what Jesus' sonship means. How will Jesus reveal his sonship? How will he fulfil his filial duty in the mission given him? How will he use the power and authority he enjoys as God's Son—in the service of God, or in self-service? Jesus has gone for many days without food and drink. Thus, it would be to his own

APPENDIX 4. THE TEMPTATION OF CHRIST

personal advantage to supply his needs in the desert. Instead of depending on God the Father for nourishment, Jesus is tempted to repeat the miracle of the manna for his own benefit. But this he refuses to do. By use of a citation from *Deuteronomy* 8, 3 Jesus admits his and all Israel's need of bread, but even more he declares the necessity of obedience to the word and will of God who would feed all his people. God the Father will discipline his children, but so too would he care for them (*Deut.* 8, 1–10). Thus Jesus refuses to yield to the Devil's promptings.

But the struggle continues. In another confrontation Jesus is taken to Jerusalem, the Holy City, and placed on a high point of the Temple structure. Where this is cannot be determined, and for the point of the episode it is irrelevant (*Matt.* 4, 5–7, *Luke* 4, 9–12). Jesus is challenged by the Devil to test God, much as did Israel. During the Exodus of the chosen people through the desert, an angel of God—as it was then understood—guided Israel on its way. God was always prepared to help his people when they needed him. Accordingly, Jesus should see if God the Father would send his angels to protect his Son in this instance of his need (cf *Ps.* 91, 11–13 and *Exod.* 23, 20–3 etc.). Again, almost in the style of a rabbinic disputation, Jesus answers his adversary by reference to *Deut.* 6, 16. Israel tested God and his fidelity at Massah (*Exod.* 17, 1–7. *Num.* 20, 2–13). This Jesus will not do; Jesus will not force God to use his ministers to care for his Son. If he were to test God's fidelity then his own infidelity would be exposed. Again, Jesus refuses to meet the Devil's temptation.

For the last time the adversary approaches Jesus with a supreme offer. The Devil shows him all the kingdoms of the world and their pomp and glory. He promises to give them to Jesus, being within his sphere of power and authority. However, there is a condition: Jesus must acknowledge the Devil as his lord and master. Then all will be his (*Matt.* 4, 8–10. *Luke* 4, 5–8). Instead of serving God and his Kingdom, Jesus is asked to serve the Prince of Evil and his kingdom. His mission and power would again be used in his own personal self-interest, and God is being tempted to allow this. But Jesus refuses by reference to *Deuteronomy* 6, 13: God alone is to be worshipped. As Israel, God's first-born son, committed its most heinous offence in the desert when it worshipped the molten calf as its god, so Jesus, God's Son, is tempted to do the same (*Exod.* 32. *Deut.* 9, 6–21). But he will not do this. Jesus proves his sonship in reaffirming his loyalty to God and his intention to reverence him. With this, the Devil withdraws defeated. Jesus has emerged the victor in his rededication to serve God alone.

The Synoptic tradition is uniform in presenting the temptation of Christ as a personal experience. This ordeal was something that Jesus alone had to undergo. Indeed, in the description of the content of the trials of Jesus, there is a polarized conflict between him and Satan. The physical setting is the wilderness, but the area of action is the mind and heart of Jesus. The test is to see whether Jesus of Nazareth will serve God or his own personal self-interest. In this the event is subordinated to its interpretation. Virtually nothing is reported of the details of Jesus' sojourn in the desert. As an event it takes place after his baptism and before the opening of his ministry in Galilee. Conversely, the significance of this ordeal is stressed, and the soteriological and eschatological themes centring around the ordeal of Israel in the desert suggest that Christian thought has preserved the memory of this event because of its meaning. What is this?

It has been proposed that the significance of this episode is primarily didactic. The Synoptic tradition has described the temptation of Jesus in this fashion so as to show the Christian faithful how their own Lord withstood his personal test, and thus give them an example of courage and commitment in their own trials. The Christian community needed to know how Jesus had experienced temptation and how he had remained constant in this time of personal suffering. Jesus was tempted to satisfy his physical need of nourishment and his spiritual need of independence and freedom of action. He withstood this onset of the Devil, and so gave an example to all: Christians had to submit to suffering for their way of life, and they needed to know how Jesus had been faced with the same situation and conquered his adversary (cf 1 *Cor.* 10, 1–13. *Heb.* 2, 18; 4, 15 and *Jas.* 1, 2–15. 1 *Pet.* 1, 6; 4, 12–19). At the hour of his final ordeal Jesus was tempted once again (*Luke* 22, 40–6. cf *Mark* 14, 32–42. *Matt.* 26, 36–46), and perhaps even during the course of his public ministry (*Mark* 8, 31–3. *Matt.* 16, 21–3; but cf *Luke* 4, 13). Yet, his initial victory over Satan determined the course of subsequent events. His adversary could never overcome him. In this the Christian could base his hope and trust in God; he too could stand fast in his trials and remain obedient to the divine will.

It has also been suggested that the significance of this episode is primarily apologetic. The Christian community knew quite well that Jesus of Nazareth had not been received by his own countrymen. The Jews would not believe in him. Rather, they sought to put him to the test, seeking wonders and signs of him (*Mark* 8, 11. *Matt.* 12, 38–9; 16, 1–4. *Luke* 11, 16 & 29. cf *John* 7, 3–5 and *Mark* 3, 21–7). But he refused to satisfy their demands; he repudiated such desires for extraordinary feats as diabolical. Thus the temptation of Jesus portrays his rejection of the sign-seeking of his contemporaries. The Christian community must be reminded that Jesus did not meet the contemporary Jewish demands for a messianic wonder-worker because he would not. Such was not God's will.

Certainly these didactic and apologetic elements cannot be ignored in any search for the significance of Jesus' temptation in the desert. However, it is doubtful that they reveal the basic significance of this episode. They suggest that the ordeal of Jesus was recounted for the benefit of the Christian community, whether didactic or apologetic. Yet these various temptations were hardly the type which the ordinary Christian would have to endure, and so the discovery of their overriding didactic value is problematical. Similarly, these trials of Jesus were scarcely able to explain why he did not work any wonders, for in fact he did perform great signs and deeds. But he always sought faith from those who experienced or witnessed them. This key element does not even appear in the episode, and so it is uncertain how

APPENDIX 4. THE TEMPTATION OF CHRIST

valuable this would appear as an apologetic motive for the Christian community.

Rather, it seems that the primary significance of Jesus' temptation is Christological. The baptism of Jesus has revealed and declared him to be the *Son of God*. All possible Old Testament themes are introduced into this setting to show that this event enjoys divine authentication. It is God himself who manifests Jesus as his Son; it is God himself who anoints him with the Spirit. Jesus' sonship is a call to action and a mission to fulfil the special will of God the Father. Jesus must proclaim the inbreaking of the Kingdom of God and offer God's gift of salvation to Israel, and indeed, through Israel, to all men. The use of the Old Testament suggests that his work is to be as Messiah and Servant. Hence, Jesus must be brought into direct confrontation with that power which has kept man from the Kingdom of God and the grace of salvation; Jesus must challenge the power of Satan and reveal his own power and authority as greater; Jesus must show himself to be the *Mightier One*. Hence, endowed with the Spirit to assist him to carry out the functions of Messiah and Servant, Jesus must go to face Satan and the evil forces of his kingdom. As Messiah, Jesus must conquer; as Servant, Jesus must obey. Here is the context of the temptation: Jesus must encounter Satan to reveal the meaning of his sonship; the Synoptic tradition describes Jesus' meeting with Satan as a Christological conquest of his adversary through obedience and service to the will of God.

In the desert, Israel was put to the test and rebelled against God. Now Jesus, revealed and consecrated as the Son of God, is also put to the test. He is tempted to pervert his soteriological and eschatological role as Messiah and Servant into one of self-glorification and self-interest. He is tempted to repeat the manna-wonder in the desert, as was expected of the Messiah; he is tempted to use the guidance and direction of God's angels in the display of spectacular power-authority, rather than accepting their leadership in the desert; he is tempted to renounce his task of conquest, one expected of the Messiah, and instead worship his adversary as did Israel in the desert. In each instance Jesus is tested to renounce his role of Messiah and to refuse to serve God as he should; Jesus is tempted to repudiate his function as Messiah and to rebel against his mission of a dutiful and suffering servant. But he refuses to do this. Unlike the Israel of old, he will not disobey and rebel against the will of God. Perhaps even more, unlike the Adam of old, he will not use his power to turn the desert into a new garden of paradise —with food and drink at the disposal of a mere word; he will not use his power and authority to obtain a false immortality and independence of God in casting himself from the Temple; he will not use his power and authority to make himself another god—master over the kingdoms of the world. Israel and even Adam were sons of God. Yet both rejected their position as sons: they would not obey the commands of God; they rebelled against his authority. Jesus would not do this. He chose to remain a dutiful Son by accepting his role as Messiah and Servant. In this decision he reveals his power over Satan. By refusing to disobey God the Father, Jesus leaves

Satan powerless over him. His messianic victory over the Devil and his kingdom is brought about through his Servant's obedience. The rebellion of the chosen people in the desert is rectified by the obedience of Christ the anointed Son of God. Now, in the light of this victory Jesus is prepared to go forth to reveal the meaning of the Kingdom of God. This is the Christological significance of the temptation of Jesus.

It cannot be denied that the present form and content of the temptation of Christ in the desert as described in the Synoptic Gospels manifests the insights, reflections and traditions of the primitive Christian community and its Christology. Do they also reflect the mind of Jesus? The answer to this question remains qualified. As with the baptism of Jesus—so with his temptation. If Jesus of Nazareth understood the meaning of his personal filial mission as that of the Messiah and Servant of God, then he could very easily have seen the necessity of facing the trials demanded of his role at the beginning of his ministry. He could have grasped the soteriological and eschatological necessity of remedying the disobedience of Israel by his own representative and dutiful obedience. If this be admitted, then the Christological formulations of the primitive Church which appear in the Synoptics' presentation of the baptism and temptation of Christ could have their foundation in Jesus' personal experience and self-consciousness. If this is so, then Jesus' mission is truly based upon his own understanding of his personal relationship to God and his task as the revealer of his Kingdom.

Appendix 5
THE WORKS AND THE WORDS OF CHRIST
(3a. 42–44)

AFTER HIS temptation in the wilderness and his personal victory over Satan, Jesus of Nazareth returned to Galilee, his homeland. There he began with his proclamation that the Kingdom of God was at hand (*Mark* 1, 15. *Matt.* 4, 17). Indeed, the Synoptic Gospels present his witness of the Kingdom as central to their entire account of his activity—and to the very mystery of his person. What does this mean?

By the time Jesus inaugurated his public ministry the term *Kingdom of God* had attained a certain uniformity of meaning in contemporary Judaistic thought. In its broadest sense it designated the active revelation and presence of God in cosmic and human history as Lord and King. Since this revelation of God's kingly power and authority was for the salvation and judgment of men the Kingdom of God was a soteriological and eschatological reality. What the Synoptic tradition has done is to relate the salvific and judicial aspects of the Kingdom to the mission and the person of Jesus.

The Kingdom of God revealed his saving activity; it was soteriological in character. Judaism had long awaited the reorientation and reconciliation of all creation back to God. This was to take place in the future when God would choose to act. However, Christian thought, as reflected in the Synoptic tradition, proclaims that the soteriological events had already begun in the person and mission of Jesus of Nazareth. This revelation of God's saving presence was found in the words of Jesus, but most especially in his *works*. His activity was seen to have manifested God's power to save all those in need. Accordingly the Synoptic tradition portrays much of Jesus' public revelation of the Kingdom of God as a *challenge to Satan* and his kingdom of evil. In the world-view of Judaism, Satan and the forces of evil were held to be directly or indirectly responsible for all the disorders affecting cosmic and human history. Thus Jesus must confront Satan and reveal the even mightier works of God and his kingly power. This Jesus did in overcoming Satan at the time of his own personal temptation. This he did in overcoming and rectifying the disorders of nature, the disorders of human life, whether physical or mental, the disorders of sin, whether corporate or personal. The works of Jesus as recorded in the Synoptic tradition all serve to manifest the saving or soteriological presence of God in history.

There was no restriction placed upon this revelation. Certainly Israel constituted the chosen people of God, and so it was to Israel that Jesus was sent. Almost all of his public ministry was confined to Galilee, Judaea and Jerusalem—the land and city of God. Nevertheless, Jesus did not confine his saving works to the Jews alone. The Synoptic tradition shows that he envisaged his work as a *mission to mankind*. He was prepared to help all who needed him, whether Jew or gentile. There was no systematic work among the gentiles, but these he assisted when they declared their need. In his view all men were in the power of Satan and in the grip of sin. They needed his soteriological help. Indeed, salvation was at hand in the work of Jesus of Nazareth.

The Kingdom of God revealed his end-time activity; it was eschatological in character. Judaism expected a future reorientation of all creation back to God. But here too Christian thought, as reflected in the Synoptic tradition, saw the end-time appearing in the revelation of Jesus. This revelation of God's eschatological presence was found in the works of Jesus, but most especially in his *words*. His teaching was seen to proclaim the beginning of the end, and the advent of the forthcoming judgment. Accordingly, the Synoptic tradition describes much of Jesus' public revelation of the Kingdom of God as a *demand for perfection*. Men must prepare themselves before the judgment of God. Again and again the words of Jesus emphasize the need for preparation so as to survive the approaching ordeal and enter into the full possession of the Kingdom of God. Since Jesus was himself a Jew and since he spent almost all his time labouring among the Jews, he would have to assume an attitude with respect to the covenant Law of Moses. This was imperative because orthodox Jews saw the Law as their way of perfection, their guarantee of future deliverance. Obedience to the demands of the Law would mean their successful judgment and justification. This was not the outlook of Jesus. Rather he viewed the Law as a very real threat to salvation and judgment. Careful and exact obedience to the demands of the Law built up a false sense of security and fostered a confident self-righteous blindness to the fundamental obligations of the covenant. But his way of perfection meant a return to the sense of dependence on God and fulfilment of the radical and universal demands of the Law. This was found in the original purpose of the Law and ultimately revealed by Jesus himself. This was done directly—in clear contrast or opposition to his opponents, the Scribes and Pharisees; and this was done indirectly—in the context of parables whose life-situations would offer a provocation to reflection concerning the meaning and demands of the sovereign rule of God. Thus, his teaching was an appeal for a perfect way of life now that the Kingdom of God was at hand.

Again, there was no limitation placed upon this revelation. All men would have to undergo the eschatological judgment of God. Israel constituted the chosen people of God, but this would only add to their responsibility. The Jews as well as the gentiles must be prepared to acknowledge their need of God's grace and mercy. The future judgment awaited them all. Jesus' words revealed much of the eschatological situation of all men living in the period of tension between the present and the future. The Kingdom of God is present now in a small and hidden way, but it is growing and leading up to the future judgment when the just would enter into the full and final possession of the Kingdom of God and receive the *gift of eternal life*. The present would determine the future, and the future would fulfil the present.

APPENDIX 5. THE WORKS AND WORDS OF CHRIST

Judgment was at hand in Jesus of Nazareth. In this setting his mission unfolds.

The baptism of Jesus has proclaimed his sonship and the temptation has put it to the test. Now Jesus emerges as the obedient and dutiful Son of God who is to reveal the full meaning of God and his Kingdom (cf *Matt.* 11, 27-9. *Luke* 10, 21-2). Since in the world-view of contemporary Judaism Satan and the forces of evil exercised a preponderant influence over the present age, the Kingdom of God—when it would be revealed—must challenge the kingdom of Satan. The supremacy of God over all creation must be manifested. Accordingly to fulfil his representative mission of proclaiming the inbreaking of the Kingdom of God, the Synoptic tradition describes Jesus as endowed with power and authority which he was to use in revealing the works of God (e.g. *Matt.* 7, 29; 9, 6; 10, 1; 11, 27-9; 21, 23-7; 28, 18-20). In the possession of such might he would be able to bring to a completion his victory over Satan gained at the temptation.

It is the saving works of Jesus which reveal his personal power and authority and manifest the inbreaking of the Kingdom of God in his mission. As the dutiful Son of God Jesus as Messiah must lead the people of God to victory over Satan and all the forces of evil at his disposal. Hence, he must perform works able to assist those in need of God's salvific help. Thus Jesus' works were *signs* of the advent of the Kingdom of God; they were extraordinary deeds performed to reveal God's power and willingness to save those in stress. Jesus' works had cosmological and soteriological proportions; they revealed his power and authority over those forces opposed to God and his dominion in cosmic and human history. Thus, Jesus' power and authority are revealed in his control over the great forces of nature; he subdues them and brings them into the service of men (*Mark* 4, 35-41; 6, 45-52). Jesus shares in God's control over nature! But more especially the saving power and authority of Jesus are manifested in his curing and healing of the sick. The Galilean ministry contains several examples of Jesus rectifying the disorders of mind and body of those whom he encountered or those who were brought to him (*Mark* 1, 29-34 & 40-5; 3, 1-6; 5, 21-42; 7, 31-7; 8, 22-6 etc.). Such deeds manifested his mercy and compassion but basically the presence of God in Jesus his Son. And since Satan and the forces of evil were believed to be radically responsible for such human woes, Jesus is also described as overpowering demons and breaking their dominion over the possessed. Such evil powers recognize and understand the meaning of Jesus' mission and person; they see only too well a real threat to their own power and kingdom; they desire only to be left alone by Jesus (*Mark* 1, 24; 3, 11; 5, 7. cf *Jas.* 2, 19). The traditions which describe Jesus of Nazareth in combat with demons and exercising authority over them serve to proclaim the fact that the Kingdom of God is present in the activity of the *Mightier One* (*Mark* 1, 21-39; 3, 7-12; 5, 1-20; 7, 24-30; 9, 14-29). The reign of Satan has been broken by Jesus (*Mark* 3, 21-30. *Matt.* 12, 22-32. *Luke* 11, 14-26). His coming has marked the presence of the Kingdom of God and the downfall of Satan (*Luke* 10, 17-20; 11, 20. cf 1 *John* 3, 8). All of God's revelation in the past history of Israel was a promise of the mighty deeds to be performed by Jesus (*Matt.* 11, 2–6. *Luke* 7, 18–23).

The works were not great displays of a wonder-worker's technique nor were they evidence or proof of his unique relationship to God. Rather, they were signs of God's present involvement in cosmic and human history in the person and mission of his Son. Their meaning could be perceived only by faith, a personal trust in Jesus and his preparedness to save those in need. Even the language of the Greek text reflects this. Those who are healed of some sickness or demon-possession are saved (*Mark* 5, 28; 6, 56. *Matt.* 9, 21–2. *Luke* 8, 36–50); those who are preserved in or restored to life are saved (*Mark* 3, 4. *Matt.* 8, 25; 10, 22; 24, 13 & 22; 27, 40); those who seek to enter the Kingdom of God are saved (*Matt.* 19, 25. *Luke* 8, 12; 13, 23). Indeed the name *Jesus* means saviour (*Matt.* 1, 21. cf *Luke* 1, 31); the birth of Jesus was that of a saviour (*Luke* 2, 10–11); his mission was that of salvation (*Luke* 2, 29–32). Hence, his works are the mysterious revelation of God's saving power and the presence of his Kingdom.

Because of the universality of the power of Satan and his kingdom, all men would be in need of God's salvific help. Thus, the Synoptic tradition shows that Jesus' mission would be oriented to the salvation of all. However, this would be brought about in accordance with God's total plan of salvation. Since Israel was God's chosen people, so Israel would have to be the first to hear the good news of salvation and the inbreaking of the Kingdom of God.

The historical mission of Jesus of Nazareth was confined almost exclusively to the traditional limits of the old Israel and restricted to its people living there. He was sent by God the Father to proclaim the gospel of salvation to the House of Israel (*Matt.* 15, 24. cf 10, 5–6). Accordingly the Synoptic tradition describes much of Jesus' person and activity in the context of the religious atmosphere of Israel. He came to fulfil Israel's hope of salvation, and the allusions to the Old Testament and its sacred history serve to point out how he did this.

It is true that the Synoptic tradition concentrates on Jesus' soteriological and eschatological mission to Israel. His work in Galilee is oriented to the Jews (*Mark* 1, 15–9, 50. *Matt* 4, 12–18, 35. *Luke* 4, 14–9, 50). However, it is not confined to them; Jesus did not deny his salvific assistance to those non-Jews who sought it. Thus the Synoptic tradition records instances of his helping the gentiles. When he travelled through Galilee he cured the young son or servant of a Roman centurion who asked for his help (*Matt.* 8, 5–13. *Luke* 7, 1–10). When he travelled briefly through the region to the north of Galilee in the territory of Tyre and Sidon Jesus cured the daughter of a gentile woman who needed his help (*Mark* 7, 24–30. *Matt.* 15, 21–8). When he travelled through the area to the east of Galilee in the Greek-speaking Decapolis he cured the sick and the possessed there (*Mark* 5, 1–20; 7, 31–7. *Matt.* 15, 29–31). Indeed, this missionary work of Jesus in Galilee, with its contacts with the gentiles, was interpreted by the Synoptic tradition as the fulfilment of prophecy (*Matt.* 4, 12–16) and as the will of God (*Luke* 4,

APPENDIX 5. THE WORKS AND WORDS OF CHRIST

16-30). However, what was distinctive of this mission (unlike that of the Church) was that this work among the gentiles was not carried on in any *systematic* way. Jesus of Nazareth had no programme for the conversion of the gentile peoples, and during his lifetime he confined his salvific work to those pagans who came near him.

The active evangelization of the gentiles was only undertaken by the Church after the death of Jesus. Indeed, it was authenticated by a command ascribed to the Risen Christ (*Matt.* 28, 18-20. *Luke* 24, 44-9). But the question remains: did Jesus of Nazareth foresee the evangelization and conversion of the gentile nations? The Synoptic tradition suggests that this was so. The works and words of Jesus indicate that he recognized the fact that his mission to Israel had failed in great part. The initial enthusiasm which greeted his ministry in Galilee began to wane. Many of his contemporaries could find no real satisfaction for their own needs and demands in his message of the Kingdom of God. In Jerusalem this opposition was to terminate in his death. The Jews, as a group, would not believe in him. In this atmosphere of impending failure Jesus is recorded to have spoken in judgment against Israel. Because the people of God would not respond to him their inheritance would be given to others. God would constitute a new people of his own. The Kingdom of God would be given to others.

The figures of speech used by Jesus to warn the Jews of the divine wrath and judgment are traditional. In the future many would come to feast in the Kingdom of God with Abraham, while his natural sons would be excluded (*Matt.* 8, 11-12. *Luke* 13, 28-9. cf *Matt.* 3, 7-9. *Luke* 3, 7-8). Outsiders would be called to the eschatological banquet, while those originally invited would be kept out (*Luke* 14, 15-22. cf *Matt.* 22, 1-14). The vineyard of God would be taken from those who first worked it, and then given to others (*Mark* 12, 1-12. *Matt.* 21, 33-43. *Luke* 20, 9-18). The Temple of God at Jerusalem would be cleansed and prepared for Jew and gentile alike (*Mark* 11, 15-19. *Matt.* 21, 12-13. *Luke* 19, 45-8). Indeed, as a sign of the end of the present age, the Gospel would be preached to all nations (*Mark* 13, 10. *Matt.* 24, 14). Thus, in line with the prophetic tradition of the Old Testament, Jesus could see the salvation of God as proclaimed to the gentiles as well as the Jews (cf *Luke* 2, 29-32; 3, 4-6).

★ ★ ★

However, his activity would also have to be accompanied by his teaching; works must be complemented by words. In line with the traditions of Judaism, Jesus could still proclaim God's future judgment of his people. But, given the advent of the Kingdom of God, the present would assume the character of an intermediate period of eschatological tension. It would be a time of intense preparation for God's judgment. For this reason he would have to teach his disciples how to prepare for this ordeal. He would have to show them the meaning of God's sovereign rule and his demands placed upon those who would enter his Kingdom. As God was perfect, so would he demand perfection of his followers (*Matt.* 5, 48).

Jesus had to speak to his disciples of the meaning of God. Certainly he could describe God as the King and Lord of his subjects and in this context delineate his role as Judge (*Matt.* 18, 23-35; 22, 1-14). But the perfection of God was revealed in Jesus' calling him *Father*. First and foremost God's fatherhood designated a unique and special relationship to Jesus as his Son (*Matt.* 11, 27. *Luke* 10, 22). Jesus could address God as Father in a completely distinctive way; he called God *Abba* (*Mark* 14, 36). This term of affection and endearment was used by the Jews to speak of natural or even adopted human fathers—but never was it applied to God. Similarly Jesus could also describe God as the Father of his disciples. As their Father, God was greater than they, he lived in heaven far above the cares of the world (*Mark* 11, 25. *Matt.* 5, 16, 45 & 48; 6, 1, 9 & 26. *Luke* 11, 13). But Jesus indicated that God as Father was concerned and involved in the lives and events of those living in the world. He would act as a thoughtful and loving Father who would help and guide his needy children (*Matt.* 6, 32. *Luke* 12, 30), and he would forgive his children their offences when they sought pardon of him (*Mark* 11, 25-6. *Matt.* 6, 14-15). God was deeply interested in the salvation of men.

To establish the meaning of this interest in the salvation of men, a new revelation of the will of God the Father would be imperative. Every kingdom had its way of life and its demands, and so too would the Kingdom of God. Accordingly the Kingdom of God would have its *Law*, which would be the fulfilment of the past and the promise for the future. This revelation of the law of the Kingdom of God assumed two forms in the teaching of Jesus: a direct and an indirect one, the *precept* and the *parable*.

The words of Jesus often took the form of a precept. The Synoptic tradition contains many sayings and statements of Jesus, in isolation or in collections, which reveal the will of God for those living in his Kingdom. They are God's demands, endowed with his power and authority. They revealed to the new people of God what he desired of them in their new eschatological existence in the Kingdom. This revelation of Jesus would often entail a reformulation of the old covenant law which was binding on the old people of God. He proclaimed the *fulfilment* of the Old Law in his own person and mission. Now that the Kingdom of God was at hand there would be new eschatological demands placed upon the new people of God. This fulfilment of the old covenant law did not mean its abolition. Rather, it was to be absorbed and transformed into the new eschatological demands of the Kingdom of God (*Matt.* 5, 17-18. cf *Luke* 16, 17). This reconstitution of the Old Law meant its universalization and radicalization in the New Law of the Kingdom. The radical meaning and basic purpose of the Old Law was a promise of salvation. Jesus taught the universal need of salvation, the universal reality of sin, the universal mercy of God's salvific grace, the universal extent of God's eschatological judgment. His new demands were eschatological, a transcendent movement beyond the old into the new Kingdom of God (*Matt.* 5-7. *Luke* 6, 20-49).

The revelation would likewise place a new responsibility upon those who

APPENDIX 5. THE WORKS AND WORDS OF CHRIST

acknowledged it. The New Law of the Kingdom placed radical and universal demands on its members. Jesus revealed God as someone perfect, as a Father who asked for a perfect obedience from his children. These demands of God the Father are total; they require a response from the whole man, exteriorly and interiorly. This is the meaning of the new and perfect justice of the Kingdom of God (*Matt.* 5, 16 & 48; 6, 1, 4, 6 & 18; 13, 43. cf *Luke* 6, 36). The precepts of the Kingdom require a universal obedience, one which characterizes the eschatological life of Jesus' disciples living in a new period of salvations history.

The words of Jesus often took the form of a parable. The Synoptic tradition also contains many stories and similitudes of Jesus which contain an important insight into the nature of God the Father and the life of his Kingdom. The parables of Jesus are simple stories or illustrations from human life and experience. They are images from daily events in the lives of Jesus' fellow-countrymen. Usually these assume the form of a riddle which contains some odd or extraordinary element that would offer a point of comparison to some feature of the Kingdom of God. Something in the parable would suggest to the listener that salvation was at hand, that judgement was imminent, that God was merciful, that God was just, that decision and conversion were imperative. This form of expression was not unique to Jesus, but rather it was well represented in the ancient Semitic love of analogy. Yet Jesus employed this form of teaching more than any of his contemporaries because it suited the richness and complexity of the meaning and demands of the Kingdom of God which was at once present and future, human and divine. Indeed, Jesus could use the parable to describe the entire course of the Kingdom of God as it grew in strength and extent until the consummation of all things (*Mark* 4, 1–34. *Matt.* 13, 1–52. *Luke* 8, 4–18; 13, 18–21). The Synoptic tradition shows that many of the parables were subject to rethinking and reinterpretation in the process of time and in the subsequent understanding and experience of the Church. Yet in this was the mystery of the Kingdom of God revealed (*Mark* 4, 10–12. *Matt.* 13, 10–15. *Luke* 8, 9–10).

It was especially in his parables that Jesus of Nazareth proclaimed the significance of the approaching eschatological judgment. Thus the storm is coming (*Matt.* 7, 24–7. *Luke* 6, 47–9); the conflagration is imminent (*Luke* 12, 49–50; 17, 28–9. cf *Matt.* 13, 47–50); the fig-tree is about to be uprooted (*Luke* 13, 6–9. cf *Matt.* 7, 19); the final reckoning is under way (*Matt.* 25, 14–30. *Luke* 19, 11–27). Jesus' words issue a warning: the eschatological judgment is already at hand, and men must prepare themselves for the forthcoming crisis (*Matt.* 22, 1–13. *Luke* 14, 15–24. *Matt.* 25, 1–12. cf *Luke* 13, 25–7). In face of such an ordeal a determined response and resolute action are essential (*Matt.* 5, 25–6. *Luke* 12, 57–9; 16, 1–9 & 19–31). The Kingdom of God places all men under the imperative of God's judgment.

Indeed, this judgment was in the process of realization now that Jesus was proclaiming the Gospel. But, its consummation was still in the future; only then would those who responded to Jesus' demand for a perfect justice receive the fullness of the gift of eternal life. Accordingly the Synoptic tradition retains the future orientation of Judaism and uses the wealth of imagery from the Old Testament and the Apocalyptic literature to describe the future end of the world-order. The 'apocalyptic discourse' of Jesus must be placed in this context (*Mark* 13, 5–37. *Matt.* 24, 4–36. *Luke* 21, 8–36). The figures of speech are used not to outline a sequence of events, but rather to set a mood and establish an attitude: the eschatological drama has begun, the signs of the end are already appearing, the judgment approaches.

The distinctive element in this eschatological situation is the role of Jesus of Nazareth. The final judgment has been inaugurated by him in the present, and it will be completed by him in the future. As God's eschatological representative, the Son of Man will come again in the future to judge all men (*Mark* 13, 24–7 = *Matt.* 24, 29–31 = *Luke* 21, 25–8. *Matt.* 13, 36–43; 25, 31–46. *Luke* 17, 22–37. cf *Mark* 14, 62 = *Mark* 26, 64 = *Luke* 22, 69). At this final judgment the fate of all would be sealed. The faithful and just who acknowledged and followed Jesus would enter into the full possession of the Kingdom (*Mark* 9, 47; 10, 23–5. *Matt.* 5, 20; 7, 21; 18, 3; 19, 23–4. *Luke* 18, 24); they would enter into eternal life (*Mark* 9, 43–5. *Matt.* 18, 8 & 9; 14, 17); they would inherit the Kingdom (*Matt.* 25, 34); they would inherit eternal life (*Mark* 10, 17. *Matt.* 19, 29. *Luke* 10, 25; 18, 18). Salvation and judgment were already at hand in the person and mission of Jesus. Yet they would await their fulfilment in the future. When this would happen is not known (*Mark* 13, 30–2 = *Matt.* 24, 34–6 = *Luke* 21, 32–3). Indeed, there is considerable uncertainty in the Synoptic tradition as to the relationship of the present to the future judgment. However, there is uniformity in its expectation of the return of Jesus to bring the Kingdom of God to its full realization. Then the just will receive their reward and the wicked will pay for their crimes (*Matt.* 5, 25–6; 13, 43; 18, 34–5. *Luke* 12, 57–9; 14, 14). In all this there were many analogies used to describe the imperative of judgment and the gift of eternal life which awaited men in the future.

The teaching showed that God demanded much more of men now that his Kingdom was at hand. Jesus' disciples lived eschatologically between the past and the future. Indeed, it was Jesus' authoritative teaching that was to guide and direct his followers during the course of their life in the Kingdom which was yet both promise and fulfilment. The teaching revealed God's demand for a perfect justice, a perfect way of life. On this men would be judged.

This teaching, whether in the direct form of a precept or in the indirect form of a parable, was universal and general in character. Jesus always avoided giving any detailed precise or circumstantial exposition of his message. He refused to formulate any systematic summary of his teaching because of the danger that this would become but another legal code and thereby lose its eschatological character. He demanded perfection from all those who lived under God's dominion. In that sense he demanded more than they could ever give. His teaching must always have the character of an eschatological imperative, it must always ask for more from the individual;

APPENDIX 5. THE WORKS AND WORDS OF CHRIST

it must always force him to look to the future and trust in God's grace. Accordingly, he restricted himself to the elucidation of the fundamental principles and demands of the Kingdom of God.

Thus the Synoptic tradition shows how the soteriological and eschatological character of the Kingdom of God is revealed during the course of the mission of Jesus Christ, yet its diverse aspects of the Kingdom cannot be separated one from another. Together the works and words of Jesus constitute the totality of the revelation of the Kingdom. They are mutually complementary and mutually authenticating. So it was in the history of Israel when God manifested his power and his will through the same prophetic representative. God acted and spoke through his mediators in the past, and so he would do the same through his Son (cf Heb. 1, 1-3). Some of the oldest stories retained in the Synoptic tradition combine both elements: Jesus' works and words explain each other and reveal the saving will of God (e.g. *Mark* 1, 21-8; 2, 1-12; 3, 1-6; 7, 24-31). Similarly there can be layer collections of Jesus' sayings which are immediately complemented by his wondrous deeds (*Matt.* 5-7 and 8-9). The fullness of the Gospel of the Kingdom was revealed in teaching and preaching, in healing the sick and casting out demons (*Matt.* 4, 23-4; 9, 35-6. cf *Mark* 6, 7, 12 & 13. *Matt.* 10, 1, 7 & 8. *Luke* 9, 1, 2 & 6). Indeed, the Johannine tradition offers a constant combination of both elements in its contemplation of Christ's *Signs*. Therefore, salvation and judgment, works and words, are intimately interconnected in the mission and in the person of Jesus of Nazareth. His revelation of the Kingdom of God as saving-judging, as present and future, has its source in Jesus' unique sense of being the Son of God. Jesus himself makes his mission a soteriological and eschatological reality.

Appendix 6
THE TRANSFIGURATION
(3a. 45)

THE MISSION of Jesus centred on Galilee and the Jews who lived there. To a people eager to see and hear the works and words of God, Jesus proclaimed the Good News of the inbreaking of the Kingdom. During the first few months of his public ministry Jesus was accorded a spontaneous and popular welcome by the Jews of Galilee. Indeed, his fame even began to spread beyond its confines so that the people of the surrounding areas including Judaea and Jerusalem began to hear of Jesus of Nazareth (*Mark* 1, 28; 3, 7–8. *Matt.* 4, 24–5. *Luke* 4, 37; 5, 15; 7, 16–17). However, this was not to continue for long. On the one hand Jesus did not fit the popular image of a national hero. The Kingdom of God was associated with the restoration of the power and might of Israel over the nations, and its Messiah-King was expected to take up arms against its foes. Galilee had long been a seat of strong resistance to the Roman occupation and there had been founded in that region a para-military group, the Zealots, dedicated to the forceful expulsion of the Romans from the Promised Land of God. It seems that some of them thought that Jesus of Nazareth might be their divinely appointed leader and two of them, Simon and Judas, apparently became associated with his closest followers (*Mark* 3, 18–19. *Matt.* 10, 4. *Luke* 6, 15–16. *Acts* 1, 13). Nevertheless, he did not live up to their expectations. He did not assume the leadership of such patriotic elements in Galilee, nor is there any indication from his attitudes is recorded in the Gospel traditions that he ever advocated a violent confrontation with the enemies of Israel (cf *Matt.* 5, 9 and *Luke* 9, 52–5). Jesus did not see this as the task of the Messiah-King of the Jews, and he would not use his power and authority against Israel's oppressors (cf *John* 6, 15; 18, 36). Hence he soon began to lose support among those who wanted him to lead the struggle against Rome.

He did not fit the popular image of a religious leader. It is true that some of the people, encouraged by his works and words, saw him as a divinely constituted representative of God—and so declared him to be a prophet (cf *Mark* 8, 28. *Matt.* 16, 14. *Luke* 9, 19 and *Matt.* 21, 11. *Luke* 7, 16; 24, 19–21). Yet there were others who could not see Jesus as any such figure. A prophet was expected to be a servant of the Mosaic Law and represent God within its context. The Law was always generated as the supreme organ of divine revelation and all of Israel's religious leaders should be spokesmen of the Law. Not so Jesus of Nazareth! Many of his followers soon discovered that he assumed a position of personal authority above the Law, speaking of its renewal and fulfilment in terms of his own person and mission. The official leaders of Judaism, the Scribes, Pharisees and Sadducees, soon understood quite well that Jesus' outlook and conduct would

APPENDIX 6. THE TRANSFIGURATION

involve the complete revision of the Law and the cult as they interpreted it. To them this was an intolerable blasphemy and they refused to admit Jesus' right to speak for God. He rapidly lost any support he might have had among the leaders of the Jews and their strong influence over the people was sufficient to discourage and eliminate any large-scale acceptance of his person and mission. Rather they began to oppose him ever more actively and their opposition was eventually to bring about his death. *Mark* 2, 1-3, 6; 7, 1-23; 11, 27-12, 40. cf *John* 5, 18; 7, 1-44; 8, 20-40, 59; 10, 31-9; 11, 45-53). The Synoptic tradition does not trace any real decline in the public image of Jesus, but it does symbolize what began to take place in its brief description of his rejection at Nazareth (*Mark* 6, 1-6. *Matt.* 13, 53-8. cf *Luke* 4, 16-30). This episode shows that his own countrymen who should have been able to recognize what he sought to accomplish would not honour him as a prophet. He was not what they expected and not what they wanted.

From this point on Jesus begins to reorient the course of his public ministry. While still remaining in his homeland, he leaves more frequently, occasionally crossing the Sea of Galilee to the adjacent territory to the east (*Mark* 6, 45-56. *Matt.* 14, 22-30) and even travelling to and through the confines of Tyre, Sidon and the Decapolis (*Mark* 7, 26-8, 26. *Matt.* 14, 21; 16, 12). At the same time he concentrates more energetically on the formation of his immediate followers. The crowds are far less numerous, but his personal disciples remain with them. They become the object of his attentions and they begin to respond. This is evidenced in the so-called Confession of Peter at Cæsarea Philippi (*Mark* 8, 27-33. *Matt.* 16, 13-23. *Luke* 9, 18-22). Something of the significance of the mystery of Jesus' mission and person was revealed to Peter, the representative of the Twelve. He proclaims Jesus of Nazareth to be the Messiah, the Christ, the Son of the Living God. He was the great soteriological and eschatological representative of God. And yet there was no suspicion of how much suffering this representative function would entail. Jesus tried to speak to his disciples of what he would have to undergo, but no Jew could conceive of a Messiah who would have to suffer. This Peter and the others would have to learn, and God would have to reveal it to them. This was the reason for the Transfiguration of Christ (*Mark* 9, 2-8. *Matt.* 17. 1-8. *Luke* 9, 28-30. cf. II *Pet.* I, 16-18).

Once again the Synoptic tradition presents an episode which serves to reveal something of the mystery of the person and mission of Jesus. In a context offering a thematic parallel to his baptism, Jesus is reconsecrated and reconfirmed to the task and destiny of the Son of God (*Mark* 9, 7. *Matt.* 17, 5. *Luke* 9, 35). However, now this is revealed to Jesus and his closest disciples, Peter, James and John. They too hear this declaration of Sonship and they are given some indication of what this means. Jesus is the focal point of this setting, but the Transfiguration is for the benefit and instruction of his disciples. They must witness something of the glory of his sonship, but they must also see that it will be revealed only by way of suffering. The Synoptic tradition does this in terms suggestive of the experience of Moses and even Elijah who received the revelation of God on a mountain in the Sinai Desert and then proceeded to comply with the revealed will of God and communicate it to his people at a cost of great personal suffering. At the Transfiguration Jesus receives the divine proclamation of his sonship and he hears from Moses and Elijah what this would entail. His disciples witness this scene, and so they are prepared to hear from Jesus more of the mystery of his sonship. How is this described?

He went up to a high mountain where the entire episode is situated (*Mark* 9, 2. *Matt.* 17, 1. *Luke* 9, 28). This was not unusual since he was accustomed to withdraw to the hills or mountains of Galilee during the course of his public ministry when in need of repose and refreshment (*Mark* 3, 13; 6, 46). But there was more here, for a mountain always represented a place of great sanctity. There he prayed as was his custom at moments of great importance; here he received the special revelation of God (*Luke* 9, 28–9. cf 3, 21; 5, 16; 6, 12; 9, 18; 11, 1; 22, 39–46). Here also he would communicate the special revelation of God to his disciples (*Mark* 3, 7–12; 13, 3. *Matt.* 5, 1–2; 24, 3; 28, 18–20. cf II *Pet.* 1, 18. *Apoc.* 21, 10).

In this setting two great figures from the past appear to Jesus—Moses and Elijah, the representatives of the Law and the prophets. Both had received the revelation of God on a mountain in the Sinai Desert and both had the subsequent mission of carrying out the will of God communicated to them there (*Exod.* 19, 3; 24, 15–18. II *Kgs.* 2, 16). Both knew of the suffering that their work would entail. Moses had to endure the resistance of the people of Israel in their frequent disobedience and stubborn refusal to serve God; Elijah had to face the threats and danger to his life from the royal court of Israel when he tried to carry out his God-given mission. Both are described as speaking to Jesus and what they say is only suggested: he will have to suffer at Jerusalem (*Luke* 9, 30–1).

To show that God was involved in this setting the Synoptic tradition speaks of a cloud which surrounded Jesus and those with him (*Mark* 9, 7. *Matt.* 7, 5. *Luke* 9, 34). Again, a cloud suggested the presence of God. For in such a manner he had appeared to his chosen people during the course of their history (*Exod.* 24, 15; 40, 35. I *Kgs.* 8, 10. II *Macc.* 2, 8. cf I *Cor.* 10, 1–5). So it was when Moses was brought into the presence of God and when he received the revelation of God at Mount Sinai (*Exod.* 24, 15–18). From this cloud a voice declared Jesus to be the Son of God in a close parallel to the voice at the baptism (*Mark* 9, 7. *Matt.* 17, 5. *Luke* 9, 35. cf II *Pet.* 1, 17–18). Both Moses and Elijah had heard the voice of God on the mountain (*Exod.* 24, 16. I *Kgs.* 19, 12–18). Now Jesus and his disciples receive the witness of God and his revelation of the character of his Son.

Even more. Not only was the presence of God surrounding them on the mountain of the Transfiguration, it was also within Jesus, Moses and Elijah. This was the very glory of God which was revealed in them (*Luke* 9, 32. cf II *Pet.* 1, 17). When God revealed himself at Sinai, his glory or visible presence manifested in light was in the cloud (*Exod.* 24, 15–16. *Deut.* 5, 24). So too was God's glory with his people in the desert (*Exod.* 16, 7–10)

APPENDIX 6. THE TRANSFIGURATION

as it was in the tent of his presence (*Exod.* 29, 43; 40, 34–8. *Lev.* 9, 6–23. *Num.* 14, 10, 16, 19; 17, 7; 20, 6). It was this presence of God within Jesus that brought about his Transfiguration, a change in form whereby the divine presence was manifested (*Mark* 9, 2. *Matt.* 17, 2. cf *Rom.* 12, 2. II *Cor.* 3, 18). When Moses had talked to God and received his revelation of the Law, his face became radiant (*Exod.* 34, 29). But for a moment Jesus was given a new form. God's presence within him altered his appearance. His face shone with a sun-like brilliance; his clothes reflected a dazzling white light (*Mark* 9, 3. *Matt.* 17, 2. *Luke* 9, 29). Momentarily Jesus appeared to be a heavenly being clad in the white garments of the heavenly court (cf *Dan.* 7, 9. *Mark* 16, 5. *John* 20, 21. *Apoc.* 2, 17; 3, 4–5; 4, 4; 6, 2 & 11; 7, 9 & 13; 14, 14; 19, 11 & 14; 20, 11). At this instant something of Jesus' unique relationship to God was revealed to his disciples.

What were they to do? They had seen the brightness of his face, the splendour of his garments, the celestial figures of Moses and Elijah talking with him, the bright cloud and the voice from its midst. In fear and dismay they fall on their faces before the presence of God (*Matt.* 17, 6. *Luke* 9, 34). Then, apparently grasping some significance in this event, Peter suggests the erection of three tents so that the divine presence might be fittingly preserved as it was in the desert (*Mark* 9, 5–6. *Matt.* 17, 4 & 6. *Luke* 9, 33). Then the glory and revelation of God would always be with them (cf *Exod.* 33, 7–16). But the disciples misunderstood the situation and asked for something that could not yet be (*Luke* 9, 33); they did not really see that his glory could not be fully and permanently revealed until he had suffered for them. As later at Gethsemane they did not understand what Jesus' mission would involve (*Mark* 14, 32–42. *Matt.* 26, 36–46. *Luke* 22, 40–6). Hence, the heavenly voice adds one significant command beyond what had been communicated at the baptism. Truly Jesus is the Son of God, the Messiah-Servant (*Ps.* 2, 7. *Isa.* 42, 1). But now his disciples are commanded to listen to Jesus and hear what he has to say to them (*Mark* 9, 7. *Matt.* 17, 5. *Luke* 9, 35. cf *Deut.* 18, 15–18). They must be prepared to follow him in his ordeal; they must be prepared to see his glory through the path of suffering. This is the meaning of the episode given them by Jesus as they descend from the mountain (*Mark* 9, 9–13. *Matt.* 17, 9–13). The Baptist, the successor of Elijah, had proclaimed the presence of the Mightier One in Jesus of Nazareth. But his victory over the forces of evil would be by way of suffering and death. This they must understand.

Thus the Transfiguration is an especially important event in the Synoptic tradition. The historical context behind this episode has always been problematical. The high mountain, the cloud, the voice and the brilliant light are all suggestive of similar experiences in the lives of Moses and Elijah. But the factual details have been lost in the course of time and in the literary traditions of Mark, Matthew and Luke. It is rather the significance of this event that has been retained by the Christian community and has become the object of prayerful meditation. During the final days of the ministry in Galilee his disciples are enabled to grasp something of the mystery of his mission and person. Again Jesus is declared to be the Son of God in terms which combine the functions of the Messiah and Servant of God. The Transfiguration serves to reconfirm the meaning of the baptism: his mission is to mean that the victorious triumph of the Messiah must be brought about through the dutiful suffering of the Servant. Humiliation is his way to exaltation, and his disciples must learn this. But there is even more. At his baptism Jesus was consecrated as the Son of God and given the Spirit to assist him to fulfil his divinely appointed task. His person remained hidden in mystery. At his Transfiguration halfway through his mission, more is added. For a moment the glory of the divine presence within Jesus is revealed to his disciples. In a mysterious way Jesus the human being is also Jesus the heavenly being. The Transfiguration is at once the fulfilment of Jesus' baptism in the past, and the promise of his resurrection and parousia in the future. Only then will this momentary glimpse of the glory of Jesus be made permanent; only then will the ultimate reality of his sonship be revealed. Before that time he must suffer, and so at the Transfiguration there is the revelation that this glory will be manifested through suffering. The disciples must realize that he will follow in the path of Moses and Elijah. From this moment on Jesus turns to Jerusalem where his destiny awaits him (*Mark* 10, 1. *Matt.* 19, 1. *Luke* 9, 51. cf *Luke* 13, 33).

Biblical Index

Old Testament
Baruch
  3, 38 55
Canticle of Canticles
  6, 8 45
Daniel
  2, 11 53
  13, 45 29, 31
  13, 52 97
Deuteronomy
  5, 12 65
  19, 15 157
  32, 4 143
Ecclesiastes
  4, 12 77
Exodus
  14, 21 145
  14, 22 33
  19, 16 145
  20, 8 65
  24, 12 103
  31, 13 65
  33, 20 163
Ezekiel
  1, 1 29, 37
Genesis
  1, 20 145
  1, 24 145
  1, 44 129
  2, 2 65
  2, 7 141
  3, 1 85
  3, 5 85
  3, 23 77
  18, 17 111
  19, 17 77
  19, 22 111
  41, 46 29
  49, 10 13
Hosea
  2, 14 53
  4, 10 57
Isaiah
  8, 14 95
  47, 13 129
  49, 6 91
  53, 3 107
  66, 19 93

Jeremiah
  1, 5 31
Job
  31, 28 87
  33, 14 161
  37, 18 35
  39, 25 85
Joshua
  3, 4 33
  3, 15-16 145
I Kings
  18, 10 131
  18, 45 145
II Kings
  2, 8 145
  2, 11 159
Leviticus
  11 67
Malachi
  4, 4 3
Numbers
  4, 5 101
  11, 16 97
Proverbs
  9, 3 105
  9, 17 99
  30, 8 63
Psalms
  114, 3, 5 33
II Samuel
  5, 4 29
Sirach
  2, 1 73
  15, 9 123, 127
Wisdom
  1, 4 139
  1, 5 43
  7, 13 99
  8, 1 145
Zechariah
  13, 2 125

New Testament
Acts
  1, 1 67, 81
  1, 10-11 125
  2, 3 39

BIBLICAL INDEX

Acts (cont.)
  4, 13   139
  6, 2   63
  8, 16–17 17
  10, 43 157
  12, 2   159
  14, 21 151
  19, 1–5 17
Apocalypse
  2, 26–28 93
  5, 6   41
Colossians
  1, 20   124
  3, 3   127
I Corinthians
  1, 12   7
  1, 24   145
  2, 6   97
  2, 8   123, 127
  9, 22   59
  9, 27   81
  10, 2   33
  10, 4   41
  10, 32 95
  14, 22 109
II Corinthians
  3, 3   105
  3, 18   157
  6, 5–7 79
  8, 9   63
  13, 4   129
Ephesians
  4, 13   29
  5, 25   43
Galatians
  3, 5   109
  4, 4–5 67
  5, 3   67
Hebrews
  2, 3   7
  2, 4   139
  4, 15   73, 75
  9, 10   27
  10, 1   103
  10, 19 35
  12, 2   77, 107
  12, 18 147
James
  1, 17   41
  4, 6   33

I John
  3, 2   161
  3, 8   71
John, Gospel of
  1, 6–7 3
  1, 14   39
  1, 16   39
  1, 17   9
  1, 23   7
  1, 26   15
  1, 27   17
  1, 33   7, 23
  1, 35   113
  2, 10   141
  2, 11   113, 115
  3, 5   19, 33
  3, 13   35
  3, 17   137
  3, 22   15
  3, 29   11
  4, 2   17
  4, 7   91
  4, 48   107
  5, 14   143
  5, 17   67
  5, 19   117
  5, 21   117
  5, 36   109, 117
  5, 37   49, 51
  6, 19   151
  7, 23   69, 143
  8, 59   141, 151
  9, 3   137
  9, 6   141
  9, 16   69
  9, 32   117
  10, 31 151
  10, 38 109
  10, 39 151
  10, 41 7
  11, 41–2 111
  11, 47 107
  12, 20–5 93
  12, 31 125
  13, 1   97
  14, 5   149
  14, 6   27
  14, 10 111, 119
  14, 12 115
  15, 24 119
  16, 12 101, 161

210

16, 13   47
18, 6   139
18, 20   99
18, 37   55
20, 12–13 125
20, 29   77
21, 6   145
21, 15   159
21, 25   103
Luke, Gospel of
1, 76   3
1, 79   103
2, 9   125
3, 3   25
3, 16   15
3, 21   13, 29, 35, 37
3, 22   39, 45
3, 23   29
4, 1–2   59
4, 3   125
4, 13   79
4, 29–30 151
4, 30   139
4, 40   141
4, 41   71, 123, 125
5, 4   113, 145
6, 12   57
6, 19   117
8, 2   65
9, 27   153
9, 30   157
9, 31   159
11, 15   111, 113
11, 53–4 95
12, 3   97
13, 15   69
14, 5   69
14, 30   59
16, 16   5
21, 15   139
21, 33   101
23, 44–5 129
24, 26   149
Mark, Gospel of
1, 4   9, 25
1, 5   9, 13
1, 7   15
1, 8   11
1, 9   33
1, 10   35, 37
1, 13   59, 75, 79, 81

1, 24   125
1, 27   117
1, 34   123
1, 38   63
3, 22   113
4, 21   99
5, 19   137
6, 5   109
6, 6   111
6, 31   57
6, 48   151
6, 56   119
7, 3   3
7, 37   137
8, 22   137
8, 23   141
8, 26   137
9, 24–6 123
11, 13   143
Matthew, Gospel of
1, 21   xiii
3, 4   9, 57, 87
3, 6   3, 9
3, 11   7, 9, 11, 15, 19, 27, 41
3, 13   23, 25
3, 15   25
3, 16   33, 35, 37
3, 17   49
4, 1   71, 73
4, 1–2   59
4, 2   81
4, 2–3   73, 79
4, 5   75
4, 11   81
4, 18   113
5, 1   57
5, 17   67
5, 22   95
5, 28   95
5, 32   95
5, 34   95
5, 39   95
5, 44   95
7, 29   91, 103
8, 15   141
8, 16   117
8, 20   63
8, 26   147
8, 31   123
8, 32   145
9, 2   137

Matthew, Gospel of (cont.)
9, 8   123
9, 9   139
9, 10   55
9, 14   61
9, 30   137, 143
10, 5   13, 93
10, 9   63
10, 16 42
10, 27 97
11, 9   5
11, 11 17
11, 19 59
11, 29 63
12, 1–8 66
12, 5   69
12, 24 113
12, 38–9 129
13, 34 99
14, 15 83, 145
14, 19 111
14, 25 151, 153
15, 11 67
15, 12 97
15, 14 97
15, 22 91
15, 24 91, 93
15, 32 83, 145
16, 1–4 129
16, 4   107
16, 18–19 159
16, 21 149
16, 28 153
17, 2   149, 153
17, 6   161
17, 7   163
17, 26 145
18, 16 157
19, 12 57
21, 9   157
21, 12 139
21, 19 143
21, 25 7
24, 30 107
27, 51 145
27, 51–2 147
28, 19 49, 93
Philippians
2, 7   39
2, 8   93
3, 21   151, 157
Romans
1, 32   67
5, 2   55
6, 3   39
8, 2   105
8, 29   51
10, 8   17
10, 15 91
10, 17 77
13, 1   93
14, 17 59
15, 8   93
15, 20 91
I Timothy
1, 15   55
5, 1   95
6, 17   63
II Timothy
2, 2   99

Author Index

Ambrose, St
  De Spiritu Sancto 17
  Expositio Evangelii secundum Lucam 23, 27, 57, 73, 77, 81, 87, 125
  Sermo de Tempore XII 25
Anonymous
  De Infantia Salvatoris 113
Aristotle
  De Cælo et Mundo 45, 129
  De Partibus Animalium 25
  Peri Hermeneias 47
  Physics 23
  Politics 53
Athanasius, St 127
Augustine, St
  Contra Faustum Manichæum 21, 59, 69, 131
  De Agone Christiano 45, 47, 95
  De Civitate Dei 73, 75, 125
  De Consensu Evangelistarum 87, 103, 105, 115
  De Diversis Quæstionibus LXXXIII 61
  De Doctrina Christiana 59
  De Sermone Domini in Monte 87
  De Trinitate 41, 45, 47, 73, 123
  Epistolæ 19, 35, 83, 117, 119, 153
  Quæstionum Evangeliorum Libri Duo 59, 101
  Sermon on Epiphany 33
  Tractatus in Joannis Evangelium 5, 11, 13, 15, 19, 25, 45, 93, 99, 101, 103, 119, 139, 141, 143, 147
Bede, the Venerable
  Expositio Evangelii secundum Lucam 15, 125, 127, 153
  Expositio Evangelii secundum Marcum 11, 27, 61, 81, 127, 141, 151, 161
  Homilia in festo circumcisionis 9
Catena aurea
  listed under
    Augustine, St 141
    Bede, the Venerable 15
    Chrysostom, St John 45, 55, 141
    Rabanus 43
    Remigius 55
    Theophylactus 127
    Victor of Antioch 125
Chrysostom, St John
  Homilia de Baptismo Christi 25, 27
  Homilies on the Gospel of John 15, 49, 115, 141, 143
  Homilies on the Gospel of Matthew 5, 9, 21, 23, 29, 31, 37, 39, 41, 43, 57, 59, 61, 67, 75, 77, 79, 81, 89, 101, 109, 111, 117, 127, 133, 135, 139, 143, 145, 147, 153, 159
Cyril of Alexandria, St
  Homilies on the Gospel of Luke 117, 127, 141

AUTHOR INDEX

Damascene, St John   153
Dionysius, the Pseudo-Areopagite
  De Cælesti Hierarchia   93
  De Divinis Nominibus   131
  Epistola ad Caium   153
  Epistola ad Polycarpum   129, 131, 133
Euclid   151
Fulgentius, St   51
Gregory Nazianzen, St
  Orations   25, 27, 29, 31
Gregory the Great, St
  Homilies on Ezechiel   97
  Homilies on the Gospel   5, 9, 61, 71, 73, 75, 79, 83, 115
  Moralia   85, 99, 155
Hilary, St
  Commentary on St Matthew   51, 71, 73, 79, 101, 147, 159, 161
Jerome, St
  Commentary on Joel   17
  Commentary on St Matthew   21, 37, 49, 55, 63, 65, 83, 93, 101, 131, 139, 141, 143, 151, 153, 157, 159, 163
  Contra Vigilantium   65
  Epistolæ   17, 33
  Expositio in Marcum   11, 127
Leo, Pope St
  Discourses   85, 111
Maximus, St   135
Origen
  Commentary on St John   139
  Commentary on St Luke   75, 89
  Commentary on St Matthew   131, 135, 155
Peter Lombard   19
Polycarp, St   129
Scotus Erigena   5
Victor of Antioch   125

General Index

A

Abraham 168
Adam 77, 85, 193
analogy, use of xiv

angels 123, 125, 157, 159
apostles 17, 45, 115

B

body, glorified 153, 155, 157, 159

C

character 19
circumcision 9, 11, 23, 25, 67

covenant, old and new 171, 172, 175
creation, new 175

D

David 175-6
day of judgment (*see* judgment)
deluge 177
desert ideal 187-9
devil (*see* Satan)

disciples (*see* apostles)
divine power 37, 59, 109, 111, 113, 115, 117, 125, 139, 145
divinity of Christ xvii-xviii, 47, 49, 51, 55, 111, 115, 117, 121, 129, 135

E

Elijah 33, 157, 159, 166, 167, 168, 170, 173, 206-7
eschatalogical representative 202

eschatalogy (*see* judgment and prophet)
Essenes (*see* Qumran)
exodus 33, 174, 177, 188, 189

F

faith xv-xvi, 17, 19, 31, 35, 43, 77, 107, 109, 125, 141

fasting 79, 81

G

gentiles 13, 93, 95, 195-6, 198-9
glorified body 153, 155, 157, 159
glory 149, 151, 153, 155, 157, 161, 163

grace 9, 21, 27, 31, 33, 39, 109, 161, 163

H

Holy Spirit (*see* spirit of God)
humanity of Christ xvii-xviii, 31, 55, 111, 115, 135, 141, 183

humility 31, 33, 65

I

idolatry 87, 188

incarnation 55, 59

GENERAL INDEX

J

John the Baptist 87, 165 ff, 171, 173, 178, 187, 189
judgment, eschatalogical 45, 153, 167, 168, 169, 171, 172, 196, 197, 200, 201–2
justification 137, 139, 141

K

Kingdom of God 33, 195, 196, 197, 200–3

L

Law (*see* Old Law and New Law)

M

Moses 157, 159, 166, 189, 205–7
mountain theophany 206

N

New Adam 189
new covenant 171, 175
New Law 3, 5, 7, 21, 105, 200, 201
Noah 175, 177

O

Old Law 3, 21, 27, 29, 65 ff, 85, 105, 196, 200
original sin (*see* sin)

P

parables of Jesus 99, 101, 201
passion of Christ 35, 37, 39, 93, 149
penance 5, 9, 11, 25
Peter 205, 207
Pharisees 3, 5, 97, 168, 183, 196, 204
poverty 61 ff, 184
power of God 37, 59, 109, 111, 113, 115, 117, 125, 139, 145
prayer 37, 57, 117
precepts of Jesus 200–1
promise 175
prophet, eschatalogical 167–8, 170, 173, 185, 199

Q

Qumran 165, 169, 171, 172, 178, 184, 187, 189

R

reason and faith xiv–xvi, 35, 107, 109
remission of sins 9, 11, 27, 43, 55, 143

S

sacrament xiii, 5, 7, 11, 19, 21
Sadducees 168, 204
salvation 137
Satan 73, 75, 77, 79, 83, 85, 87, 111, 112, 125, 127, 190 ff, 195, 197
senses of Scripture xiii–xvi
servant of God 175, 176, 208
sin 9, 23, 27, 37, 75, 77, 83, 85, 87, 143
spirit of God 33, 39, 40, 41, 43, 45, 47, 49, 73, 77, 109, 174–5, 189, 208

GENERAL INDEX

T

Trinity 49, 163

truth 47, 99, 107

W

water symbolism 168, 177–8

wisdom 31, 101, 137, 139, 141

Z

Zealots 204

VOLUMES

General Editor: THOMAS GILBY, O.P.

PRIMA PARS
1. Christian Theology (1a. 1) Thomas Gilby, O.P.
2. Existence and Nature of God (1a. 2–11) Timothy McDermott, O.P.
3. Knowing and Naming God (1a. 12–13) Herbert McCabe, O.P.
4. Knowledge in God (1a. 14–18) Thomas Gornall, S.J.
5. God's Will and Providence (1a. 19–26) Thomas Gilby, O.P.
6. The Trinity (1a. 27–32) Ceslaus Velecky, O.P.
7. Father, Son, and Holy Ghost (1a. 33–43)
8. Creation, Variety, and Evil (1a. 44–9) Thomas Gilby, O.P.
9. Angels (1a. 50–64) Kenelm Foster, O.P.
10. Cosmogony (1a. 65–74) W. A. Wallace, O.P.
11. Man (1a. 75–83) Timothy Suttor
12. Human Intelligence (1a. 84–9) P. T. Durbin
13. Man Made to God's Image (1a. 90–102) Edmund Hill, O.P.
14. Divine Government (1a. 103–9)
15. The World Order (1a. 110–19) M. J. Charlesworth

PRIMA SECUNDÆ
16. Purpose and Happiness (1a2æ. 1–5) Thomas Gilby, O.P.
17. Psychology of Human Acts (1a2æ. 6–17) Thomas Gilby, O.P.
18. Principles of Morality (1a2æ. 18–21) Thomas Gilby, O.P.
19. The Emotions (1a2æ. 22–30) Eric D'Arcy
20. Pleasure (1a2æ. 31–9)
21. Fear and Anger (1a2æ. 40–8) J. P. Reid, O.P.
22. Dispositions (1a2æ. 49–54) Anthony Kenny
23. Virtue (1a2æ. 55–67) W. D. Hughes, O.P.
24. Gifts and Beatitudes (1a2æ. 68–70)
25. Sin (1a2æ. 71–80) John Fearon, O.P.
26. Original Sin (1a2æ. 81–5) T. C. O'Brien
27. Effects of Sin (1a2æ. 86–9)
28. Law and Political Theory (1a2æ. 90–7) Thomas Gilby, O.P.
29. The Old Law (1a2æ. 98–105) David Bourke
30. The Gospel of Grace (1a2æ. 106–14) Cornelius Ernst, O.P.

SECUNDA SECUNDÆ
31. Faith (2a2æ. 1–7)
32. Consequences of Faith (2a2æ. 8–16)

VOLUMES

33 Hope (2a2æ. 17-22) W. J. Hill, O.P.
34 Charity (2a2æ. 23-33)
35 Consequences of Charity (2a2æ. 34-46)
36 Prudence (2a2æ. 47-56)
37 Justice (2a2æ. 57-62)
38 Injustice (2a2æ. 63-79)
39 Religion and Worship (2a2æ. 80-91) Kevin O'Rourke, O.P.
40 Superstition and Irreverence (2a2æ. 92-100) T. F. O'Meara, O.P. and M. J. Duffy, O.P.
41 Social Virtues (2a2æ. 101-22) T. C. O'Brien
42 Courage (2a2æ. 123-40) Anthony Ross, O.P. and P. G. Walsh
43 Temperance (2a2æ. 141-54) Thomas Gilby, O.P.
44 Well-Tempered Passion (2a2æ. 155-70) Thomas Gilby, O.P.
45 Prophecy and other Charisms (2a2æ. 171-8) Roland Potter, O.P.
46 Action and Contemplation (2a2æ. 179-82) J. R. Aumann, O.P.
47 The Pastoral and Religious Lives (2a2æ. 183-9)

TERTIA PARS
48 The Incarnate Word (3a. 1-6)
49 The Grace of Christ (3a. 7-15)
50 The One Mediator (3a. 16-26) Colman O'Neill, O.P.
51 Our Lady (3a. 27-30) T. R. Heath, O.P.
52 The Childhood of Christ (3a. 31-7)
53 The Life of Christ (3a. 38-45) S. R. Parsons, O.P.
54 The Passion of Christ (3a. 46-52) T. A. R. Murphy, O.P.
55 The Resurrection of the Lord (3a. 53-9)
56 The Sacraments (3a. 60-5)
57 Baptism and Confirmation (3a. 66-72)
58 The Eucharistic Presence (3a. 73-8) William Barden, O.P.
59 Holy Communion (3a. 79-83)
60 The Sacrament of Penance (3a. 84-90) R. R. Masterson, O.P. and T. C. O'Brien